Women and Work in Ireland

This book chronicles the evolution of women's participation in the labour force in Ireland over the last five decades. This was largely spearheaded by married women and mothers, leading to many related social issues including childcare, flexible working, the sharing of domestic work and work-life balance. The book presents empirical data on these topics, drawn from the author's research spanning several decades, and shows how attitudes have evolved and influenced the development of social policy.

The book begins by exploring the factors which predisposed some married women to enter the workplace in the early 1970s while most did not and examines the relative well-being of housewives and employed married women. It demonstrates the effects the anti-discrimination legislation of the 1970s had on women's perceived discrimination over time, showing that women initially denied their own discrimination. The history of childcare policy is examined from the early Government Working Party reports of the 1980s to the evolution of childcare policy in Ireland. Issues of work-life balance are presented through cross-cultural comparisons from Ireland and several European countries, and key questions are asked, such as "are men who work part-time seen as less serious about their careers?" The concluding chapter focuses on how women's role in the workplace impacts on men and gender relations. Questions are posed concerning the ways in which men's roles need to adapt and the extent to which workplaces and social policy also need to change to accommodate men and women's needs for work-life balance.

The book will be of interest to social scientists and to students. It will be a valuable resource for courses in the sociology of work and the family, gender studies, social psychology and Irish studies. By providing quantitative data in an accessible form, it will also provide a valuable case study for courses in social research methods.

Margret Fine-Davis is Senior Research Fellow (Emerita), Department of Sociology, Trinity College Dublin. Her research focuses on changing gender-role attitudes and social-psychological and policy issues related to women's employment in Ireland and Europe. Her books include *Gender Roles in Ireland: Three Decades of Attitude Change* (Routledge, 2015) and *Changing Gender Roles and Attitudes to Family Formation in Ireland* (Manchester University Press, 2016).

Routledge Advances in Sociology

Neurodiversity Studies
A New Critical Paradigm
Edited by Hanna Bertilsdotter Rosqvist, Nick Chown and Anna Stenning

The Class Structure of Capitalist Societies
Volume 1: A Space of Bounded Variety
Will Atkinson

Studies on the Social Construction of Identity and Authenticity
Edited by J. Patrick Williams and Kaylan C. Schwarz

Globalisation, Tourism and Simulacra
A Baudrillardian Study of Tourist Space in Thailand
Kunphatu Sakwit

Thinking Through Dilemmas
Schemas, Frames, and Difficult Decisions
Lawrence H. Williams

Classifying Fashion, Fashioning Class
Making Sense of Women's Practices, Perceptions and Tastes
Katherine Appleford

Women and Work in Ireland
A Half Century of Attitude and Policy Change
Margret Fine-Davis

For more information about this series, please visit: www.routledge.com/Routledge-Advances-in-Sociology/book-series/SE0511

"Over the last half century social scientists throughout the Western world have studied women's participation in the paid labor force, along with its antecedents, correlates, and consequences. In this exemplary monograph, one of Ireland's leading scholars focuses the spotlight on her adopted country, Eire, sharing with us both the methods and the findings of five decades of meticulous survey research."

Faye J. Crosby, *Distinguished Professor of Psychology Emerita, University of California, Santa Cruz*

"In this fascinating book, M. Fine-Davis, a top scholar in the field of European social policies, brilliantly demonstrates how and why women's roles and status have so dramatically been changing in Ireland from the 1970s onwards. She adopts a systemic approach and underlines the catalytic effect of EU membership and the key role played by the women's movement. Based on a rich set of data, this book also provides a rigorous analysis of how social attitudes, trends in women's labour force participation and developing social policy intersected. In the end, a must-read book for academics and their students working in these fields."

Jeanne Fagnani, *Emeritus Senior Research Fellow, National Centre for Scientific Research (CNRS-University of Paris 1, Sorbonne)*

"This books tells a well-evidenced story of five decades of change in women's participation in the Irish labour force, from the 1970s onwards, and unpacks the ramifications for workplace discrimination, women's well-being, childcare and the division of labour. It provides a fascinating case study of how Irish social policy plays catch-up with changing behaviours and attitudes and demonstrates Ireland's ongoing, albeit uneven, progress in casting off the patriarchal legacy that limits equality for women and work."

Jacqueline Scott, *Emerita Professor of Empirical Sociology, University of Cambridge*

"Drawing on an extensive range of data, Margret Fine-Davis rigorously examines the evidence as regards continuities and changes in attitudes, patterns and policies around women and paid work in Ireland from the 1970s to the present day, locating these in an international context. There have been many welcome changes (not least the ending of the Marriage Bar in the 1970s). But this book also documents disquieting continuities including an inadequate child care system and substantial inequalities in the distribution of domestic tasks and child care: such continuities being very much in evidence in the COVID-19 situation."

Pat O'Connor, *Professor Emeritus of Sociology and Social Policy, University of Limerick and Visiting Professor, Geary Institute, University College Dublin*

Women and Work in Ireland

A Half Century of Attitude and Policy Change

Margret Fine-Davis

Routledge
Taylor & Francis Group
LONDON AND NEW YORK

First published 2021
by Routledge
2 Park Square, Milton Park, Abingdon, Oxon OX14 4RN

and by Routledge
605 Third Avenue, New York, NY 10017

First issued in paperback 2022

Routledge is an imprint of the Taylor & Francis Group, an informa business

Publisher's Note
The publisher has gone to great lengths to ensure the quality of this reprint but points out that some imperfections in the original copies may be apparent.

British Library Cataloguing-in-Publication Data
A catalogue record for this book is available from the British Library

Library of Congress Cataloging-in-Publication Data
A catalog record for this book has been requested

ISBN: 978-0-367-56491-9 (pbk)
ISBN: 978-1-138-02975-0 (hbk)
ISBN: 978-1-315-10367-9 (ebk)

DOI: 10.4324/9781315103679

Typeset in Goudy
by Apex CoVantage, LLC

This book is dedicated to the memory of
Monica Barnes, T.D.,
who was a Member of Dáil Éireann, 1982–1992, 1997–2002
and Chair of the Joint Oireachtas Committee on Women's Rights, 1987–1992.
She was a mentor and role model to me and many others, and an inspiring leader and voice for women's rights and social change.

Contents

List of figures and tables

Figures

Tables

Preface

As an American social psychologist, I have had a unique opportunity to witness the transformation of Ireland from a traditional Catholic state to a modern, more pluralistic one, which in some ways is now ahead of America in its liberalism – for example, by being the first country to have voted for the equal rights of same sex couples to get married, and indeed to elect a gay Taoiseach (Prime Minister). I came to Ireland from New York in the beginning of 1973, when this transformation was just beginning to get underway. The issue of contraception was in the news all of the time, taking up the letters columns of the main newspapers on a daily basis. At an anecdotal level, one woman, when at a gynaecologist's office to obtain family planning, was told by the doctor: "But you don't know if you need it, you haven't demonstrated your fertility!" There was no equal pay, and one could read job advertisements in the newspapers with different pay scales for men and women, and indeed for married men vs. others. In fact, very few married women were working in Ireland when I arrived – just 7.5%. I planned to do a PhD in Psychology at Trinity College on comparative theories of attitude change, but was delighted instead to be allowed by the head of the department, Professor Derek W. Forrest (1926–2015), to do my PhD dissertation on what really interested me, namely attitudes towards the role and status of women in Ireland, with particular reference to employment status of married women. I am grateful to the Irish Department of Labour for supporting the fieldwork for this dissertation, which took place in 1975. One of the articles which emerged from this research was "Social-psychological predictors of employment status of married women in Ireland," *Journal of Marriage and the Family*, *1979*, *41*(1), 145–58. This article helped to identify the characteristics of married women which determined whether or not they were in the labour force. It forms the basis of Chapter 3, with permission from the *Journal*.

I have had the privilege to participate in this society in ways that I could not have imagined had I remained in my home country. For example, I was invited by the minister of state at the Department of Labour, Brendan Daly, T.D., to be an independent member of the Working Party on Child Care Facilities for Working Parents in 1981, where I sat with other members, including those representing the Social Partners – the Irish Business and Employers Confederation (IBEC) and the Irish Congress of Trade Unions (ICTU) – Government departments and other organisations. The subject of childcare is something which has interested me for the last forty years and is the focus of Chapter 6 in this book. In this context, I carried out a nationwide survey of the attitudes of mothers to childcare and employment which forms an annex to the Working Party's Report (1983). I am grateful to the Working Party and the Department of Labour for asking me to carry out this research and for funding it. I include some of the data from this early survey in Chapter 6. I continued my work on childcare and in 2007 was asked to write a briefing paper for the Irish Congress of Trade Unions (by David Joyce, equality officer, and Sallyanne Kinahan, assistant general secretary) on childcare policy in Ireland. I also include material from this briefing paper in Chapter 6.

My work in Ireland grew to include the growing area of social indicators, and subjective social indicators in particular. In this context I was an Irish delegate to the Working Party on Social Problem Indicators in Contemporary Europe of Statistical Office of the European Communities from 1975, together with my late husband and collaborator, Professor Earl E. Davis (1932–1992), he representing the Economic and Social Research Institute and I the Institute of Public Administration. Two harmonised surveys were carried out in the then eight member countries of the European Economic Community (EEC), the second on the quality of working life in 1978. We added a special section to the Irish survey, which had to do with women and work and related social attitudes. Some of the resulting data formed the basis of a chapter in a book: "Housework vs. employment: Quality of working life and psychological well-being among Irish married women," in M. Safir and M. Mednick et al. (Eds.), *Women's Worlds: From the New Scholarship*. NY: Praeger. This chapter is largely reproduced in Chapter 4 of this book, with permission from the publisher.

This early work from the 1970s and 1980s helps to set the stage for the developments which occurred in the subsequent decades.

The mid 1970s were a time of great social change, stimulated in no small part by Ireland's membership of the European Community from 1973 onwards. This led directly to the enactment of equal pay and equal opportunity legislation (the Anti-Discrimination (Pay) Act of 1974 and the Employment Equality Act [1977]), as all members of the then European Economic Community were required to implement EEC directives agreed by the European Community. Through my work on *Attitudes toward the role of women: Implications for Equal Employment Opportunity* (1977) for the Department of Labour, I had the opportunity to meet with the Minister for Labour, Michael O'Leary, T.D. (1936–2006), and John Horgan, his social and economic advisor, on these issues, and as is often the case when academics interact with politicians and civil servants, it helps to root the academic work in political reality.

It was of particular interest to explore whether the anti-discrimination legislation, i.e., the Anti-Discrimination (Pay) Act of 1974 and the Employment Equality Act (1977), had had any impact on women's perceived discrimination during this period. Initial comparisons were made in 1986 with the 1975 data, enabling us to compare the level of discrimination experienced by women in 1975 with that experienced in 1986. These items were then replicated in a study carried out in 2005, so that we were able to see how women's experience of discrimination had changed over a thirty-year period of time. The results comparing the data from the 1975 and 1986 studies were presented in Volume II (*Issues Related to Equal Employment Opportunity*) of a series of three reports (*Changing Gender Role Attitudes in Ireland: 1975–1986*) published by the Joint Oireachtas Committee on Women's Rights of the Irish Parliament in 1988. I wish to acknowledge here the funding from the Joint Oireachtas Committee on Women's Rights which supported this research and, in particular, the support, encouragement and guidance of Monica Barnes, T.D. (1936–2018), chair of the Joint Oireachtas Committee at this time. When the study was being discussed prior to funding, Monica Barnes was vice-chair and Maire Geoghegan-Quinn, T.D. (the first woman to be appointed a cabinet minister in the history of the Irish state) was chair. I recall meeting with both of them in the Dáil to discuss the parameters of the study, and Maire Geoghegan-Quinn said she would be in favour of supporting the research as long as the sample were to be increased to include a rural sample as well as a Dublin sample. This not only led to a more representative sample, as the 1975 data were from Dublin only, but also to a larger sample. I am grateful for her intervention at that stage since it led to better quality data for these and subsequent comparisons. Data from this early period is scarce, and we are fortunate that our legislators saw the usefulness of obtaining such data at that time. The Joint Oireachtas Committee reports are paperbacked and are not widely circulated in Ireland, let alone abroad. For this reason, I felt it would be useful to reproduce the key findings from Volume II in this book. These are included in Chapter 5, which deals with perceived discrimination by women in the workplace and barriers to career advancement over time.

The 2005 data were from a separate subsequent survey, which was part of the Work-Life Balance Project. This project was funded by the European Social Fund through the EQUAL Community Initiative, administered through the Department of Enterprise, Trade and Employment. Their support is gratefully acknowledged. In the course of this study we replicated the earlier measures of perceived discrimination and barriers to career advancement, thus enabling us to examine how attitudes had changed in these areas over three points in time: 1975, 1986 and 2005. These data were not published as part of the Work-Life Balance report and hence are being published for the first time here, together with the earlier data from 1975 and 1986. In addition, other data are included from the Work-Life Balance study focusing on attitudes to flexible working and related social policy issues, such as paternity leave. I wish to gratefully acknowledge the collaboration of my colleagues on this project: Mary McCarthy, Grace Edge, Mairéad O'Sullivan, Ciara O'Dwyer, and Keeley Wynne.

The issues of work-life balance and flexible working are the main focus of Chapter 7. In this chapter we also refer to cross-cultural comparisons carried out in the context of a four-country comparative study of working parents. This study,

Fathers and Mothers: Dilemmas of the Work-Life Balance, was carried out in Ireland, France, Italy and Denmark by four main collaborators: Jeanne Fagnani (Centre National de la Recherche Scientifique MATISSE, University of Paris-1 – France), Dino Giovannini (Department of Social, Cognitive and Quantitative Sciences, University of Modena and Reggio Emilia – Italy), Lis Højgaard (Institute of Political Science, University of Copenhagen – Denmark) and myself, with the collaboration of Hilary Clarke (Centre for Gender and Women's Studies, Trinity College Dublin). This study was supported by the European Commission, Directorate General, Employment and Social Affairs; and the Irish Department of Justice, Equality and Law Reform, who provided national co-funding through the National Development Plan (NDP) 2000–2006. We are most grateful to these bodies for this support. Our work on this study was initially presented as a report to the European Commission. It was later published as a book by Kluwer (2004) and subsequently published in Italian by Il Mulino in 2007 through the efforts of Dino Giovannini in order to make the results more accessible to an Italian audience. We refer to some of the key findings from the 2004 volume in Chapter 7, with permission from Kluwer.

In the case of all of these studies, the sampling, fieldwork and data analyses were carried out by the Economic and Social Research Institute (ESRI), Dublin. The earlier studies from the 1970s and 1980s were overseen by Professor Brendan Whelan, then head of the survey unit. The later studies, including the Fathers and Mothers study and the 2005 Work-Life Balance study, were overseen by Professor James Williams when he was head of the survey unit of the ESRI. I am indebted to both Professors Whelan and Williams, whose expertise was invaluable in bringing these studies to fruition. More recently, Bertrand Maitre, senior research officer in the ESRI, carried out further analyses of the 2005 data to make it comparable to the earlier data sets. I am most grateful for his assistance. I am also grateful to the Central Statistics Office for carrying out a special run on the 2016 Quarterly National Household Survey data on childcare.

Chapter 8 discusses the implications of the previous chapters for men, for gender relations and for social policy. We draw upon the international literature and in particular refer to the work of Helen Russell and Frances McGinnity and their colleagues at the ESRI, Dublin, on a range of subjects relating to women, employment, caring and domestic work. We also draw upon some of the cross-cultural findings from the Fathers and Mothers study in relation to men and women's reciprocal perceptions concerning their contributions to childcare and domestic work. Some more recent data from a nationwide study of 1,404 Irish men and women in the childbearing age group concerning attitudes to changing gender roles, family formation and relationships are also included here. This study, carried out in 2009–2010, was supported by the Family Support Agency. Their support is gratefully acknowledged. Following a report to the Family Support Agency in 2011, the results were then published as a book in 2016. Some findings are presented here with permission from Manchester University Press.

Thus, this volume brings together selected findings from social research carried out over a significant period in Ireland's history, one in which the role and status of women changed dramatically. We hope that these findings help to paint a picture of how attitudes and behaviour changed and policy tried to catch up with them. It is an unfolding story.

I wish to express my thanks to Prof Daniel Faas, former Head, and Prof Richard Layte, Head, of the Sociology Department, Trinity College, for their ongoing encouragement and facilitation of my research. My thanks also go to Amanda Holzworth for her meticulous work, particularly on the tables, on several preceding publications which fed into this volume and for her work on this book itself. Finally, I wish to thank Dr Gerald Morgan, Director of the Chaucer Hub, for his encouragement of this work and, as he is a noted medieval English scholar, for his occasional helpful comments on grammar and style.

Margret Fine-Davis
Dublin, 17 April 2020

Chapter 1

Background and introduction

Until relatively recently Ireland was a more traditional society relative to many other Western countries and for centuries women's role in Ireland was a traditional and subordinate one, influenced in large part by the power and authority of the Catholic Church (Chubb, 1971; Flanagan, 1975; Mac Curtain and Ó Corráin, 1978; Robinson, 1978; Whyte, 1980; Inglis, 1987, 1998; Hornsby-Smith and Whelan, 1994; O'Connor, 1998; Garvin, 2004; Craven, 2006, 2010; Ferriter, 2009). It was not always thus. Ó Corráin observed that while early Irish society up through the sixth and early seventh centuries was patriarchal, from the late seventh and early eighth century the situation changed fairly rapidly. Women were granted extensive rights during this period, particularly with regard to marriage, divorce and property rights under secular law and this held until the middle ages (1978, p. 1). The wide ranging and flexible grounds for divorce available to women under the Brehon Laws "served as a guarantee of extensive women's rights and protected women in a way which was remarkably different from the customs of other European countries" (Ibid., p. 8). Ó Corráin believes that historical developments which followed, beginning with the Norman invasion in 1169 and followed by the imposition of English law in the early seventeenth century, had the effect of curtailing the natural development of these Gaelic customs:

> As a result, in its attitude to women and their place in society – as in its attitude to many other matters – modern Ireland enjoys no continuity with its Gaelic past.
>
> (Ó Corráin, 1978, p. 11)

Since Ó Corráin wrote in the late 1970s, many changes have taken place in Ireland, which have given Irish women some of the rights which they had under the Brehon Laws, including divorce, finally enacted in 1995. However, in the last several hundred years women's role in Ireland has been traditional in comparison with many other Western countries, and it is only in the last fifty years that significant reforms and policy changes have taken place to modernise the position of women and the society as a whole in the area of gender equality. It is this time period up to the present day on which we focus in the book, and our substantive focus is on the area of work, specifically women's entrance into the workforce in significantly greater numbers from the 1970s onwards and the social policy issues which ensued in response to this new situation. We take a social-psychological approach, focusing on social attitudes and how they have changed over time. We also take a social policy approach, juxtaposing social attitudes and attitude change with relevant social policy developments of the day, both in terms of policies of Government, the Social Partners and other relevant non-Governmental bodies and in terms of legislation, both Irish and that emanating from the European Community.

Up until the early 1970s, while it was acceptable for single women to participate in the workforce, it was unusual for married women to do so. Their proper role was seen to be in the home. This was explicitly expressed in the Irish Constitution (1937):

> 2.1 In particular, the State recognises that by her life within the home, woman gives to the State a support without which the common good cannot be achieved.
> 2.2 The State shall, therefore, endeavor to ensure that mothers should not be obliged by economic necessity to engage in labour to neglect of their duties in the home.
>
> (Article 41.2, Constitution of Ireland, 1937)

Because married women were expected to make their lives in the home, it probably did not seem unreasonable to create a social order which actually provided obstacles to their participation in employment. These included a lack of contraception, so that women could control neither the number nor the spacing of the children they had, nor did they have the option of having no children if that was their wish. There was a lack of equality in the workplace, notably in the area of pay. It was normal to see job advertisements in the newspapers with different pay scales which favoured men, particularly married men, who were seen as having to support families and hence be entitled to a higher wage. The tax laws also were designed to discourage married women from working, as their income was added to that of their husband and taxed at his highest marginal rate. In the early 1970s the highest marginal rate was 70%, and there was at times a 10% surtax, bringing the highest marginal rate at that time to as much as 77%. Thus married women whose husbands earned salaries taxed at the highest marginal rate could expect to take home just 23% of their salary. Clearly this was a disincentive to working. Indeed Walsh and O'Toole pointed out in 1973:

> A substantial reduction in the tax liability of working wives would be the most appropriate policy for the Government to pursue in this area at present. This policy would extend the effective freedom of choice of married women regarding entry to the labour force, by allowing them to retain a larger proportion of their gross pay. It is likely that some who are now deterred from

> working by the burden of taxation at a high marginal rate, in addition to child-care etc. expenses, would find it worthwhile to work if their tax liability were substantially reduced.
>
> (1973, p. 143)

As there were very few childcare centres, if a woman worked outside the home she would have to arrange and pay for her own childcare. If these obstacles were not enough there was also a "marriage bar" in place up until 1973, which required that women had to give up their jobs upon marriage if they were employed in the public service, in teaching and in some other employments (see Daly, 1978, for a discussion of this). Thus, it was a determined woman indeed who would face all of these obstacles and go out to work in the Ireland of the early 1970s and before.

The social change which began in the 1970s and gained momentum in the following decades was a major upheaval for the society, having profound effects and changing it in ways that would be impossible to reverse. The women's movement, which was occurring internationally since the late 1960s, emerged in Ireland in the early 1970s, and it was one of the prime catalysts for social change in women's roles in this country. Also, significantly, Ireland joined the European Community in 1973, and this too had a catalytic effect in spurring a period of rapid social change which impacted on women's roles. These two major influences independently, and undoubtedly synergistically as well, had a profound effect on gender-role attitudes and behaviour in the country and indeed on the emergence of related social policy responses.

All of these influences were reinforced by a series of administrative and legislative changes which had significant implications for the role and status of women. These began with the removal of the marriage bar (1973), followed in rapid succession by legislation for equal pay (passed in 1974, implemented in 1975), employment equality (1977), contraception (1979) and taxation of married women (1980). Legislation concerning equal pay and equal employment were direct results of EU membership, as they followed EU directives. There was extensive public debate on contraception in the 1970s. In 1971 senator and barrister Mary Robinson, later to become Ireland's first woman president, attempted to introduce a contraception bill into the Senate but was not allowed to. However, in 1973 in the McGee case, the Supreme Court ruled that contraceptives could be imported for personal use. This decision helped, through a series of interim steps over several years, to precipitate legislation in 1979 in this area. In 1980 there was also a significant change to the tax code which removed the discriminatory tax laws which had served to discriminate against married women (see Scannell, 2000). Further significant changes followed, including the legalisation of divorce (1995), following two national referenda in 1986 and 1995, the latter successful by a very small margin (O'Connor, 1998).

All of these changes profoundly affected the role and status of women in Ireland and removed impediments to their freedom and labour force participation. They also greatly facilitated their participation in the labour market. Increasing numbers of married women entered the labour force from the 1970s onwards (Callen and Farrell, 1991), and this trend has continued to the present day. As a result of this, new issues came to the fore, including the need for childcare, flexible working and work-life balance, and these key policy issues still remain central to the equality agenda not only in Ireland but also in Europe and elsewhere.

This book is about the evolution of women's participation in the labour force over the course of the last five decades of social change in Ireland, the social-psychological factors surrounding it and the policy issues generated by it. The book presents empirical data spanning a 35-year period, with some of this data in the form of replicated measures over time, providing a rich tableau of attitudes concerning women and work in Ireland over time, thus enabling us to see how attitudes have evolved in a number of key areas, together with related policy developments. Several of the surveys referred to used large nationwide representative samples (Fine-Davis, 1983a, 1983b, 2016; Fine-Davis et al., 2005). Others were based on stratified samples (e.g., Fine-Davis, 1988a, 1988b, 1988c), re-weighted wherever possible so as to be comparable to the nationwide samples. The measures used in these studies tap a very wide range of issues concerning women and work and related policy issues. The studies and their methodologies are described in Chapter 2.

The data presented in Chapters 3 through 8 provide an historical overview of the major trends in women's labour force participation and corresponding social attitudes of the day and how these intersected with developing social policy. On the basis of empirical data over time, the book describes women's journey into the world of work, from a subordinate role to a more equal role and sometimes to a leadership role. It begins by looking at what predisposed some married women to enter the labour force in the early 1960s while the majority stayed at home. Who were those 5% of married women who were working outside the home in the early 1960s when it was more usual for women to be housewives and stay at home? It tells the story of the women – particularly the married women who entered the labour force beginning in the 1970s – and explores what made them different from their non-employed counterparts. Chapter 3 presents the research which examined the determinants of married women's labour force participation at this time (Fine-Davis, 1979). It explores which social-psychological characteristics of married women determined whether or not they became employed. The findings from this analysis highlight the characteristics of employed and non-employed married women in the mid-1970s, at the very beginning of Irish women's influx into the labour market. The predictor variables explored included women's own attitudes to labour force participation and gender roles, their perception of the attitudes of their 'important others' (i.e., mother, father, close friend, husband) towards their actual or potential employment and their attitudes to contraception (not yet legally available in Ireland at that time), among others.

While just a very small proportion (precisely 5.2%) of married women were in the labour force in 1961, this rose to 7.5% in 1971, and from that point onwards their participation continued to increase at a very rapid rate and stood at 54% in

2009, with an even higher rate (72.6%) amongst those in the childbearing age group 25–34. Apart from women in the workforce generally, women have also made strides in the political arena: women now comprise one-third of the Irish cabinet, the first woman president of Ireland was elected in 1990 (Smyth, 1992) and two of the last three presidents of Ireland have been women. Thus Irish women's progress in the labour force and indeed in leadership roles has been quite remarkable over such a relatively short period of time.

A key focus of the book is on well-being, and Chapter 4 looks at the effects of employment on married women's well-being, comparing it with that of non-employed married women (Fine-Davis, 1985). The question of whether employment of married women led to greater well-being was a subject of debate beginning in the 1970s (e.g., Oakley, 1974; Hoffman and Nye, 1974; Ferree, 1976), and this controversy in the literature continued into the 1980s and 1990s (e.g., Adelmann, 1988; Hoffman and Youngblade, 1999). The data presented are contextualised in this literature.

Chapter 5 charts the progress of women in the labour force, looking at such issues as discrimination in the workplace (in areas such as hiring, pay, promotion, etc.) and barriers to women's career advancement. It does this from the point of view of employed women as well as others in society, comparing the perceptions of employed women with those other groups. Results from the 1970s and 1980s showed that employed women were less likely to report experiencing discrimination in employment – though they felt other women experienced it – whereas other groups were more likely to see it. Reflecting on these surprising findings might lead one to ask: were women *denying* their own discrimination? Comparisons were made at three points in time (1975, 1986 and 2005) to see to what extent attitudes tapped in 1975 before the equality legislation was introduced changed in later years as a result of equality legislation and other changes in society.

The issue of childcare is examined in Chapter 6, with attitudes to childcare presented from studies going back to the 1970s and 1980s (Fine-Davis, 1983a, 1983b, 1988a) up to more recent times (Fine-Davis et al., 2005; Fine-Davis, 2016), showing the extent to which attitudes have changed or remained the same over the past four decades. The book then examines the policy debates surrounding childcare (e.g., Fine-Davis, 2004; Bradley, 2011; Mahon and Bailey, 2015) and shows how childcare policy has evolved over time (e.g., Hayes, 2002; Fine-Davis, 2007), from virtually no policy to one which aspires to meet expectations of the EU and the OECD (2003, 2006), as well as a more demanding population.

Chapter 7 focuses on the increasingly recognised policy issue of work-life balance. Attitudinal data concerning people's attitudes to flexible working and work-life balance are presented from several surveys, including a nationwide Irish survey (Fine-Davis et al., 2005), as well as a comparative European survey of working parents with young children (Fine-Davis et al., 2004). This study, which included Ireland, France, Italy and Denmark, explores attitudes of working parents towards flexible working and other related issues as well as the relationship between flexible working arrangements and well-being. Current Irish attitudes to work-life balance issues are included from a more recent study (Fine-Davis, 2016) and compared with findings from earlier studies. The relationship between work-life balance policies and employee well-being cross-culturally is a particular focus of this chapter, continuing the focus on well-being which was addressed in Chapter 4.

The concluding chapter (Chapter 8) focuses on the future and what all of this means in terms of gender relations and, more particularly, men's roles. This chapter engages with the evolution of thinking in this area, particularly in relation to discussion of the male role and social policy (e.g., McKeown et al., 1998; Hearn, 2001; Esping-Andersen, 2009; Haas, 2014). It synthesises key findings from the preceding chapters and poses questions concerning how women's role in the workplace impacts on men. To what extent do men need to adapt their role to better fit with women's changing roles? To what extent should workplaces change to accommodate men and women's needs for work-life balance and childcare responsibilities? To what extent has policy responded to these issues and to what extent and in what ways does it need to respond more fully?

We are fortunate to have a rich set of survey data covering a range of issues related to women and work in Ireland and related gender and policy issues. These span the years 1975 to 2010 – a 35-year period which captures a key phase of social and attitude change in Ireland. The social-psychological data on women and work over time is presented against the backdrop of changing gender-role attitudes (Fine-Davis, 2015) and social policy developments which emerged in response to women's increasing labour force participation, as well as to external influences, such as EU directives. Policy developments, from the early 1970s to the present, are documented so that the book provides an overview of five decades of social change from 1970 to 2020, showing how social attitudes and behaviour preceded and often precipitated social policy developments.

References

Adelmann, P. K. (1988). *Employment and Psychological Well-Being in Women: A Meta-Analysis*. Presented at the Annual Convention of the American Psychological Association, New York.

Bradley, S. (2011). *Inside the Black Box: An Exploration of the Impact of Action and Activity in the Inner Spheres of Policy Making on Early Childhood Education and Care Policy*. PhD dissertation, Dublin Institute of Technology, Dublin.

Callen, T. and Farrell, B. (1991). *Women's Participation in the Irish Labour Market*. Dublin: National Economic and Social Council.

Chubb, B. (1971). *The Government and Politics of Ireland* (2nd ed.). Oxford: Oxford University Press. London and New York: Longman, 1982.

Craven, E. V. (2006). *An Analysis of the Social, Religious and Gender Role Attitudes of Catholic and Protestant Women in the Republic of Ireland: A Comparative Study*. PhD dissertation, Centre for Gender and Women's Studies, Trinity College Dublin.

Craven, E. V. (2010). *A Comparison of the Social, Religious, and Gender Role Attitudes of Catholic and Protestant Women in the Republic of Ireland*. Lewiston, Queenston and Lampeter: The Edwin Mellen Press.

Daly, M. E. (1978). Women, work and trade unionism. In: M. MacCurtain and D. Ó Corráin (Eds.), *Women in Irish Society: The Historical Dimension*. Dublin: Arlen House, pp. 71–81.

Esping-Andersen, G. (2009). *The Incomplete Revolution: Adapting to Women's New Roles*. Cambridge: Polity Press.

Ferree, M. M. (1976). Working class jobs: Housework and paid work as sources of satisfaction. *Social Problems*, 23 (4), 431–441.

Ferriter, D. (2009). *Occasions of Sin: Sex and Society in Modern Ireland*. Dublin: Profile Books.

Fine-Davis, M. (1979). Social-psychological predictors of employment status of married women in Ireland. *Journal of Marriage and the Family*, 47 (1), 145–158.

Fine-Davis, M. (1983a). *Women and Work in Ireland: A Social Psychological Perspective*. Dublin: Council for the Status of Women.

Fine-Davis, M. (1983b). Mothers' attitudes toward child care and employment: A nationwide survey. In: Working Party on Child Care Facilities for Working Parents, *Report to the Minister for Labour*. Dublin: Stationery Office, pp. 73–168.

Fine-Davis, M. (1985). Housework vs. employment: Quality of working life and psychological well-being among Irish married women. In: M. Safir, M. Mednick, D. N. Israeli and J. Bernard (eds.), *Women's Worlds: From the New Scholarship*. New York: Praeger, pp. 105–116.

Fine-Davis, M. (1988a). Changing gender role attitudes in Ireland: 1975–1986. Vol. I: Attitudes Toward the Role and Status of Women, 1975–1986. In: *First Report of the Second Joint Oireachtas [Parliamentary] Committee on Women's Rights* (Pl. 5609). Dublin: The Stationery Office, May.

Fine-Davis, M. (1988b). Changing gender role attitudes in Ireland: 1975–1986. Vol. III: Attitudes Towards Moral Issues in Relation to Voting Behaviour in Recent Referenda. In: *Third Report of the Second Joint Committee on Women's Rights* (Pl. 5796). Dublin: The Stationery Office, July.

Fine-Davis, M. (1988c). Changing gender role attitudes in Ireland: 1975–1986. Vol. II: Issues Related to Equal Employment Opportunity. In: *Second Report of the Second Joint Committee on Women's Rights* (Pl. 5673). Dublin: The Stationery Office, June.

Fine-Davis, M. (2004). The childcare policy debate in Ireland. *Administration*, 52 (2), 36–56.

Fine-Davis, M. (2007). *Childcare in Ireland Today*. Briefing Paper to the Irish Congress of Trade Unions. www.ictu.ie/download/pdf/briefing_paper_on_childcare_final_draft_14_june_2007_mfd.pdf.

Fine-Davis, M. (2015). *Gender Roles in Ireland: Three Decades of Attitude Change*. London: Routledge.

Fine-Davis, M. (2016). *Changing Gender Roles and Attitudes to Family Formation in Ireland*. Manchester: Manchester University Press.

Fine-Davis, M., Fagnani, J., Giovannini, D., Højgaard, L. and Clarke, H. (2004). *Fathers and Mothers: Dilemmas of the Work-Life Balance – A Comparative Study in Four European Countries*. Dordrecht, Boston and London: Kluwer Academic Publishers.

Fine-Davis, M., McCarthy, M., Edge, G. and O'Dwyer, C. (2005). *Work-Life Balance and Social Inclusion in Ireland: Results of a Nationwide Survey*. Dublin: National Flexi-Work

Partnership (Centre for Gender and Women's Studies, Trinity College Dublin; IBEC; ICTU; FÁS, Age Action Ireland and Aware).

Flanagan, D. (1975). The more subtle discrimination. *Studies* (Autumn), 231–242.

Garvin, T. (2004). *Preventing the Future: Why Was Ireland Poor for so Long?* Dublin: Gill & Macmillan.

Haas, L. (2014). *Paid Parental Leave for Fathers? Lessons from Sweden*. Guest Lecture, Trinity College Dublin, 21 October.

Hayes, N. (2002). *Children's Rights – Whose Right? A Review of Child Policy Development in Ireland*. Studies in Public Policy 9. Dublin: The Policy Institute, Trinity College Dublin.

Hearn, J. (2001). *Men and Gender Equality: Resistance, Responsibilities and Reaching Out*. Keynote Paper, Men and Gender Equality, 15–16 March 2001, Örebro, Sweden.

Hoffman, L. W. and Nye, F. I. (1974). *Working Mothers*. San Francisco: Jossey-Bass.

Hoffman, L. W. and Youngblade, L. M. (1999). *Mothers at Work: Effects on Children's Well-Being*. Cambridge: Cambridge University Press.

Hornsby-Smith, M. P. and Whelan, C. T. (1994). Religious and moral values. In: C. T. Whelan (Ed.), *Values and Social Change in Ireland*. Dublin: Gill & Macmillan, pp. 7–44.

Inglis, T. (1987). *Moral Monopoly: Catholic Church in Modern Irish Society*. Dublin: Gill and Macmillan.

Inglis, T. (1998). *Moral Monopoly: The Rise and Fall of the Catholic Church in Modern Ireland* (2nd ed.). Dublin: University College Dublin Press.

Mac Curtain, M. and Ó Corráin, D. (Eds.) (1978). *Women in Irish Society: The Historical Dimension*. Dublin: Arlen House.

Mahon, E. and Bailey, J. (2015). The incomplete revolution: Development of childcare policies in Ireland. In: D. Kutsar and M. Kuronen (Eds.), *Local Welfare Policy Making in European Cities*. Social Indicators Research Series No. 59. New York and Heidelberg: Springer, pp. 149–160.

McKeown, K., Ferguson, H. and Rooney, D. (1998). *Changing Fathers? Fatherhood and Family Life in Modern Ireland*. Cork: The Collins Press.

Oakley, A. (1974). *The Sociology of Housework*. London: Martin Robertson & Co. Ltd.

O'Connor, P. (1998). *Emerging Voices: Women in Contemporary Irish Society*. Dublin: Institute of Public Administration.

Ó Corráin, D. (1978). Women in early Irish society. In: M. MacCurtain and D. Ó Corráin (Eds.), *Women in Irish Society: The Historical Dimension*. Dublin: Arlen House, pp. 1–13.

OECD (2003). *Babies and Bosses – Reconciling Work and Family Life: Vol. 2 Austria, Ireland and Japan*. Paris: Organisation for Economic Co-operation and Development.

OECD (2006). *Starting Strong II: Early Childhood Education and Care*. Paris: Organisation for Economic Co-operation and Development.

Robinson, M. (1978). Women and the new Irish state. In: M. MacCurtain and D. Ó Corráin (Eds.), *Women in Irish Society: The Historical Dimension*. Dublin: Arlen House, pp. 58–70.

Scannell, Y. (2000). The taxation of married women – Murphy v. Attorney General (1982). In: E. O'Dell (Ed.), *Leading Cases of the Twentieth Century*. Dublin: Round Hall Sweet and Maxwell, pp. 327–352.

Smyth, A. (1992). A great day for the women of Ireland . . . The meaning of Mary Robinson's presidency for Irish women. *The Canadian Journal of Irish Studies*, 18 (1), 61–75. Women and Irish Politics, July.

Walsh, B. M. and O'Toole, A. (1973). *Women and Employment in Ireland: Results of a National Survey*. Paper No. 69. Dublin: The Economic and Social Research Institute.

Whyte, J. H. (1980). *Church and State in Modern Ireland 1923–1979* (2nd ed.). Dublin: Gill and Macmillan.

Chapter 2

Method

Overview of studies: 1975–2010

This chapter presents an overview of the various studies which provided the empirical data for the book, as well as key methodological information for each study, including sampling, data collection procedures, etc. Selected results from seven studies are presented in Chapters 3–8. These include seven separate attitudinal surveys carried out over a 35 year period (1975 to 2010). Several of the surveys had comparable measures of attitudes related to women and work. The surveys took place in **1975** (Fine-Davis, 1976, 1977, 1979a, 1979b, 1983a, 2015), **1978** (Fine-Davis, 1983b, 1984, 1985a, 1985b, 2015), **1981** (Fine-Davis, 1983c), **1986** (Fine-Davis, 1988a, 1988b, 1988c, 2015), **2002** (Fine-Davis et al., 2004), **2005** (Fine-Davis, McCarthy, Edge, et al., 2005) and **2010** (Fine-Davis, 2011, 2016).

Attitudes towards the role and status of women

The initial study carried out in 1975 focused on attitudes towards the role and status of women in Ireland, with particular reference to employment status of married women. The focus on married women's employment status was chosen due to their very low participation rate at the time of the research, which began in 1973. The most recent census data (1971) at that time revealed that this stood at just 7.2%, a very low figure compared to other Western countries. In addition to collecting detailed data on attitudes to the role and status of women and gender roles, the study gathered data on selected issues related to women and work, including perceived discrimination in the workplace. This initial study provided baseline data at an early period in Irish history when women's issues were just coming to the fore.

Women, work and well-being

The initial 1975 study was followed by several subsequent studies. The first of these was carried out in 1978 in the context of an Irish nationwide survey of the quality of working life which was part of an eight-nation harmonised survey of subjective social indicators, sponsored by the Statistical Office of the European Communities, in the then eight member nations of the European Community. This survey provided data cross-culturally on quality of working life and also enabled the author to add an additional set of attitudinal items specifically concerning women and work in Ireland (Fine-Davis, 1983b). This eight-nation survey also offered the opportunity to examine the data relating to women, work and well-being cross-culturally (Fine-Davis, 1984, 1985a) as well as to compare men and women (Fine-Davis, 1985c). Cross-national comparisons were carried out for the European Commission (Bureau for Questions Concerning Employment and Equal Treatment of Women, Directorate-General Employment, Social Affairs and Education). These data were presented to the Commission as a report (Fine-Davis, 1984) and also appeared in summary form in a journal article (Fine-Davis, 1985a). The Irish data from this survey also provided the opportunity to compare the effects of employment and non-employment on married women's well-being (Fine-Davis, 1985b), an issue which was a focus of much research in the United States and elsewhere at that time (e.g., Hoffman and Nye, 1974; Cochrane and Stopes-Roe, 1981; Adelmann, 1988). A chapter presenting these results was included in a book (Safir et al., 1985), which brought together work in the newly emerging field of women's studies, following the First International Interdisciplinary Congress on Women, held in Haifa in 1981. This was followed by a second conference held in Groningen, the Netherlands, and we hosted the Third International Interdisciplinary Congress on Women at Trinity College Dublin in 1987. This series of international congresses on women's scholarship has continued to the present day.

A third major survey was conducted in Ireland in 1986 with a grant from the Joint Oireachtas Committee on Women's Rights of the Irish Parliament. This was designed to replicate and extend the original 1975 research to see to what extent attitudes towards the role of women had changed, as well as to explore new emerging issues. While the original 1975 study was on a Dublin sample, the 1986 survey was extended to include a national sample. The results of this study were presented in a series of three reports published by the Joint Oireachtas Committee on Women's Rights, which documented major attitudinal change during the period 1975–1986 and also included data on newer social issues such as divorce and abortion (Fine-Davis, 1988a, 1988b, 1988c). Results from the first report (Fine-Davis, 1988a) concerning changing gender-role attitudes and from the third report focusing on attitudes to divorce, abortion and other moral issues (Fine-Davis, 1988c) were included in the author's recent book (Fine-Davis, 2015).

Equal employment opportunity

In Chapter 5 of the present book, data are presented from the second report of the Joint Oireachtas Committee on Women's Rights, which dealt with issues related to equal employment opportunity (Fine-Davis, 1988b). In particular we present data over time on perceived discrimination and barriers to women's career advancement from 1975 to 1986, a period in which key legislation in the area of employment opportunity was passed in Ireland, including equal pay and equal opportunity. These same measures were replicated again in an Irish nationwide representative sample in the context of a survey of work-life balance (Fine-Davis, McCarthy, Edge, et al., 2005). The more recent data from 2005 are unpublished and hence this time series, covering a 30-year time span with three points in time – 1975, 1986 and 2005 – is presented for the first time.

Childcare

The issue of childcare was the focus of a nationwide survey of mother's attitudes to childcare (Fine-Davis, 1983c) commissioned by the Government Working Party on Child Care Facilities for Working Parents (1983) and conducted in 1981. Selected data from this study are presented in Chapter 6. In addition, selected data on childcare are also presented from three other studies: (1) the 1978 survey of the quality of working life (Fine-Davis, 1983b), (2) a cross-cultural comparative study conducted in 2002 in Ireland, France, Italy and Denmark (Fine-Davis et al., 2004) and (3) the 2005 Irish nationwide study (Fine-Davis, McCarthy, Edge, et al., 2005). Results from these four studies will enable us to explore attitudes to childcare over time, from 1981 to 2005. The comparative aspects of childcare provision, attitudes to childcare and the relationship between childcare and work-life balance in four European countries will be highlighted (Fine-Davis et al., 2004). In addition, we will also refer to selected data on attitudes to childcare obtained in a more recent study of attitudes to family formation carried out in 2010 (Fine-Davis, 2011, 2016).

Work-life balance and flexible working

Attitudes to work-life balance and flexible working were addressed in the earlier studies conducted in 1978, 1981 and 1986, as well as in the more recent studies conducted in 2002, 2005 and 2010. Where we have cross-cultural comparative data, notably in the 2002 study (Fine-Davis et al., 2004), this is included and highlighted.

The variables in the first four studies included measures of gender-role attitudes and stereotypes as well as attitudes to several of the major social policy issues of the day: maternal employment, equal pay, equal opportunity, taxation of married women, contraception, divorce and abortion. These issues resulted in developments in public policy over this period, including in many cases, legislation. The availability of comparable attitudinal data at several points in time over this key period of social change enables us to see to what extent attitudes may have stimulated legislation and public policy and to what extent changes in legislation and public policy may have in turn facilitated further attitude change. The passage of legislation concerning equal pay (implemented in 1975), employment equality (1977), contraception (1979) and taxation of married women (1980) after collection of baseline data in 1975 offered a unique natural experiment which made it possible to examine attitudes towards these issues both before the legislation and at two points afterwards. We examined these effects in my earlier book (Fine-Davis, 2015). While we could not definitively attribute causation here, we could assume that public attitudes contributed to a readiness to enact legislation, and changes in legislation and related public policies were likely in turn to have facilitated further attitude change. In this book we will be focusing on different policy issues, including perceived discrimination in the workplace and educational system, perceived barriers to career advancement, work-life balance and childcare. We have data on these issues from several surveys spanning a number of decades. Hence, we will be able to see how attitudes towards these issues have evolved over time and how they have interfaced with – and possibly stimulated – policy developments over this same time period.

The series of studies which forms the basis of this volume is unique in that it includes an extensive range of measures, the majority of which have been developed in Ireland, yielding results which are robust and reliable over a significant time period. The advantage of having a differentiated set of items from the early period is that it provides a baseline against which to measure the effects of key legislation relating to gender equality which was passed in the period 1975–1980 in the immediate aftermath and allows for the measurement of change over time.

The studies carried out in 2005 and 2010 contain extensive data on attitudes to work-life balance and related social policies, and the study from 2010 includes newer measures of gender-role attitudes, including those eliciting a "response" to changes in men's and women's roles. Thus, the combined data sets offer a unique opportunity to measure attitude change over a considerable period of time, whilst also examining attitudes to newer issues as they have emerged.

The methodology of each of the studies is described here chronologically.

1975 Study: attitudes towards the role and status of women in Ireland

Pilot and pre-test

The 1975 study of attitudes towards the role and status of women in Ireland was one of the first of its kind to be carried out in Ireland. The main purpose of the study was to examine attitudes towards the role of women, with particular focus on employment status of married women. Thus, careful preliminary work was necessary, including review of literature of related work in other countries and well as an in-depth pilot study. The pilot study was carried out in April 1975 with 27 subjects varying in sex, age, socio-economic status and marital status. Face-to-face interviews were conducted using a semi-structured questionnaire to try out the questions as well as to gain new insights and perspectives on attitudes towards gender roles. Interviews lasted approximately one hour. For a fuller description of this phase of the research see Fine-Davis (1976).

The pilot study was followed by an instrument pre-test using a stratified sample of 122 male and female Dublin adults. The instrument consisted of 60 attitude statements presented in Likert format concerning the role and status of women in Ireland. Many of the items were selected from instruments developed in the United States (i.e., Kirkpatrick, 1936; Levinson and Huffman, 1955; Spence and Helmreich, 1972). Spence and Helmreich's (1972) Attitude towards Women Scale was the most widely used instrument at that time. When they carried out their study, Spence and Helmreich reported a dearth in the literature of scales measuring attitudes towards the status of women. Although they drew in part upon the work of Kirkpatrick (1936), they found that his items were in general quite outdated and that male-female relationships and sex-role behavior in the United States had changed considerably from 1936 to 1972. However, in the context of the present study – Ireland in the mid-1970s – many of Kirkpatrick's much earlier items were still relevant, and indeed many of Spence and Helmreich's that were relevant in the United States in 1972 were not yet appropriate for Ireland. Therefore, a careful selection of items was necessary. Some of these were modified and others newly developed – in part on the basis of the pilot interviews – in an attempt to elicit attitudes particularly relevant to the Irish context.

The pre-test data were factor analysed to examine the dimensionality of the attitudes as well as for purposes of data reduction (Fine-Davis, 1976). On the basis of this analysis, 33 items were selected for inclusion in the main test instrument. In general, items were selected on the basis of having high loadings on the resulting factors; however, in some cases an item was retained because of the interest and importance of its content even if it was not among the highest loading items. Factor analysis was also carried out in the main 1975 study (Ibid.), and these results were published in Fine-Davis (1983a). The relationship between attitudes to gender roles and personality characteristics was presented in Fine-Davis (1979a). These results were also included in my book which measured attitude change from 1975 to 2005 (Fine-Davis, 2015). What we are presenting here are the data from the 1975 study on predictors of employment status of married women in Chapter 3 (initially published in Fine-Davis, 1979b) and also the data on perceived discrimination from this earlier study as well as from subsequent studies (1986 and 2005) to allow us to see if and how these attitudes had changed over time (in Chapter 5).

Sample and sampling procedures

The main 1975 study was based on a sample of 420 Dublin adults, aged 18 to 65, who were selected using stratified quota sampling procedures. Names and addresses from high- and low-SES neighbourhoods, randomly selected from the Dublin Electoral Register, were used as starting points, in order to optimise randomness. The sample was stratified on the basis of sex, age, socio-economic status and marital status. In order to examine the effect of employment status on married women's attitudes, the sample included an oversampling of married women (N = 240) who were stratified by both employment status and presence or absence of dependent children.

The research design of the main study consisted of two overlapping or "nested" factorial designs that would permit the use of analysis of variance. Given the nature of the research design which necessitated obtaining respondents with very specific combinations of characteristics (e.g., an employed, married woman over 35 of lower socio-economic status with dependent children), it would have been quite inefficient, if not impossible, to utilise strictly random sampling procedures. Stratified quota sampling thus seemed the most appropriate procedure to use; however, within this framework, attempts were made to optimise randomness in subject selection.

Each of 13 interviewers was given six starting points (names and addresses randomly selected from the Dublin Electoral Register). Three of the six were in high-SES neighbourhoods and three in low. Interviewers were instructed to start with the initial name and address and then if that person did not satisfy the characteristics required by their quota, to go from one house to the next on the same side of the street to locate respondents to fill their quotas. Once a completed interview was obtained, the interviewer was instructed to skip five houses. This was to reduce the likelihood of respondents knowing one another as well as to spread the sample out geographically. Once five interviews were obtained in one area, the interviewer was instructed to move to a new starting address. Interviewing was conducted in the evening as well as during the day to facilitate contact with males and employed females.

Each of the stratification categories was defined as follows:

1 *Socio-economic status* was based on own or, in the case of married women, husband's occupational status in terms of the Hall-Jones Scale (Hall and Jones, 1950) Scale of Occupational Prestige, as adapted to the Irish context by Hutchinson (1969). Categories 6, 7, and 8 (skilled manual, semi-skilled manual, and unskilled manual routine) were classified as "low SES," and categories 1–5 (professionally qualified/high administrative, lower professional/ managerial and executive, supervisory – higher grades, supervisory – lower grades, and routine grades – non-manual) were classified as "high SES." This dichotomy was essentially based on a blue collar / white collar distinction and a manual/non-manual distinction.
2 *Age:* The age range of respondents was 18 to 65; as 65 is the usual retirement age, it was used as the upper age limit, since employment status was part of the factorial design. Respondents were dichotomised at age 35, since it was felt that any higher age, such as 40, would probably not adequately reflect age-related attitudinal differences. Thus, those aged 18–34 constituted the "young" group and those 35–65 constituted the "old" group.
3 *Employment status:* The factorial design required that all males and single females be employed. However, married women were stratified by this

characteristic, with half being employed and half non-employed. Employment was defined as "paid employment outside the home." No lower limit of hours worked was placed. This flexible definition of employment was based on (1) the realisation that it would be difficult to obtain the necessary number of married females in all of the appropriate categories if the definition were too stringent, (2) the fact that part-time work is quite a common form of employment for married women and therefore should not be excluded from study and (3) the belief that a job that may take a woman outside the home for even a few hours may be just as psychologically meaningful for her as a job that involves a greater number of hours outside the home.

4 *Presence or absence of dependent children:* This stratification characteristic was also applied only to married women. "Dependent children" was defined as children in primary school or younger. The rationale for this was based on the assumption that children of post-primary school age are usually more self-sufficient, and their care would not likely be as significant a factor for the mother as in the case of younger children. The women "without dependent children" included both women without any children and women with one child or more of post-primary school age, but with no children of primary school age or younger.

A breakdown of the sample by demographic characteristics may be thus summarised as follows: The total sample of 420 consisted of 300 females and 120 males. The 300 females consisted of 240 married women and 60 single women, all of whom were stratified by age and socio-economic status. The 240 married women were further stratified by employment status and presence or absence of dependent children. The 120 males, of whom 60 were married and 60 were single, were further stratified by age and socio-economic status.

Instrument and data collection procedures

The main test questionnaire included the following sets of variables:

a *Attitudes towards the role and status women.* A set of 33 items measuring attitudes towards the role and status of women constituted the main focus of the study. These were presented in modified Likert format, i.e., a six-point scale ranging from "strongly disagree" to "strongly agree," with three levels of agreement (strong, moderate and slight) and three levels of disagreement. The scale was constructed in such a way as to encourage an "agree" or "disagree" response and to discourage a "don't know" response. The scale was however coded as if it were a seven point scale with a code of '4' being the theoretical midpoint. This code accommodated those respondents who insisted on making a mark in between the two sides of the continuum, indicating a "don't know" response.

b *Social-psychological and personality characteristics.* A set of 33 items measuring social-psychological and personality constructs was also presented in a similar Likert format ranging from "strongly disagree" to "strongly agree."

The questionnaire was administered to the respondents in their own homes by trained interviewers of the survey unit of the Economic and Social Research Institute (ESRI), Dublin. The Likert items were self-administering, and the remaining sections were administered by the interviewer. All of the questionnaires were completed in September and October 1975.

1978 Study: study of the quality of working life and attitudes to social issues in Ireland

Sample

Several key items measuring attitudes towards gender roles from the original 1975 study were replicated in a larger nationwide representative study (N = 1,862) of the quality of working life and attitudes to social issues in Ireland carried out in 1978 (Fine-Davis, 1983b) as part of a harmonised cross-national survey of social indicators of working life sponsored by the Statistical Office of the European Communities. The sample was of the adult population of the Republic of Ireland living at non-institutional addresses.

The sample was selected using a computer-based system (RANSAM) which employs the Electoral Register as the sampling frame; the procedure also relies on supplementary information about the population in order to improve the efficiency of the estimates derived from the sample (Whelan, 1977, 1979). The refusal rate was 5%, which is quite low by international standards, but quite typical for Irish surveys at that time. The sex ratio and other demographic characteristics of the sample were found to correspond fairly closely to official statistics. The questionnaires were administered to respondents in their own homes by trained interviewers. The data from Likert items reported here were self-administered by the respondents. All interviews were carried out in September–October 1978.

Instrument

The 1978 questionnaire included an extensive set of items on the quality of working life and measures of well-being including self-assessed health, satisfaction with health, work satisfaction and life satisfaction, as well as attitudinal measures related to social issues including childcare. We will be referring to some of these data in relation to comparisons between employed and non-employed married women in relation to the quality of their working life and their objective and subjective well-being, discussed in Chapter 4. We shall also be referring to some of the data concerning childcare in Chapter 6.

1981 Study: mothers' attitudes toward childcare and employment – a nationwide survey

Sample

The 1981 survey of mothers' attitudes to childcare and employment (Fine-Davis, 1983c) was carried out on behalf of the Working Party on Child Care Facilities for Working Parents (1983). The objective in sampling was to generate two national random samples, one of employed women with at least one child under 15 (approximately 600 respondents) and one of non-employed women, also with one or more children under 15 (approximately 400 respondents), yielding a total sample of approximately 1,000 respondents.

The sample was selected using the RANSAM procedure, a computer-based system for drawing national random samples, which was developed at the Economic and Social Research Institute (Whelan, 1977, 1979) and has been used successfully to draw samples in numerous nationwide surveys (Whelan, 1977, p. 8). This procedure utilises the Electoral Register as the sampling frame, while also making use of "supplementary information about the population in order to improve the efficiency of the estimates derived from the sample" (Ibid., p. 2).

It was evident at the outset that the sample of employed mothers would be more difficult to contact than the non-employed because they constitute a relatively small proportion of the total population. The pilot survey carried out prior to the main survey had suggested that approximately 8% of women on the Electoral Register would be employed with children. It was therefore decided to randomly select 75 polling districts throughout the country from the Electoral Register, with 100 women selected from each of these, resulting in an initial sample of 7,500. It was hoped to obtain the necessary 600 employed mothers as well as 400 non-employed mothers from this larger initial pool. However, contrary to the initial estimates based on the pilot survey, this procedure generated a sample of only 339 employed mothers. Thus, in order to bring the number in this group up to the desired level, a supplementary quota sample was selected in each area. This quota sample of 242 respondents was selected so as to correspond in occupational status to the original random sample. Comparisons of the two samples indicate a very close similarity on most characteristics, such as number and ages of children, husband's occupational status, perceptions of husband's attitudes, etc.; however, there was a slightly greater tendency for the quota sample to have a higher level of education, occupational status and income than the random sample, as well as a greater likelihood of having a child who was not yet in school, particularly in the under-two age group. The resulting sample of 581 employed mothers is therefore slightly weighted in a higher socio-economic status direction, a fact which should be borne in mind in interpreting the results.

The final sample consisted of 581 employed mothers and 440 non-employed mothers, resulting in a total sample of 1,021 respondents.

Table 2.1 Breakdown of initial national random sample by reasons for response and non-response

	No.	%
Available for interview		
Employed with child(ren) under 15 (all interviewed)	339	5.0
Non-employed with children) under 15 (440 interviewed)	2,058	30.1
Without child(ren) under 15	4,428	64.9
Sub-total:	**6,825**	**100.0**
Unavailable for interview		
Away throughout survey period	314	46.5
Unable to contact	201	29.8
Deceased	55	8.1
Too ill to be interviewed	22	3.3
House vacant	11	1.6
Refusals	15	2.2
Other (e.g., working at home, etc.)	57	8.4
Sub-total:	**675**	**100.0**
Total:	**7,500**	

Source: Fine-Davis (1983c), Table 1, p. 91.

Although we shall be solely concerned with the data from these 1,021 respondents who were interviewed, the breakdown of the initial random sample of 7,500 women, aged 18 and over, is of interest in terms of the indication it provides as to the proportion of women in the population who may have needed to avail of childcare facilities at that time due to their employment. As may be seen from Table 2.1, 6,825 of the 7,500 were available to be interviewed, and thus this figure will be considered the sample of the population. Of this 6,825, 339 or 5% were found to be employed with one or more children under 15 years of age. This, then, was the potential target group for childcare, i.e., 5% of all women 18 years and over. Of the remaining women, 30.1% had one or more children under 15 years of age, but were non-employed, and 64.9% had no children in this age group.

It is interesting to note that the target group for women requiring childcare was so small, a mere 5% of all women 18 years and over.

Questionnaire

Pilot test

Two forms of the questionnaire were developed, one for employed mothers and one for non-employed mothers. Initial drafts of the questionnaires were developed taking into account the concerns of the Working Party. After several revisions, the questionnaires were pilot tested on 52 respondents in different parts of the country. Twenty-five of the pilot interviews were carried out by the ESRI's field staff in Dublin and Kilkenny. These were supplemented by 27 additional interviews carried out by the National Manpower Service in Limerick, Thurles and Ennis and by members of the Working Party and Department of Labour in Clare and Dublin. All pilot interviews were conducted in late August 1981.

Main questionnaire

On the basis of the pilot survey, the two forms of the questionnaire were revised a final time, prior to going into the field for the main survey. The final questionnaires consisted of several sections, some unique to employed mothers, some unique to non-employed mothers, and the remainder common to both.

Employed mothers were asked questions about their employment: the type of work they did, the pattern of hours they worked, the reasons they worked, etc. They were also asked detailed questions about their childcare arrangements. Separate questions were asked about childcare arrangements for (a) infants and preschoolers and (b) school-age children. The mothers' level of satisfaction with aspects of their childcare arrangements was also ascertained.

Both employed and non-employed mothers were asked about their preferred childcare arrangements for (a) infants and toddlers and (b) preschool-age children, including preferred location and type of personnel. Questions concerning after-school and holiday care for school-age children were also asked. Both groups were asked about who they felt should finance childcare and how much they themselves would be willing to pay in this regard. Finally, a series of questions was asked concerning potential changes in the workplace and in the community which might assist working parents. A special section for non-employed mothers was included which contained questions concerning previous labour force participation, reasons for leaving the labour force and attitudes and intentions towards future labour force entry or re-entry.

Data collection procedures

The questionnaires were administered to the respondents individually in their own homes by experienced interviewers of the field staff of the Economic and Social Research Institute's survey unit. Prior to going into the field, the interviewers were briefed in an all-day session on the questionnaire, as well as on criteria for selecting respondents for interview. In addition to verbal instructions, detailed written instructions were also provided. All interviews were conducted in September–October 1981.

1986 Study: changing gender-role attitudes in Ireland, 1975–1986

Sample

The 1986 study was a replication and extension of the original 1975 Dublin study. The replication was to enable attitude change to be measured over the intervening years, and the extension was to provide policy makers with a picture of attitudes in the country at large and in particular to include rural respondents to allow for rural/urban comparisons. This was an express wish of the Joint Oireachtas Committee on Women's Rights, a committee of the Irish Parliament (Dáil), which supported the study. The sampling and data collection procedures were identical to those used in the original study except for the addition of 300 rural subjects and a consequent slight diminution of the number of urban subjects, from 420 to 300, resulting in a total of 600 respondents – 300 urban and 300 rural. "Rural" was defined as a village or open country or a town of between 1,000 to 3,000 inhabitants. All 26 counties in Ireland were included except for Longford and Laois. Cities and towns with populations over 3,000 were left out of the sample, apart from Dublin. Thus, this sample provided a clear comparison between rural and urban, with urban being defined as Dublin. The sample was limited to adults between the ages of 18 and 65.

The sample was based on stratified quotas, so as to meet the requirements of a factorial design. For this reason, it does not constitute a national representative sample; however, every attempt was made to maximise randomness in subject selection within the context of the stratification design. There were a total of 83 sampling points (starting points) – 30 in rural areas and 53 in Dublin. Starting addresses were generated from the Electoral Register by means of the Economic and Social Research Institute's (ESRI) sampling system, RANSAM (Whelan, 1977, 1979). In addition, when percentage results for the total sample are presented they have been re-weighted so as to reflect the exact proportions of the groups as they actually exist in the population. Thus, any re-weighted results presented are representative of the groups which were studied in the survey, i.e., men and women aged 18–65 from Dublin and rural Ireland. The survey includes employed and non-employed married women, employed single women, and employed married and single men. It does not include other groups such as the retired, the unemployed or non-employed single women. Thus, the results may be generalised to the groups studied, but not to the country as a whole. Differences measured between groups are quite reliable indicators since the sampling techniques used to obtain respondents within categories were essentially random, using strict quota sampling procedures. The sampling, fieldwork and data processing for the study were carried out by the survey unit of the Economic and Social Research Institute. The 1986 survey was carried out in September–December 1986.

Instrument

The content of the 1986 questionnaire was identical to that used in the 1975 study with regard to the key sets of items, and additional items concerning more current issues were added. Extensive measures were included on attitudes to divorce and abortion, and these have been reported on in Fine-Davis (1988c, 2015). In addition a set of items on perceived barriers to women's career advancement was added. These data constitute one of the main subjects of Chapter 5, together with data on perceptions of discrimination in the workplace.

2002 Study: *Fathers and mothers: dilemmas of the work-life balance* – a comparative study in four European countries

Collaborators, research design and sampling

The Fathers and Mothers Study was a cross-cultural collaborative study between four principal investigators from France (Dr Jeanne Fagnani, Centre National de la Recherche Scientifique, MATISSE, University of Paris – 1), Italy (Prof. Dino Giovannini, Department of Social, Cognitive and Quantitative Sciences, University of Modena and Reggio Emilia), Denmark (Prof Lis Højgaard, Institute of Political Science, University of Copenhagen) and Ireland (myself, Centre for Gender and Women's Studies, Trinity College Dublin) with the collaboration of Hilary Clarke, Trinity College Dublin. The sample of the Fathers and Mothers study consisted of 400 male and female respondents, with 100 from each of four countries (Ireland, France, Italy and Denmark). Each of the respondents was employed and living in a couple with a partner/spouse who was also employed and had at least one child under six.

The sample was stratified by sex, socio-economic status and employment in the public vs. the private sector. The schema used for measuring socio-economic status was that of the Hall-Jones classification of occupational status (Hall and Jones, 1950; Hutchinson, 1969). This has eight levels of occupational status, ranging from unskilled manual to professionally qualified / high administrative. These sampling parameters held for all of the four countries participating in the study and hence the samples are comparable. All of the Irish respondents were from Dublin, and the samples from the other three countries were also from major cities, i.e., Paris, Copenhagen and Bologna. Respondents were located for the research through employers in the public and private sectors, through community agencies and through childcare centres. The stratification design for the total sample is illustrated in Table 2.2 and that for each of the four individual countries is illustrated in Table 2.3.

Table 2.2 Sample design, Fathers and Mothers Study: four countries (N = 400)

		Public sector	*Private sector*		
Male	Low SES	50	50	100	200
	High SES	50	50	100	
Female	Low SES	50	50	100	200
	High SES	50	50	100	
	Total	**200**	**200**	**400**	

Source: Fine-Davis et al. (2004), Table 7.1, p. 89.

Table 2.3 The individual country samples, Fathers and Mothers Study (N = 100)

		Public sector	*Private sector*		
Male	Low SES	12–13	12–13	25	
	High SES	12–13	12–13	25	50
Female	Low SES	12–13	12–13	25	
	High SES	12–13	12–13	25	50
	Total	**50**	**50**	**100**	

Source: Fine-Davis et al. (2004), Table 7.2, p. 90.

Questionnaire

The questionnaire was designed to explore people's attitudes and experiences in coping with balancing work and family, with particular reference to the different perspectives of men and women. Attitudes towards and experience of different workplace social policies were also explored. In developing the questionnaire an extensive review of the literature in the four countries was carried out. There was, in addition, an international search for relevant items. The authors actively collaborated in the development of the questionnaire, and the final set of items includes some replicated from other studies by the authors and others, as well as the adaptation of some previous items and the creation of some new items. Some of the main areas of the questionnaire are summarized later. We have drawn upon some of the key findings in relation to sharing of domestic work and childcare and also in terms of attitudes to flexible working, and the relationship between flexible working and well-being.

You and your children

Extensive data were collected concerning who usually carried out various household and childcare tasks in the home – the respondent, his/her partner, both of them or someone else. Three questions were included concerning desires about time: (1) the extent to which the respondent would like to spend more or less time with the family, (2) whether they would like their partner to spend more or less time with the family and (3) the extent to which they would like more or less personal time. Detailed information was collected on childcare arrangements, including what arrangements were used when usual arrangements fell through. The cost of childcare was obtained as well as overall satisfaction with childcare arrangements.

The workplace

Several sets of attitudinal items were included in a section on the workplace. These were designed to ascertain the attitudes in the workplace towards working parents and the possible barriers to reconciling work and family. Respondents were also asked about the extent of potential flexibility in the workplace and then the actual flexibility they took advantage of at work.

Combining work and family

In this section respondents were asked a series of questions concerning combining work and family. They were asked about their working hours in relation to their childcare arrangements and how easy or difficult they found combining work and family. The measure of ease vs. difficulty in combining work and family was a key dependent measure in the study.

Well-being

The final section of the questionnaire concerned respondents' overall well-being in several key life domains. These included satisfaction with health, work, family life, relationship with spouse/partner and satisfaction with life in general. These items were designed to be key dependent measures of well-being.

Translation of the questionnaire into four languages

The questionnaire was translated from the English into the languages of the other three participating countries – French, Danish and Italian – and the interviews were conducted in the native language of respondents by native speakers. The English version of the questionnaire may be found in Fine-Davis et al. (2004, Appendix B). The translated versions may be found in Fine-Davis et al. (2002).

Data collection

Interviews

Interviews were carried out by interviewers on a one-to-one basis. Each interview took approximately 45 minutes. Interviews were generally carried out in the workplace, although some were carried out in the respondents' homes and a few were carried out in the workplace of the interviewer, i.e., at the university.

Data analysis

The approach taken in the study was to examine percentage results first, by country and sex. Where applicable, Chi-Square tests were carried out. The next main set of analyses carried out was analysis of variance. The stratification design of the sample, with the systematic variation of the key independent variables of (1) country, (2) sex, (3) socio-economic status and (4) public vs. private sector, enabled us to carry out both three- and four-way analyses of variance using various combinations of these variables. This allowed us to examine the main effects of each of these variables, while controlling for the effects of the other variables.

It also allowed us to examine any significant interaction effects between these independent variables in determining the dependent variables. In order to examine the relationships between variables, correlational analyses were carried out, as well as multiple regressions. These tools were primarily used to examine the relationship of a wide range of potential "predictor" variables to key dependent measures, including ease vs. difficulty in combining work and family and five global measures of well-being. Data entry and analysis were carried out by the survey unit of the Economic and Social Research Institute, Dublin.

Generalisability of the findings to the larger population

It should be borne in mind that the samples, while systematically stratified and comparable from country to country, were nevertheless small. Furthermore, they were of city populations – Paris, Bologna, Copenhagen and Dublin. Thus, while we can be confident of the differences and relationships found in our sample, where these were statistically significant, we cannot generalise to the larger population with samples of this size. Thus, the results hold for our sample and they are suggestive of trends, which are likely to occur in larger samples. Data would need to be collected on larger representative samples in order to generalise to whole countries. However, where possible, we have compared the data obtained in the present study with comparable data obtained on larger, more representative samples. It was the purpose of this study to develop and pilot an instrument in the area of reconciliation of work and family life which could be used in larger, more representative samples. Our nationwide study on work-life balance carried out in Ireland (Fine-Davis, McCarthy, Edge, et al., 2005) replicates some of the measures developed in this study on a larger sample.

2005 Study: study of work-life balance and social inclusion in Ireland

Sample and sample selection

The sample used in the 2005 study of work-life balance (Fine-Davis, McCarthy, Edge, et al., 2005) was a random, nationally representative sample of the adult population living in private households. As in the case of the 1978 sample, the institutional population was excluded from the sampling frame.

The sample for the 2005 study was also selected by the survey unit of the ESRI using its computer-based, random sampling procedure, RANSAM (Whelan, 1977, 1979), which uses the Electoral Register as the sampling frame. Sample selection was on a two-staged clustered basis. At the initial stage of selection a set of primary sampling units (or sampling points) were selected based on district electoral divisions or parts thereof. The primary sampling units were formed on the basis of a minimum population criterion, in this case 1,000 persons. When the primary sampling units were selected a random systematic sample of respondents was selected from within each for contact by the interviewer.

The specific respondent within a household selected for interview was identified on the basis of the "next birthday" rule. This was used as a simple but highly effective selection of respondent from all adults in the household. The target respondent was identified as the household member who had the next birthday – regardless of their age on the birthday. This provides a random sample of respondents within households.

A total of 2,200 names were issued to interviewers. Questionnaires were successfully completed with 1,218 respondents (a total of six of these were not included for analysis due to missing information in important areas of the questionnaire), resulting in a final sample of 1,212. The gross response rate for successfully completed surveys was 55%. If one includes only the households successfully contacted in the course of fieldwork, the figure rises to a response rate of 67%.

Re-weighting the data

The purpose of sample weighting is to compensate for any biases in the distributional characteristics in the completed sample as compared to the population of interest, in this case the population of all adult persons who are resident in private households in the Republic of Ireland. The weighting adjustment is used to account for biases that occur because of sampling error, due to the nature of the sampling frame or as a result of differential response rates within different groups of the population.

Regardless of the source of the discrepancy between the sample and population distributions we used the statistical adjustment or re-weighting procedure to adjust the distributional characteristics of the sample in terms of characteristics such as age, sex, economic status and so on in order to match the corresponding structures in the population. This is achieved by comparing sample characteristics to external population figures. These latter were principally derived from the *Census of Population 2002* supplemented with figures from the most recent record of the *Quarterly National Household Survey* (QNHS) – both conducted by the Central Statistics Office.

The variables used in the weighting scheme in the current project were:

- number of adults in the household (5 categories)
- gender by age cohort (10 categories)
- gender by marital status by age (12 categories)
- gender by age by highest level of educational attainment (12 categories)
- gender by age by region (18 categories)
- gender by age by principle economic status (21 categories)

The weighting procedure involved constructing weights so that the marginal distributions of each of the characteristics of responding individuals were equal to the distribution of characteristics for the population. To achieve this we used a so-called minimum information loss (minimum distance) algorithm to adjust an initial weight so that the distribution of characteristics in the sample matched those of the set of control totals.

Data collection procedures

The data were collected on a face-to-face basis by experienced interviewers from the ESRI's standing panel of field staff. Approximately 60 interviewers – both male and female, distributed throughout the country – were used in the survey. Interviewers working on the project attended a dedicated training session at which the survey, its design, protocols and implementation were explained by the survey unit staff and the research team from Trinity College.

Interviewers were allocated 20 names in each work assignment or cluster. The interviewer approached the household and presented his/her photo I.D. card along with a brochure explaining the survey. The "next birthday rule" was explained and the target respondent identified for interviewers. The interview may have taken place on the first call or a visit arranged for a time convenient for the respondent.

A total of four calls were made to each household – the initial call plus three call-backs. The timing and day of the week of call-backs was changed on each attempt to visit the household. All questionnaires were completed on a paper-and-pencil basis with subsequent entry onto the ESRI's computer system by their data-entry staff. All questionnaires were extensively checked before data entry. Questionnaires took approximately 45 minutes to complete. All interviews took place in the respondent's home during the period September 2004 to January 2005.

Instrument

The questionnaire was designed to explore people's experiences and attitudes as they related to work and work-life balance. Some sections were for all respondents, some were for the employed only and some were for people who were not currently in employment.

A literature review was carried out prior to designing the questionnaire, and some of the questionnaire items were taken from various sources including Fine-Davis (1983a, 1983b, 1983c, 1988b), Davis and Fine-Davis (1991) and Fine-Davis et al. (2004). Many of the items were newly developed on the basis of the results of the pilot research (Fine-Davis, McCarthy, O'Dwyer, et al., 2005; Fine-Davis, O'Dwyer, et al., 2005).

The questionnaire covered many different areas; however, we shall summarise here only those sections which we will be discussing in the book.

Attitudes to working arrangements

A set of 26 attitudinal statements, developed on the basis of the research carried out in the pilot projects on flexible working described earlier, was designed to tap attitudes to flexible working, work-life balance, gender and caring, etc. The items were presented in Likert format on seven-point scales, ranging from strongly disagree (1) to strongly agree (7).

Caring responsibilities

This section ascertained the household configuration, the numbers of children in the household and their ages and the extent of caring commitments for children. Those with children aged 0–5 years were asked about their childcare arrangements, including who cares for them, how much it cost per week and level of satisfaction with these arrangements.

The employed with care responsibilities were asked how they coped when their usual care commitments broke down and if their hours/schedule created problems with their childcare or other childcare arrangements. Attitudes of supervisor, employer and colleagues were ascertained concerning how well they took into account the respondent's caring commitments. Finally respondents were asked their opinions about paternity leave and parental leave.

Work and work arrangements (of the currently employed)

This section obtained information on the employee's working hours and working arrangement. It included their experience, if any, of different forms of flexible working arrangements; the rationale behind their choices; and their perceptions of its effect on their well-being, career, promotion opportunities and work effectiveness. It also elicited their satisfaction with their existing working arrangements and their ideal working arrangements.

Work-life balance and well-being

The last section of the questionnaire focused on respondents' work-life balance and quality of life in various life domains. Specifically, respondents were asked how easy or difficult it was to combine their job with their family or personal life, how satisfied they were with their work-life balance and what changes they might like, e.g., more time with family, personal time, etc. The issue of stress was also explored, i.e., whether respondents felt under stress, and what were the main sources of stress. The issue of overall satisfaction with their life in general, together with items on their health, and satisfaction with relationships and financial situation were also assessed.

Data analysis procedures

Factor analyses were carried out on the main sets of Likert items, including that which measured attitudes to working arrangements, in order to examine the structure of attitudes in this area. Composite scores were created based on the resulting factors, and these were then examined as dependent variables in a four-way analysis of variance design, which systematically varied four demographic variables as the independent variables. These were gender, employment status, socio-economic status and age. Correlational analyses were also carried out on a range of variables. In particular we examined people's actual situations on the one hand and their well-being on the other.

Data analysis was carried out by the survey unit of the Economic and Social Research Institute in collaboration with the project's research team.

2010 Study: changing gender roles and attitudes to family formation

The qualitative study

An in-depth qualitative study was carried out in late 2008–early 2009 as a precursor to the quantitative study. The purpose of the qualitative study was to obtain in-depth qualitative information and insights into current attitudes to gender roles and gender relations and attitudes to family formation and childbearing. The results of the qualitative study played an essential role in identifying key issues for inclusion in the questionnaire to be administered in the quantitative study (Fine-Davis, 2011, 2016).

The sample used in the qualitative study consisted of 48 adults selected to mirror the types of respondents which were to be included in the main quantitative phase. The sample was stratified by gender, age (20–34 / 35–55 years), family status (single / cohabiting / married and living with spouse), socio-economic status and geographic location (Dublin / other towns and cities / rural areas).

Most of the questions were open-ended and designed specifically for this study. Interviews were carried out on a one-to-one basis in a variety of locations. They were conducted primarily in the respondent's home, the interviewer's home or in Trinity College Dublin. All interviews were tape recorded. Interviews lasted from 39 minutes to one hour and 58 minutes, with the average interview length being one hour. The full results of the qualitative study are contained in Fine-Davis (2009).

Pilot study

Following the development of an extensive questionnaire, a pilot study was carried out in the summer of 2010 on a stratified sample of 150 male and female respondents in the childbearing age group and in various marital statuses throughout the country. The results of the pilot were used in developing the questionnaire to be used in the main study. Factor analyses were carried out to identify underlying dimensions of attitudinal items and to provide an empirical basis for retaining the best items for inclusion in the main questionnaire.

Main study

Research design and sample

The population under investigation was adults of child-bearing age (20–49 years) in the Republic of Ireland. A stratified sampling design was employed. This was based on gender, family status (single, cohabiting, married), age (20–34 and 35–49 years), having one or more children or not, and rural vs. urban location. "Single" was defined as not living with a partner; it did not refer to marital status *per se*. "Married" was defined as married and living with one's spouse. Presence of a child was defined as the respondent having given birth, fathered or adopted one or more children; it did not require that the child be resident with the respondent. This design was employed so that the sample would include people in all possible combinations of these characteristics, including married with children, married without children, single with and without children, etc., as this would allow for the use of analysis of variance – one of the primary multivariate statistical techniques used in the study. A major goal in creating this design was to allow for comparisons between single, cohabiting and married people, while controlling for the effects of gender, age and other key demographic variables.

A multi-staged quota controlled sampling design with randomly selected starting addresses from the Geo Directory was used. This was based on a total of 200 randomly selected sampling points throughout the country with six interviews conducted per point. A "random walk" from the random starting point was adopted within each sampling point. A total of 1,254 interviews were conducted during the main fieldwork phase, with the additional 150 pilot survey questionnaires boosting the final sample to 1,404. Because of the comparability of the questionnaires and the quality of responses elicited at the pilot stage, the pilot data were thus incorporated into the final dataset prior to analysis.

In order to obtain the final sample of 1,404 a total of 10,596 contacts were made. Of these, 38% were ineligible, 32% were not at home and 1% was derelict properties. Twenty-eight per cent of the total contacts were eligible, i.e., they fulfilled the characteristics of the quota sample design. Of these eligible respondents, there was a 51% response rate in urban areas and a 42% rate in rural areas, for an overall response rate of 47%.

Data collection procedures

All interviewing was conducted on a face-to-face basis in respondents' homes by experienced and pre-briefed interviewers from Behaviour and Attitudes. Computer Aided Personal Interviewing (CAPI) was utilised. Some of the sections of the questionnaire were self-completed by respondents on the laptops – Computer Aided Self-Completion Interviewing (CASI). This protected the privacy of the respondent in providing answers to more sensitive questions and, accordingly, enhanced data quality. Fieldwork for the main survey took place from mid-August to early November 2010. The average interview time was 45 minutes.

Instrument of main study

The questionnaire used in the main study included, *inter alia*, the following sections: (1) demographics, (2) attitudes to relationships, (3) relationships and relationship history, (4) attitudes to having children, (5) attitudes to gender roles and (6) attitudes to work-life balance and related social policies.

Most of the items were developed on the basis of the qualitative study, while others were replications of items used in previous research by the author and others. Some of the items concerning gender-role attitudes were replicated from Fine-Davis (1983a, 1988a), while some items concerning work-life balance were replicated from Fine-Davis et al. (2004) and Fine-Davis, McCarthy, Edge, et al. (2005). Selected items measuring attitudes to childcare and other family policies were replicated from Fine-Davis (1983b, 1983c); Fine-Davis et al. (2004); and Fine-Davis, McCarthy, Edge, et al. (2005). Likert items were used extensively. These were presented on seven-point scales ranging from "strongly disagree" to "strongly agree." Within each set, items were presented in a randomised order for each respondent so that there would be no ordering effects.

Weighting of the sample and comparison with population estimates

In line with best practice in all sample surveys, the completed sample was statistically adjusted or re-weighted to ensure that it reflected the socio-demographic structure of the relevant sub-group of the population under investigation. Forty-eight individual weighting variables were set which reflected the population breakdown of 20- to 49-year-olds in terms of gender, age, family status, presence of children and area. Additional educational and SES (occupational status) weights were applied. All population figures were derived from the 2006 Census of Population.

The completed sample, notwithstanding the quota controls, was slightly under-represented in terms of family composition by single and married respondents and over-represented in terms of cohabitees. This is due to the fact that certain groups, including cohabitees, were oversampled in order to have sufficient respondents in each cell of the design to make it possible to carry out analyses of variance. Other groups in the completed sample are largely in line with the population figures. Comparison of the re-weighted sample and the Census figures shows that the structure of the re-weighted sample is very close to the population figures. Thus, we may be confident that the re-weighted data is representative of the population in the childbearing age group.

In the final weighted sample there are 50% males and 50% females. There are 54% in the age group 20–34 and 46% in the age group 35–49. The final weighted sample consists of 45% single people, 44% married people and 11% cohabiting people.

The proportion of rural and urban respondents is 40% urban and 60% rural in the final re-weighted sample. Again, this was adjusted somewhat by the weighting to conform to the proportions of these groups in the population. The final re-weighted sample includes 46% with children and 54% people without children, reflecting a minor readjustment from the original sample.

Data analysis techniques

Factor analysis was used in the 1975 study and again in the 1978 study to confirm the factor structure of the earlier study. It was also used in the 1986 survey to explore the dimensionality of new sets of items, including items measuring new gender-role attitudes, attitudes to divorce, etc. It was used in the 2005 and 2010 studies to develop new measures of gender-role attitudes, attitudes to family formation and attitudes to social policies. Analysis of variance was the second major multivariate method used, with attitudinal measures, derived through factor analysis, as the dependent measures and demographic characteristics as the independent measures. Multiple regression was used selectively as appropriate when a larger number of independent variables were examined as predictors of a single key dependent variable. In addition to these multivariate techniques, bi-variate analyses (i.e., t-tests and correlational analysis) have been used to compare groups and to explore relationships between variables.

Comparisons of data sets

The nature of the research presented here is that it measures phenomena in a natural social setting. As such it is not amenable to a strict experimental design, with control groups, etc. However, the research designs employed in all of the studies were of a quasi-experimental design. Their major strengths involve the randomness of subject selection, the availability of data in a time series and the use of identical measuring instruments over time (Campbell and Stanley, 1963).

Chapter 5 shows how attitudes concerning perceived discrimination and perceived barriers to career advancement changed over the period 1975 to 2010. We summarise later how the various samples described previously are compared in this chapter.

Dublin samples: 1975, 1986, 2005

The first set of comparisons is for Dublin only. It includes the 1975 data for Dublin (N = 420) and the 1986 data for Dublin only (N = 300). These samples are comparable, and while they are based on stratified sampling, they include the most complete sets of variables, covering the full gamut of social policy issues relevant to gender equality at the time. They provide a comparison over an 11-year period at the first stage of social change. The Dublin data from 1986 were then compared to the Dublin data from 2005, which were extracted from the nationwide representative sample for comparative purposes.

Nationwide samples: 1986 and 2005

The second set of comparisons is for the country as a whole. It includes the datasets from 1986 and 2005. The 2005 (N = 1,212) dataset is based on a representative nationwide sample selected using probability sampling. The 1986 data for Dublin and rural Ireland (N = 600) are re-weighted to reflect the proportions of the groups studied in the country as a whole. While the 1986 sample is not strictly comparable to the 2005 sample, it is a national sample which provides a comparison point between 1986 and 2005. The advantage of the comparisons between these two datasets is that they are of the country as a whole, and in the case of the 2005 survey, the comparison includes a representative nationwide sample.

References

Adelmann, P. K. (1988). *Employment and Psychological Well-Being in Women: A Meta-Analysis*. Presented at the Annual Convention of the American Psychological Association, New York.

Campbell, D. T. and Stanley, J. C. (1963). *Experimental and Quasi-Experimental Designs for Research*. Chicago: Rand McNally.

Cochrane, R. and Stopes-Roe, M. (1981). Women, marriage, employment and mental health. *British Journal of Psychiatry*, 139, 373–381.

Davis, E. E. and Fine-Davis, M. (1991). Social indicators of living conditions in Ireland, with European comparisons. *Social Indicators Research*, 25 (2–4), 103–365.

Fine-Davis, M. (1976). *Structure, Determinants and Correlates of Attitudes Toward the Role and Status of Women in Ireland, with Particular Reference to Employment Status of Married Women*. Unpublished doctoral dissertation, Department of Psychology, Trinity College, University of Dublin.

Fine-Davis, M. (1977). *Attitudes toward the Status of Women: Implications for Equal Employment Opportunity*. Report to the Department of Labour. Dublin: Department of Psychology, Trinity College Dublin.

Fine-Davis, M. (1979a). Personality correlates of attitudes toward the role and status of women in Ireland. *Journal of Personality*, 47 (3), 379–396.

Fine-Davis, M. (1979b). Social-psychological predictors of employment status of married women in Ireland. *Journal of Marriage and the Family*, 47 (1), 145–158.

Fine-Davis, M. (1983a). A society in transition: Structure and determinants of attitudes toward the role and status of women in Ireland. *Psychology of Women Quarterly*, 8 (2), 113–132.

Fine-Davis, M. (1983b). *Women and Work in Ireland: A Social Psychological Perspective*. Dublin: Council for the Status of Women.

Fine-Davis, M. (1983c). Mothers' attitudes toward child care and employment: A nationwide survey. In: Working Party on Child Care Facilities for Working Parents, *Report to the Minister for Labour*. Dublin: Stationery Office, pp. 73–168.

Fine-Davis, M. (1984). *Women, Work and Well-Being in the European Community: Nationwide Results for 8 Countries*. V/55/85-EN. Brussels: Commission of the European Communities.

Fine-Davis, M. (1985a). Women, work and well-being in the European Community. *Social Europe* (Brussels), 2 (85), 45–49.

Fine-Davis, M. (1985b). Housework vs. employment: Quality of working life and psychological well-being among Irish married women. In: M. Safir, M. Mednick, D. N. Israeli and J. Bernard (Eds.), *Women's Worlds: From the New Scholarship*. New York: Praeger, pp. 105–116.

Fine-Davis, M. (1985c). *Working Life and Well-Being Among Men and Women in the European Community: Representative Results from 8 Countries*. V/611/86-EN. Brussels: Commission of the European Communitie].

Fine-Davis, M. (1988a). Changing gender role attitudes in Ireland: 1975–1986. Vol. I: Attitudes Toward the Role and Status of Women, 1975–1986. In: *First Report of the Second Joint Oireachtas [Parliamentary] Committee on Women's Rights* (Pl. 5609). Dublin: The Stationery Office, May, pp. 1–100.

Fine-Davis, M. (1988b). Changing gender role attitudes in Ireland: 1975–1986. Vol. II: Issues Related to Equal Employment Opportunity. In: *Second Report of the Second Joint Committee on Women's Rights* (Pl. 5673). Dublin: The Stationery Office, pp. 1–66.

Fine-Davis, M. (1988c). Changing gender role attitudes in Ireland: 1975–1986. Vol. III: Attitudes Towards Moral Issues in Relation to Voting Behaviour in Recent Referenda. In: *Third Report of the Second Joint Committee on Women's Rights* (Pl. 5796). Dublin: The Stationery Office, pp. 1–80.

Fine-Davis, M. (2009). *Attitudes to Family Formation in Ireland: Preliminary Findings – The Qualitative Study*. Report to the Family Support Agency. Dublin: Social Attitude & Policy Research Group, Trinity College Dublin.

Fine-Davis, M. (2011). *Attitudes to Family Formation in Ireland: Findings from the Nationwide Study*. Dublin: Social Attitude and Policy Research Group, Trinity College Dublin and Family Support Agency.

Fine-Davis, M. (2015). *Gender Roles in Ireland: Three Decades of Attitude Change*. London: Routledge.

Fine-Davis, M. (2016). *Changing Gender Roles and Attitudes to Family Formation in Ireland*. Manchester: Manchester University Press.

Fine-Davis, M., Fagnani, J., Giovannini, D., Højgaard, L. and Clarke, H. (2002). *Fathers and Mothers: Dilemmas of the Work-Life Balance*. Final Report to the European Commission and the Irish Department of Justice, Equality and Law Reform. Dublin: Centre for Gender and Women's Studies, Trinity College Dublin.

Fine-Davis, M., Fagnani, J., Giovannini, D., Højgaard, L. and Clarke, H. (2004). *Fathers and Mothers: Dilemmas of the Work-Life Balance – A Comparative Study in Four European Countries*. Dordrecht, Boston and London: Kluwer Academic Publishers.

Fine-Davis, M., McCarthy, M., Edge, G. and O'Dwyer, C. (2005). *Work-Life Balance and Social Inclusion in Ireland: Results of a Nationwide Survey*. Dublin: National Flexi-Work Partnership (Centre for Gender and Women's Studies, Trinity College Dublin; IBEC; ICTU; Age Action Ireland & Aware).

Fine-Davis, M., McCarthy, M., O'Dwyer, C., Edge, G. and O'Sullivan, M. (2005). *The Effects of Flexible Working on Work-Life Balance and Social Inclusion: An Evaluation of a Series of Pilot Projects*. Dublin: National Flexi-Work Partnership (Centre for Gender and Women's Studies, Trinity College Dublin; IBEC; ICTU; FÁS, Age Action Ireland and Aware).

Fine-Davis, M., O'Dwyer, C., McCarthy, M., Edge, G., O'Sullivan, M. and Wynne, K. (2005). *Men in Childcare: Promoting Gender Equality in Children – Evaluation of a Pilot Project*. Dublin: National Flexi-Work Partnership (Centre for Gender and Women's Studies, Trinity College Dublin; IBEC; ICTU; FÁS, Age Action Ireland and Aware).

Hall, J. and Jones, D. C. (1950). The social grading of occupations. *British Journal of Sociology*, 1, 31–55.

Hoffman, L. W. and Nye, F. I. (1974). *Working Mothers*. San Francisco: Jossey-Bass.

Hutchinson, B. (1969). *Social Status in Inter-Generational Social Mobility in Dublin*. Paper No. 48. Dublin: The Economic and Social Research Institute.

Kirkpatrick, C. (1936). The construction of a belief pattern scale for measuring attitudes toward feminism. *Journal of Social Psychology*, 7, 421–437.

Levinson, D. and Huffman, P. (1955). Traditional family ideology and its relation to personality. *Journal of Personality*, 23, 251–273.

Safir, M., Mednick, M., Israeli, D. N. and Bernard, J. (Eds.) (1985). *Women's Worlds: From the New Scholarship*. New York: Praeger.

Spence, J. T. and Helmreich, R. (1972). The Attitudes toward Women Scale: An objective instrument to measure the attitudes toward the rights and roles of women in contemporary society. *JSAS: Catalogue of Selected Documents in Psychology*, 2, 66–67 (Ms. No. 153).

Whelan, B. J. (1977). *RANSAM: A national random sample design for Ireland*. Seminar paper presented at the Economic and Social Research Institute, Dublin, 3 November.

Whelan, B. J. (1979). RANSAM: A random sample design for Ireland. *Economic and Social Review*, 10 (2), 169–175.

Working Party on Child Care Facilities for Working Parents (1983). *Report to the Minister for Labour*. Dublin: Stationery Office.

Chapter 3

Social-psychological predictors of employment status of married women[1]

Employment on the part of married women was an unusual behaviour in Ireland in the early 1970s – just 7.5% of married women were employed at this time. While just 5.2% of married women were in the labour force in 1961, this rose to 7.5% in 1971 (Callan and Farrell, 1991). From that point onwards their participation continued to increase at an unprecedented rate. Who were those 5% of married women who were working outside the home in the early 1960s when it was more usual for women to be housewives and stay at home? What made them different? This chapter explores the factors which made these women different in comparison to their non-employed counterparts.

This chapter presents the results of an early study, carried out in 1975, which explored a range of social-psychological characteristics of married women, both employed and non-employed, in order to determine which characteristics best predicted whether or not they were employed. This chapter thus presents the research which examined the determinants of married women's labour force participation at this time (Fine-Davis, 1979). The findings from this analysis highlight the characteristics of employed and non-employed married women in the mid-1970s, at the very beginning of Irish women's influx into the labour market. We examined women's own attitudes to labour force participation and gender roles; their personality and related social-psychological characteristics, such as religiosity, life satisfaction, etc.; their perception of the attitudes of their "important others" (i.e., mother, father, close friend, husband) towards their actual or potential employment and their attitudes to family size, as measured by their ideal and expected family size. Finally we explore attitudes towards contraception, which was not yet legally available in Ireland at that time.

We began by reviewing the literature as it was at the time that the study was carried out, namely the early 1970s. This informed our own research, both in terms of the variables which were included as potential predictors of married women's employment status and in terms of our hypotheses. However, as most of this research was carried out in the United States, it was not necessarily generalisable to Ireland. Nevertheless, it offered ideas and potential hypotheses to explore in the Irish context.

Numerous studies had identified personality correlates of attitudes towards the role of women (e.g., Worell and Worell, 1971; O'Keefe, 1972; Tangri, 1970; Fowler and Van de Reit, 1972; Cherniss, 1972; Stoloff, 1973; Ryckman et al., 1972; Pawlicki and Almquist, 1973; Joesting, 1971; Welch, 1975; Gump, 1972; Nielson and Doyle, 1975). Fewer systematic findings had been found, however, between personality characteristics and actual role behaviour reflective of such characteristics, aside from the few studies which had observed relationships between personality characteristics and effective family planning (Meleis, 1971) and membership in a women's liberation group (e.g., Pawlicki and Almquist, 1973). Thus, we felt it would be of great interest to explore whether or not personality characteristics were related to employment on the part of married women, which is a clear manifestation of sex-role–related behaviour.

While it is true that some variables had been found to be related to employment status of married women, these were largely demographic in nature or had demographic implications (e.g., attitudes to childbearing). For example, Sobol (1973) had found that the larger the expected family size, the less likely the wife was to work, and the higher the wife's education, the more likely she was to work. Other studies had also reported that working women both desired (Ridley, 1959) and indeed had (Pratt and Whelpton, 1958; Weller, 1977) fewer children than did nonworking women. Very few studies, however, had revealed actual personality or attitudinal differences between working and nonworking married women.

Two studies which had examined one or more attitudinal determinants of female labour force participation were conducted by Weil (1961) in the United States and by Walsh and Whelan (1973) in Ireland. Weil found that the husband's attitude towards his wife's outside employment was the single best predictor of whether or not his wife worked and whether she planned to work in the future. Walsh and Whelan (1973), reporting results of a primarily econometric analysis of the determinants of female labour force participation in Ireland, found that a significant predictor of participation on the part of married women was the perceived approval of the husband. In fact, together with other non-attitudinal variables, this variable's contribution to the explained variance was the greatest of any single variable.

Other variables which had been shown to differentiate between working and nonworking women were their sense of competence and their attitudes towards the woman's role (Hoffman, 1974). Mason and Bumpass (1975) found that employed married women in the United States were more likely to have egalitarian sex-role attitudes and to endorse equal opportunity. Working wives in Finland were also more likely to endorse employment of married women than were nonworking wives (Haavio-Mannila, 1972). However, according to Hoffman:

> Because of the paucity of the data, it is premature to say whether or not personality traits differentiate working from nonworking women within specific groups. Where differences have not been found, the groups compared were often too heterogeneous; where differences were clear, usually there has

been a question of cause and effect. The few longitudinal studies have not examined data germane to this question, and studies of non-college women are particularly scarce.

(1974, p. 52)

It was the purpose of the present study to (1) investigate several sets of personality and attitudinal variables together, many of which had previously been studied in isolation, in order to assess their relationship to employment status of married women; (2) correct some of the methodological flaws noted by Hoffman (1974) as existing in some of the previous research in this area and (3) carry out this study in a country, Ireland, where extremely little such research has been carried out before and which, because it is just beginning to undergo social change in this area, offered an opportunity to obtain baseline data at a unique period in its history.

Method

Pilot and pre-tests

A pilot study was conducted in April 1975, followed by a questionnaire pre-test in May 1975. A stratified sample of 122 male and female Dublin adults constituted the pre-test sample. The questionnaire to which they responded consisted largely of attitude statements concerning the role and status of women in Ireland. Many of the items were selected from instruments developed in the United States, e.g., Kirkpatrick (1936), Levinson and Huffman (1955) and Spence and Helmreich (1972). Some of these were modified, and others were newly developed in an attempt to elicit attitudes to issues particularly relevant to the Irish situation. The pre-test data were factor analysed both for purposes of examining the dimensions of the attitudes as well as for purposes of item reduction. On the basis of this analysis, items were selected for inclusion in the main test interview schedule.

A second pre-test was conducted to develop measures of general social-psychological and personality constructs in an Irish sample. A stratified sample of 412 male and female Dublin adults responded to this pre-test instrument in March 1975. Responses to the items were factor analysed, and items from several of the resulting factors were selected for inclusion in the main test instrument of the present study. The results of this pre-test as well as subsequent research along these lines are described more fully by Davis et al. (1977).

Research design and sample of main study

The sample of the main study consisted of 240 married Irish women living in the Dublin metropolitan area. The sample was stratified according to four dichotomised characteristics: (1) employment status, (2) socio-economic status, (3) age and (4) presence or absence of dependent children. This formed a 2 x 2 x 2 x 2 factorial design of subject characteristics. Each of the dichotomised independent variables was defined as follows:

Employment status was defined as "paid employment outside the home." No lower limit in terms of hours worked was placed. Therefore, employed women could have worked anywhere from a few hours per week to full time. This flexible definition of employment was based on (1) the realisation that it would be difficult to obtain the necessary number of married female subjects in all of the appropriate categories if the definition were too stringent; (2) the fact that part-time work is quite a common form of employment for married women and, therefore, should not be excluded from study and (3) the belief that a job which may take a woman outside the home for even a very few hours may be just as psychologically meaningful for her as a job which involves a greater number of hours outside the home. Thus, for purposes of the factorial design, the women were dichotomised as being "employed" or "non-employed."

Socio-economic status was based on husband's occupational status in terms of the Hall-Jones Scale (Hall and Jones, 1950) of Occupational Prestige, as adapted to the Irish context by Hutchinson (1969). Categories 6, 7 and 8 (skilled manual, semi-skilled manual and unskilled manual-routine) were classified as "low SES," and categories 1–5 (professionally qualified / high administrative, lower professional / managerial and executive, supervisory-higher grade, supervisory lower grades, and routine grades, non-manual) were classified as "high SES." Essentially, the dichotomy was based on a blue collar / white collar distinction.

The *age* range of subjects was 18 to 65. Since 65 is the usual retirement age and since employment status was part of the factorial design, 65 was used as the upper age limit. Subjects were dichotomised at age 35, since it was felt that any higher age, such as 40, would probably not adequately reflect young-old attitudinal differences. Therefore, subjects 18–34 years of age constituted the "young" group, and subjects 35–65 constituted the "old" group.

The fourth independent variable in the design was the *presence/absence of dependent children*. "Dependent children" were defined as children in primary school or younger. Thus, women "without dependent children" included both women without any children as well as women with one or more children of post-primary school age, but with no children of primary school age or younger. The rationale for defining this variable in this way was based on the assumption that children of post-primary school age usually are more self-sufficient, and, therefore, their care would not be as great a factor to the mother as if they were younger.

The factorial design consisted of 16 cells representing the systematic variation of the four independent variables described earlier. Fifteen subjects were obtained to fill each of the 16 cells, resulting in a total N of 240. Given the complex nature of the research design in terms of the necessity of obtaining subjects with very specific combinations of characteristics, it would obviously have been quite inefficient, if not impossible, to utilise strictly random sampling procedures. Given these sampling parameters, stratified quota sampling seemed the most appropriate procedure. However, attempts were made to maximize randomness in subject selection. This was achieved by the use of randomised starting points (names and addresses randomly selected from the Dublin Electoral Register). In addition, interviewers were instructed to skip five houses once a completed interview had been obtained to reduce the likelihood of respondents knowing one another and to spread the sample out geographically. Once five interviews were obtained in one area, the interviewers – of whom there were 13 – were instructed to move to a new starting address. Interviewing was carried out in the evening as well as in the daytime to facilitate contact with employed women.

Instrument

The main test questionnaire included the following sets of items:

1 *Attitudes towards the role and status of women:* Thirty-three items were used to measure attitudes towards the role and status of women. These were presented in modified Likert format, i.e., a six-point scale ranging from strongly agree to strongly disagree. The items were selected on the basis of the factor analysis of the first pre-test, described earlier. In general, items were selected on the basis of having high loadings on the resulting factors; however, in some cases, an item was retained because of the interest and importance of its content even if it was not among the highest loading items.
2 *Social-psychological and personality constructs*: Thirty-three Likert items were used to measure general social-psychological and personality constructs. These items were selected on the basis of the factor analysis of the second pre-test.
3 *Ideal and expected family size and contraceptive practice:* Ideal and expected family size were ascertained, as well as information concerning contraceptive practice.[2] Women were asked what method of birth control (if any) they and their husbands use or, in the case of post-menopausal women and women who wished to become pregnant, what method (if any) they used to use. Specific methods used were recorded and recoded into (1) no method of birth control used, (2) "natural" methods (such as the rhythm method, etc.) and (3) "artificial" methods (such as the pill, etc.). For purposes of this analysis, contraceptive use was operationalised as a code of "3"; codes of 1 and 2 (no method and natural methods) were combined.
4 *Attitudes of important others:* As was discussed earlier, the perceived approval of the husband has been found to be an important determinant of labour force participation of married women. In order to measure this variable, parallel sets of questions were developed for the employed and the non-employed wives in the sample. Employed women were asked, "How does your husband feel about your working?" They were then given five options ranging

from strong approval to strong disapproval. Nonworking wives were asked, "How do you think your husband would feel if you started working?" Again, five degrees of approval/disapproval were offered. Both groups of women were asked, "How important are your husband's views on this topic to you?" While primarily the views of the husband have been investigated in previous research concerned with employment of married women, the perceived attitudes of "important others" generally have been shown to influence behaviour (e.g., Newcomb, 1943). Thus, both groups of women were also asked about the approval and importance of their mother, father and closest friend regarding their actual or potential employment. They were also asked to rate the "importance" of each of the significant others' views in order to weight each of the approval scores by its importance as well as to obtain a global approval score weighted by importance.

Data collection procedures

The questionnaire was administered to the respondents in their homes by trained interviewers. The two sections of Likert items were self-administering and the remaining sections were administered by the interviewer. All of the questionnaires were completed in September and October 1975.

Preliminary results

Dimensions of attitudes towards the role and status of women

Several preliminary analyses were performed on the main-test data. A factor analysis was performed on the responses to the set of Likert items measuring attitudes towards the role and status of women. This was done to examine to what extent the factor structure obtained in the pre-test would hold in the main test and, if necessary, to modify the interpretation accordingly. It was also done to obtain accurate measures, reflective of the factor space of the main test sample. Principal axis factors were extracted using the principal components technique. These principal axis factors were then orthogonally rotated to simple structure using the Varimax criterion (Kaiser, 1958). After an inspection of several factor solutions, an eight-factor solution was found to provide optimal psychological interpretability. The names of these factors and an example of a high-loading item for each are listed here:

Factor I: traditional sex-role orientation (e.g., "Some equality in marriage is a good thing, but by and large the husband ought to have the main say in family matters.")

Factor II: positive attitude to contraception (e.g., "The sale of contraceptives should be legalised in Ireland.")

Factor III: belief in equal opportunity (e.g., "People should be employed and promoted strictly on the basis of ability, regardless of sex.")
Factor IV: positive attitude to maternal employment (e.g., "A woman who has a job she enjoys is likely to be a better wife and mother because she has an interest and some fulfilment outside the home.")
Factor V: belief in equal pay (e.g., "A married man should be paid more than a woman for performing the same job" – loaded negatively.)
Factor VI: belief in higher tax for married women (e.g., "It is only fair that a married couple [both working] pay more tax than two single people.")
Factor VII: perception of females as inferior (e.g., "Generally speaking, women think less clearly than men.")
Factor VIII: perception of limitations in housewife role (e.g., "Housework is basically dull and boring.")

Composite scores were computed for each factor, based on the subject's responses to the items on that factor. These composite scores were then used in subsequent analyses.

Factor analysis of measures of general social-psychological and personality constructs

The second pre-test carried out prior to the main study resulted in a number of measures of general social-psychological and personality constructs, many of which represent well-known constructs in the psychological literature. High-loading items from several of the factors which emerged in this pre-test were included in the main test and then factor analysed again. A six-factor solution provided optimal psychological interpretability. The names given to these factors with an example of a high-loading item from each are as follows:

Factor I: religiosity (e.g., "Prayer is something which is very important in my life.")
Factor II: self-deprecation with powerlessness (e.g., "I certainly feel useless at times.")
Factor III: life satisfaction (e.g., "All things considered, I would say that I am very happy with my life these days.")
Factor IV: need for order and predictability (e.g., "I always see to it that my work is carefully planned and organized.")
Factor V: trust in people (e.g., "If you don't watch yourself, people will take advantage of you" – loaded negatively.)
Factor VI: self-esteem (e.g., "I feel that I am a person of worth, at least on an equal basis with others.")

Composite scores for each of these factors were also computed for each respondent to be used in subsequent analyses.

Main results

An examination of the effects of employment status and related characteristics of married women on attitudes towards the role and status of women

Table 3.1 presents the main effects[3] of four independent variables on the eight measures of attitudes towards the role and status of women. Corroborating findings obtained both in the United States (Mason and Bumpass, 1975) and in Finland (Haavio-Mannila, 1972), the employed married women in our sample manifested significantly less traditional sex-role attitudes than non-employed married women, both in terms of overall sex-role attitudes ($F = 6.30$; $p < .05$, see Table 3.1) and more specifically attitudes to maternal employment ($F = 35.17$; $p < .001$). In addition they were more likely to support policies associated with greater equality for women. This included greater support for equal pay ($F = 4.61$; $p < .05$) and less support for higher taxes for married women. They were also significantly less likely to perceive women as inferior than were non-employed married women ($F = 4.2$; $p < .05$). This finding suggests that employment may

Table 3.1 Summary of analysis of variance results: main effects of four independent variables on eight composite scores based on the F.A. of attitudes toward the role and status of women (N = 240 married females)

Source	*Sums of squares*	*df*	*F-ratio*
a. Traditional sex-role orientation			
Main effects			
A (Dependent children)	.05	1	.03
B (Age)	32.89	1	17.58***
C (SES)	.10	1	.05
D (Employment status)	11.78	1	6.30*
Residual	419.04	224	
b. Positive attitude to contraception			
Main effects			
A (Dependent children)	5.61	1	2.62
B (Age)	59.34	1	27.75***
C (SES)	2.40	1	1.12
D (Employment status)	3.92	1	1.83
Residual	479.01	224	
c. Belief in equal opportunity			
Main effects			
A (Dependent children)	1.07	1	1.25
B (Age)	.15	1	.18
C (SES)	2.61	1	3.06
D (Employment status)	.02	1	.03
Residual	191.01	224	

Source	*Sums of squares*	*df*	*F-ratio*
d. Positive attitude to maternal employment			
Main effects			
A (Dependent children)	11.93	1	5.10*
B (Age)	31.54	1	13.48***
C (SES)	2.11	1	.90
D (Employment status)	82.25	1	35.17***
Residual	523.92	224	
e. Belief in equal pay			
Main effects			
A (Dependent children)	4.27	1	1.44
B (Age)	23.65	1	7.96**
C (SES)	.01	1	.00
D (Employment status)	13.69	1	4.61*
Residual	665.46	224	
f. Belief in higher tax for married women			
Main effects			
A (Dependent children)	.05	1	.02
B (Age)	19.55	1	6.63**
C (SES)	.13	1	.04
D (Employment status)	28.36	1	9.62**
Residual	660.50	224	
g. Perception of females as inferior			
Main effects			
A (Dependent children)	.01	1	.00
B (Age)	23.65	1	10.99***
C (SES)	3.43	1	1.59
D (Employment status)	9.08	1	4.22*
Residual	481.78	224	
h. Perception of limitations in housewife role			
Main effects			
A (Dependent children)	3.04	1	1.03
B (Age)	.15	1	.05
C (SES)	7.70	1	2.61
D (Employment status)	15.00	1	5.08*
Residual	661.87	224	

*$p < .05$. **$p < .01$. ***$p < .001$

provide psychological benefits which influence women's basic perceptions of women and, inevitably, their own sense of self-esteem, or alternatively, that higher self-esteem is itself a determining factor in the decision to seek employment. Employed married women were more likely to perceive limitations in the housewife/mother role than were non-employed married women ($F = 5.08$; $p < .05$) – a not altogether surprising finding, since one of the reasons many of the employed women chose to work was undoubtedly the fact that they were not completely fulfilled as housewives.

In addition to employment status, age was also found to be a very significant determinant of attitudes towards sex-role–related issues on the part of married women. Older married women were found to be significantly more traditional and less supportive of social change. A somewhat unexpected finding, but one which is supported by theory, was that women with dependent children were significantly more likely to be positive to maternal employment than women with no dependent children. This was true both of women who were employed and women who were non-employed. This finding would seem to support Bailyn's (1964) "traditional dream" theory which postulated that women who do not have children idealise motherhood, but after they achieve it they are more likely to want to work.

A further interesting observation was an almost total lack of effect of socio-economic background on married women's attitudes towards the role and status of women. This absence of significant differences contrasts with results using a more heterogeneous sample, which also included males and single people (Fine-Davis, 1976). This would seem to indicate that, among married women, socio-economic status is not a significant determinant of attitudes to sex-roles and social issues relevant to the status of women; on these issues, lower and upper socio-economic status women would appear to be united.

An examination of the effects of employment status and other demographic characteristics of married women on personality and related social-psychological characteristics

It was observed in the review of previous research that very few studies had been conducted concerning personality differences of employed and non-employed married women. Those which had been carried out had not adequately controlled important variables, and very few studies had included samples of non-college women. The research design employed in the present study – a factorial design which systematically varied employment status and other relevant demographic variables – enabled us to make such a comparison of the personality characteristics of employed and non-employed married women. Relevant characteristics of age, socio-economic status and presence or absence of dependent children are simultaneously controlled. Table 3.2 presents analysis of variance results for six personality and related social-psychological variables obtained as a result of the factor analysis described earlier. The dependent variables are composite scores based on these six factors.

The most important finding to emerge from this set of analyses was an observed difference in religiosity. Employed married women were found to be significantly less religious than their non-employed counterparts ($F = 14.73$; $p < .001$). This difference was particularly pronounced among younger women. The religiosity factor included items tapping several different dimensions of religiosity, suggesting that the lesser degree of religiosity manifested by employed married women

Table 3.2 Summary of analysis of variance results: main effects of four independent variables on six composite scores based on the factor analysis of general social-psychological and personality items (N = 240 married women)

Source	*Sums of squares*	*df*	*F-ratio*
a. Religiosity			
Main effects			
A (Dependent children)	.02	1	.01
B (Age)	31.97	1	25.95***
C (SES)	.32	1	.26
D (Employment status)	18.15	1	14.73***
Residual	276.00	224	
b. Self-deprecation with powerlessness			
Main effects			
A (Dependent children)	1.24	1	1.04
B (Age)	5.40	1	4.51*
C (SES)	36.04	1	30.10***
D (Employment status)	4.40	1	3.68
Residual	268.19	224	
c. Life satisfaction			
Main effects			
A (Dependent children)	.00	1	.00
B (Age)	2.97	1	4.36*
C (SES)	.07	1	.10
D (Employment status)	1.78	1	2.61
Residual	152.23	224	
d. Need for order and predictability			
Main effects			
A (Dependent children)	2.61	1	1.87
B (Age)	.60	1	.43
C (SES)	9.60	1	6.89**
D (Employment status)	2.93	1	2.10
Residual	312.19	224	
e. Trust in people			
Main effects			
A (Dependent children)	.24	1	.14
B (Age)	.15	1	.09
C (SES)	37.21	1	21.32***
D (Employment status)	1.59	1	.91
Residual	391.07	224	
f. Self-esteem			
Main effects			
A (Dependent children)	.04	1	.06
B (Age)	.78	1	1.23
C (SES)	3.83	1	6.06*
D (Employment status)	.16	1	.26
Residual	141.66	224	

*$p < .05$. **$p < .01$. ***$p < .001$.

reflected both behavioural (e.g., frequency of church attendance) as well as attitudinal (e.g., belief) components.

In addition, as may be seen in Table 3.2, a trend was detected which suggested that employed married women were somewhat less likely to be self-deprecating or to feel powerless than were non-employed married women ($F = 3.68$; $p < .06$). There was no main effect for employment status on the variable self-esteem. However, there was a main effect for socio-economic status in an unexpected direction: lower-SES married women expressed somewhat greater self-esteem than their higher-SES counterparts ($F = 6.06$; $p < .05$). A three-way interaction effect ($F = 4.33$; $p < .05$) between age, socio-economic status and employment status helped to elucidate these results. This effect indicated that young married women from lower-SES backgrounds who were not employed tended to have higher self-esteem than their employed counterparts, whereas the reverse was true among young married women of higher socio-economic status. This reversed effect may well reflect prevailing socio-cultural norms in the two groups. As noted in previous research (e.g., Yorburg and Arafat, 1975; Mason and Bumpass, 1975; Welch, 1975; Fine-Davis, 1976) traditional attitudes concerning the woman's role are, generally speaking, more strongly held by respondents from lower socio-economic backgrounds.

Thus, a lower-SES married woman who is not working is performing her role in a manner consistent with social norms and expectations. Conversely, given the somewhat less traditional attitudes held by members of higher socio-economic backgrounds regarding the woman's role, it is possible that the young married woman from such a background who is non-employed may be experiencing doubts about her role behaviour and beginning to question whether or not she should be employed, while employed women from higher-SES backgrounds may have more interesting jobs than women from lower-SES backgrounds, which could also have implications for feelings of self-esteem.

Fertility expectations and contraceptive practice

Previous research (e.g., Pratt and Whelpton, 1958; Weller, 1977) had shown that in general employed women had smaller families than non-employed women. It was not possible to test this relationship in the present study due to the nature of the stratification design, which called for an equal number of employed and non-employed married women, both with and without dependent children. It was possible, however, to see if there were differences among employed and non-employed married women with regard to their "ideal" and "expected" family size. Table 3.3 presents a comparison of employed and non-employed married women on these two variables, with age, socio-economic status and presence of dependent children controlled for. It was found that employment status did not differentiate between married women in terms of their ideal family size. The modal response to this question among all married women was four children. This figure contrasts with data from this time period (1976) from Britain which indicated

Table 3.3 Summary of analysis of variance results: main effects of four independent variables on ideal and expected family size and contraceptive use (N = 240 married women)

Source	*Sums of squares*	*df*	*F-ratio*
a. Ideal family size			
Main effects			
A (Dependent children)	.07	1	.05
B (Age)	8.07	1	5.59*
C (SES)	20.42	1	14.14***
D (Employment status)	1.07	1	.74
Residual	323.47	224	
b. Expected family size			
Main effects			
A (Dependent children)	18.15	1	6.24*
B (Age)	4.82	1	1.66
C (SES)	2.02	1	.69
D (Employment status)	22.82	1	7.84**
Residual	652.00	224	
c. Contraceptive use			
Main effects			
A (Dependent children)	.70	1	3.91*
B (Age)	4.54	1	25.16***
C (SES)	.94	1	5.20*
D (Employment status)	.94	1	5.20*
Residual	40.40	224	

*$p < .05$. **$p < .01$. ***$p < .001$.

that the ideal family size was now two to four children, with more respondents favouring two, rather than three or four.[4] Comparable data on ideal family size was not available on a national basis in Ireland at that time.

Thus, while employment status did not differentiate between married women in terms of their *ideal* family size, it did differentiate them in terms of their *expected* family size. Replicating findings of Sobol (1973) in the United States, the employed married women in our sample expected to have significantly smaller families than did the non-employed married women ($F = 7.84$; $p < .01$, Table 3.3).

Employed married women who currently had no dependent children expected to have the smallest families of all; this group of women is likely to include both older women who have completed their families as well as younger women who are practicing contraception.

Employed married women were also found to be significantly more likely than non-employed married women to use contraceptives ($F = 5.20$; $p < .05$). This finding is quite consistent with their expressed expectation of having smaller families. However, a two-way interaction effect between employment status and socio-economic status indicated that the greater likelihood of using contraceptives on the part of employed married women applied primarily to women from higher socio-economic backgrounds ($F = 3.90$; $p < .05$).

In addition to employment status, age was also found to be a significant predictor of ideal family size and contraceptive use, in the direction of older women being more likely to favour larger families ($F = 5.59$; $p < .05$) and less likely to use contraceptives ($F = 25.16$; $p < .001$) than younger women. Socio-economic status was also found to be predictive of these two variables: married women from lower socio-economic backgrounds were found to have larger ideal family sizes and to be less likely to use contraceptives. However, changing attitudes on the part of married women of lower socio-economic status were suggested by an obtained two-way interaction effect between age and socio-economic status, indicating that younger women in this group were more likely to have a smaller expected family size than were the older women in the group ($F = 4.17$; $p < .05$).

An examination of the effects of employment status and other demographic characteristics on married women's perception of the approval of important others regarding their actual or potential employment

Both the employed and non-employed married women in the sample were given parallel sets of questions concerning the perceived approval of several "important others" concerning their actual (in the case of employed women) or potential (in the case of non-employed women) employment. Perceptions of extent of approval or disapproval were ascertained for the respondent's husband, mother, father and closest friend. Each of these approval scores was weighted in terms of the importance of that individual's views to the subject. Finally, a global approval score was constructed which took into account all four of the important others (each weighted by their importance to the respondent). Table 3.4 presents analysis of variance results for these variables.

The findings to emerge from this set of analyses were quite consistent. Employed married women were found to perceive greater approval from their husbands, mothers and fathers concerning their employment than were non-employed married women concerning their potential employment. To what extent these differences reflect a process of dissonance reduction on the part of respondents as a means of rationalising their existing behaviour is open to speculation. However, an alternative explanation, namely that perceived attitudes of important others are an important factor influencing behaviour (cf. Newcomb, 1943), must also seriously be taken into consideration.

In addition to employment status, age was also found to be related to perceived approval of important others. Younger women (whether or not they were working) were more likely to perceive approval of their employment by their husbands than were older women. This suggests that male attitudes regarding employment of their wives may be changing in the direction of becoming less traditional. However, a significant interaction effect ($F = 8.21$; $p < .01$) indicated

Table 3.4 Summary of analysis of variance results: main effects of four independent variables on perceptions of the approval of important others concerning respondent's actual or potential employment (N = 240 married women)

Source	*Sums of squares*	*df*	*F-ratio*
a. Perception of husband's approval (weighted by importance)			
Main effects			
A (Dependent children)	32.26	1	.71
B (Age)	322.01	1	7.05**
C (SES)	120.42	1	2.64
D (Employment status)	1016.80	1	22.27***
Residual	10230.00	224	
b. Perception of mother's approval (weighted by importance)			
Main effects			
A (Dependent children)	.60	1	.01
B (Age)	117.59	1	2.87
C (SES)	21.60	1	.53
D (Employment status)	614.40	1	14.99***
Residual	9183.70	224	
c. Perception of father's approval (weighted by importance)			
Main effects			
A (Dependent children)	132.02	1	3.84
B (Age)	21.59	1	.63
C (SES)	8.06	1	.23
D (Employment status)	260.42	1	7.58**
Residual	7694.90	224	
d. Perception of friend's approval (weighted by importance)			
Main effects			
A (Dependent children)	3.27	1	.17
B (Age)	12.14	1	.63
C (SES)	.15	1	.01
D (Employment status)	70.41	1	3.65
Residual	4318.10	224	
e. Perception of overall approval (weighted by importance)			
Main effects			
A (Dependent children)	.50	1	.71
B (Age)	10.05	1	14.44***
C (SES)	.44	1	.63
D (Employment status)	49.23	1	70.77***
Residual	155.84	224	

*$p < .05$. **$p < .01$. ***$p < .001$.

that young women with dependent children perceived less approval from their husbands than did young women without dependent children. Interestingly enough, there was also an almost significant main effect ($F = 3.84$; $p < .06$) for presence of dependent children in the case of perception of fathers' approval. These findings, together with the interaction effect described earlier, suggest that women with dependent children may be particularly sensitive to the attitudes of their male important others. It is interesting, in this connection, that women with dependent children did not necessarily perceive less approval from their female important others (i.e., mother and closest friend) concerning employment on their part. These findings are consistent with other findings from this study which showed that males held significantly more traditional sex-role attitudes than women (Fine-Davis, 1983) and from other studies carried out in a similar time frame (1978) which also showed them to be less supportive of maternal employment (Fine-Davis, 2015).

A multiple regression analysis of predictors of employment status of married women

We have seen in the previous section that employed and non-employed married women differed on a number of characteristics. The analysis of variance model with employment status as an independent variable was used to make comparisons between the two groups of women, employed and non-employed, while controlling for other relevant demographic variables, in order to determine which variables were significantly related to employment status. However, the foregoing analyses do not tell us which variable or variables were most important in determining whether or not a married woman became employed in 1975. We shall now explore this question through the use of regression analysis. In this analysis we treat employment status as the dependent variable, rather than as an independent variable. Regression analysis will enable us to determine the extent to which certain attitudinal variables, which have been shown to be related to employment status, are predictive of employment status in a multiple regression model. This is not to say that holding certain attitudes necessarily "causes" one to become employed or to remain non-employed; it is equally plausible that one's employment status itself may influence one's attitudes. Thus, these analyses do not resolve the question of direction of causality. The most likely explanation is that there is a two-way causal chain. This question has been discussed by Weller (1977) and Hoffman (1974).

On the basis of the preceding analyses of variance, seven attitudinal variables were selected which either differentiated very significantly between employed and non-employed married women or differentiated at a moderate level of significance, but were of theoretical interest. These variables were (1) the perceived approval of important others concerning the respondent's actual or potential employment (the global measure of perceived approval of husband, mother, father and closest friend, weighted by the importance of their views to the respondent); (2) expected family size; (3) contraceptive use (artificial method vs. natural method or no method); (4) sex-role orientation (composite score on "traditional sex-role orientation"); (5) attitude to maternal employment (composite score on "positive attitude to maternal employment"); (6) extent to which limitations are perceived in housewife role (composite score on "perception of limitations in housewife role") and (7) religiosity (composite score on "religiosity").

These seven predictor variables were entered into a multiple regression analysis with employment status as the dependent variable. Table 3.5 presents the results of this analysis. These seven variables taken together yielded a multiple R of .51, which explains 26% of the variance in the dependent variable. It may be seen from an inspection of Table 3.5 that some variables which had been significant in the analyses of variance in terms of differentiating between employed and non-employed married women were not significant predictors of employment status when examined simultaneously with the other variables in the multiple regression equation. This is due to the fact that there is some common variance between some of the variables. For this reason, the next step undertaken was a stepwise multiple regression with these same seven variables. This procedure entered one variable at a time, with that predictor variable which explained the most variance entered first, that which explained the next most variance entered second, etc. Thus, the results of seven different equations, including from one variable to seven, were inspected.

Table 3.5 Multiple regression analysis of predictors of employment status of married women (N = 240)

Variables	*Multiple R*	R^2	*Beta*	*Standard error B*	*F*
1. Perceived approval of important others	.462	.213	–.37	.03	33.11***
2. Expected family size	.480	.230	.12	.02	4.33*
3. Contraceptive use	.484	.234	–.01	.07	0.05
4. Traditional sex-role orientation	.484	.234	–.08	.02	1.60
5. Positive attitude to maternal employment	.506	.256	–.16	.02	4.89*
6. Perception of limitations in housewife role	.508	.258	–.03	.02	.27
7. Religiosity	.514	.264	.10	.03	2.12

Multiple *R* for total equation		Analysis of variance for total equation				
Multiple *R*	= .514	Source	Sums of squares	*df*	Mean square	*F*
R^2	= .264	Regression	15.86	7	2.27	11.92**
Standard error	= .436	Residual	44.13	232	0.19	

$^*p < .05$. $^{**}p < .01$. $^{***}p < .001$.

Table 3.6 Summary of stepwise multiple regression of predictors of employment status of married women (N = 240)

Variables	*Beta*	*Standard error B*	*F*
1. Perceived approval of important others	−.37	.03	33.10***
2. Positive attitude to maternal employment	−.17	.02	6.84**
3. Expected family size	.12	.01	4.77*

Multiple *R* for total equation		Analysis of variance for total equation				
Multiple *R*	= .502	Source	Sums of squares	*df*	Mean squares	*F*
R^2	= .252	Regression	15.12	3	5.04	26.51**
Standard error	= .436	Residual	44.87	236	.19	

*$p < .05$. **$p < .01$. ***$p < .001$.

The equation consisting of three predictor variables yielded the optimal solution in terms of parsimony of explanation and percentage of variance explained. As may be seen from an inspection of Table 3.6, three of the original seven variables explained 25% of the variance (approximately 1% less than was explained by the original seven). By far the greatest amount of variance was explained by perceived approval of important others. It alone explained 21% of the variance (see Table 3.5). Those women who perceived approval of employment on their part from their important others were more likely to be employed than those perceiving disapproval. The next most important predictor was the respondent's own attitude to maternal employment. The more positive her attitude, the more likely she was to be employed. The third most important predictor was expected family size; those who expected to have smaller families were more likely to be employed than those expecting to have larger families.

When a four-variable regression equation was inspected, religiosity was the fourth variable entered. Its F-ratio of 2.05, while not reaching statistical significance, did indicate that religiosity explained some variance in the dependent variable in the direction of less religiosity being associated with employed status. However, its inclusion in the equation somewhat reduced the F-ratios of the two preceding variables, indicating that it was introducing enough common variance to detract from their unique significance.

In summary, it has been shown that the following factors predict a significant amount of variance in the dependent variable of the married woman's employment status: (1) her perceived approval of four of her important others (husband, mother, father and closest friend, weighted by their importance) concerning employment on her part; (2) her own attitude to maternal employment and (3) her expected family size.

The results concerning perceived approval of important others (in this case the husband) confirm those of Weil (1961) and Walsh and Whelan (1973); the results concerning the woman's own attitude also confirm those obtained by Walsh and Whelan (1973); and the results concerning expected family size replicate those of Sobol (1973). The percentage of variance explained (25%) by these three attitudinal variables exceeds that explained by a combination of attitudinal and non-attitudinal variables in the previous studies by Walsh and Whelan (18.6% was explained, of which the greatest amount of variance was due to the single variable of perceived approval of husband) and by Sobol (11% was explained by 14 variables, with the majority explained by wife's education and expected family size). These results suggest that if these three attitudinal variables were studied in a random sample of married women, together with some of the demographic characteristics found to be of importance by Walsh and Whelan (e.g., number and ages of children) and Sobol (i.e., wife's education), an even greater amount of variance in the dependent variable of employment status would undoubtedly be explained.

Notes

1 An earlier version this paper was published in Fine-Davis, M. (1979). Social-psychological predictors of employment status of married women in Ireland. *Journal of Marriage and the Family*, 47 (1), 145–158.
2 These items were not presented in sequence, but rather were imbedded in other related items.
3 Both main effects and interaction effects were examined; however, for reasons of space, only main effects are presented in tables. In general, there were very few significant interaction effects. All significant interaction effects which involved employment status are discussed in the text with accompanying F-ratios and levels of significance.
4 Data from Office of Population Censuses and Surveys, Central Statistics Office, London, as reported in "Fewer Births Trend Shown," 1976.

References

Bailyn, L. (1964). Notes on the role of choice in the psychology of women. *Daedalus*, 93, 700–710.

Callan, T. and Farrell, B. (1991). *Women's Participation in the Irish Labour Market*. Dublin: National Economic and Social Council.

Cherniss, C. (1972). Personality and ideology: A personological study of women's liberation. *Psychiatry*, 35 (2), 109–125.

Davis, E. E., Fine-Davis, M., Breathnach, A. and Moran, R. (1977). A study of the factor structure of attitudinal measures of major social psychological constructs in an Irish sample. *Economic and Social Review*, 9 (1), 27–50.

Fewer births trend shown (1976). *The Irish Times*, 5 May, p. 7.

Fine-Davis, M. (1976). *Structure, Determinants and Correlates of Attitudes Toward the Role and Status of Women in Ireland, with Particular Reference to Employment Status of Married Women*. Unpublished doctoral dissertation, Department of Psychology, Trinity College Dublin, University of Dublin.

Fine-Davis, M. (1979). Social-psychological predictors of employment status of married women in Ireland. *Journal of Marriage and the Family*, 47 (1), 145–158.
Fine-Davis, M. (1983). A society in transition: Structure and determinants of attitudes toward the role and status of women in Ireland. *Psychology of Women Quarterly*, 8 (2), 113–132.
Fine-Davis, M. (2015). *Gender Roles in Ireland: Three Decades of Attitude Change*. London: Routledge.
Fowler, M. G. and Van de Reit, H. K. (1972). Women, today and yesterday: An examination of the feminist personality. *Journal of Psychology*, 82, 269–276.
Gump, J. P. (1972). Sex-role attitudes and psychological well-being. *Journal of Social Issues*, 28 (2), 79–92.
Haavio-Mannila, E. (1972). Sex-role attitudes in Finland, 1966–70. *Journal of Social Issues*, 28 (2), 93–110.
Hall, J. and Jones, D. C. (1950). The social grading of occupations. *British Journal of Sociology*, 1, 31–55.
Hoffman, L. W. (1974). Psychological factors. In: L. W. Hoffman and F. I. Nye (Eds.), *Working Mothers*. San Francisco: Jossey-Bass, pp. 32–62.
Hutchinson, B. (1969). *Social Status and Inter-Generational Social Mobility in Dublin*. Paper No. 48. Dublin: The Economic and Social Research Institute.
Joesting, J. (1971). Comparison of women's liberation members with their non-member peers. *Psychological Reports*, 29 (3, Part 2), 1291–1294.
Kaiser, H. F. (1958). The varimax criterion for analytic rotation in factor analysis. *Psychometrika*, 23, 187–200.
Kirkpatrick, C. (1936). The construction of a belief-pattern scale for measuring attitudes toward feminism. *Journal of Social Psychology*, 7, 421–437.
Levinson, D. and Huffman, P. (1955). Traditional family ideology and its relation to personality. *Journal of Personality*, 23, 251–273.
Mason, K. O. and Bumpass, L. L. (1975). U.S. women's sex-role ideology, 1970. *American Journal of Sociology*, 80 (5), 1212–1219.
Meleis, A. I. (1971). Self-concept and family planning. *Nursing Research*, 20 (3), 229–236.
Newcomb, T. M. (1943). *Personality and Social Change*. New York: Holt, Rinehart and Winston.
Nielson, J. M. and Doyle, P. T. (1975). Sex-role stereotypes of feminists and non-feminists. *Sex Roles*, 1 (1), 83–95.
O'Keefe, B. E. (1972). Attitudes toward women's liberation: Relationships between cooperation, personality and demographic variables. *Dissertation Abstracts International*, 33 (3-B), 1293.
Pawlicki, R. E. and Almquist, C. (1973). Authoritarianism, locus of control and tolerance of ambiguity as reflected in membership and nonmembership in a women's liberation group. *Psychological Reports*, 32, 1331–1337.
Pratt, L. and Whelpton, P. K. (1958). Extra-familial participation of wives in relation to interest in and liking for children, fertility planning and actual and desired family size. In: P. K. Whelpton and C. V. Kiser (Eds.), *Social and Psychological Factors Affecting Fertility* (Vol. 5). New York: Milbank Memorial Fund.
Ridley, J. (1959). Number of children expected in relation to nonfamilial activities of the wife. *Milbank Memorial Fund Quarterly*, 37, 277–296.

Ryckman, R. M., Martens, J. L., Rodda, W. C. and Sherman, M. F. (1972). Locus of control and attitudes toward women's liberation in a college population. *Journal of Social Psychology*, 87, 157–158.

Sobol, M. G. (1973). A dynamic analysis of labour force participation of married women of childbearing age. *The Journal of Human Resources*, 8 (4), 497–505.

Spence, J. T. and Helmreich, R. (1972). The attitudes toward women scale: An objective instrument to measure attitudes toward the rights and roles of women in contemporary society. *JSAS Catalog of Selected Documents in Psychology*, 2 (Spring), 66–67.

Stoloff, C. (1973). Who joins women's liberation? *Psychiatry*, 36 (3), 325–340.

Tangri, S. S. (1970). Role-innovation in occupational choice among college women. *Dissertation Abstracts*, 30 (9-A), 4021.

Walsh, B. M. and Whelan, B. J. (1973). *The Determinants of Female Labour Force Participation: An Econometric Analysis of Survey Data.* Paper presented to the Statistical and Social Inquiry Society of Ireland, Dublin, December.

Weil, M. W. (1961). An analysis of the factors influencing married women's actual or planned work participation. *American Sociological Review*, 26, 91–96.

Welch, S. (1975). Support among women for the issues of the women's movement. *The Sociological Quarterly*, 16 (2), 216–227.

Weller, R. H. (1977). Wife's employment and cumulative family size in the United States, 1970 and 1960. *Demography*, 14 (1), 43–65.

Worell, J. and Worell, L. (1971). *Supporters and Opposers of Women's Liberation: Some Personality Correlates.* Paper presented at the Annual Convention of the American Psychological Association, Washington, DC, September.

Yorburg, B. and Arafat, I. (1975). Current sex-role conceptions and conflict. *Sex-Roles*, 1 (2), 135–146.

Chapter 4

Effects of housework vs. employment on married women's well-being[1]

During the 1970s several studies were carried out, both by psychologists and sociologists, which examined the differential satisfaction of housewives and employed married women. Some of these studies also examined the effect of social class on satisfaction with one's role. These studies addressed the basic questions: Does housework or paid employment outside the home lead to greater satisfaction? Is the housewife role more gratifying for certain groups of women (i.e., those less well educated or of lower socio-economic status) or is the converse true? Although some of these studies revealed no difference between employed married women and housewives on measures of life satisfaction (Spreitzer et al., 1975; Shaver and Freedman, 1976) and work satisfaction (Weaver and Holmes, 1975), others, using smaller, more homogeneous samples, did. In a study of U.S. women living in a working-class neighbourhood, Ferree (1976) found that full-time housewives were more dissatisfied than women who were employed. Their dissatisfaction with housework was found to be related to a sense of isolation, powerlessness, and low self-esteem. Ferree's findings corroborated earlier findings obtained by Komarovsky (1962) to the effect that less educated women were somewhat happier (or less unhappy) at home than better educated women; however, Ferree found that these less educated women were even happier if they were employed. The importance of employment status, rather than class, would appear to have been reinforced in a study of British housewives by Oakley (1974) in which no class differences in satisfaction were obtained. Both working-class and middle-class housewives were equally likely to express dissatisfaction.

In addition to looking at satisfaction, some investigators have looked at the relationship of employment status to physical and psychological symptoms and, indeed, significant differences have been found. Shaver and Freedman (1976), in a large-scale study in the United States, found that while housewives said they were as happy as employed wives, they nevertheless were more likely to report psychological symptoms such as anxiety, worry, loneliness and feelings of worthlessness. Powell's (1977) study of "empty nest" U.S. women in their fifties also found a higher level of psychiatric symptoms among full-time housewives than employed women; women employed part time occupied an intermediate position. Cochrane and Stopes-Roe (1981) in Britain also found that a higher level of psychiatric symptoms was associated with being a full-time housewife. These authors concluded that "employment offers a protection against depression for women much as it does for men" (Cochrane and Stopes-Roe, 1981, p. 379).

Further findings, consistent with the above, which are perhaps even more noteworthy, since they are based on an actual behavioural measure, were reported by Cumming et al. (1975), who analysed nationwide suicide statistics from British Columbia. These authors found that housewives were significantly more likely than employed married women to commit suicide. These findings were even stronger in an analysis of 1971, as compared with 1961 data, which the authors interpreted as indicative of the greater normative support for employment in 1971, resulting in its offering even greater protection from suicide than it did 10 years previously. Like several other investigators, Cumming et al. (1975) interpreted their findings as suggesting that housewives may be more likely to experience isolation, loneliness, and lack of social integration, and that the main benefit of employment may be affiliative rather than economic.

The present study was carried out in the late 1970s in Ireland, where employment on the part of married women was far less common than in the United States, Great Britain, or most of Western Europe. Although the labour force participation rate of Irish married women was only 16.4% in 1979, this represented a threefold increase since 1961, when the rate was only 5.2%. Several factors were responsible for this. While women have traditionally had good access to education in Ireland, many barriers to equal employment opportunity, particularly for married women, remained until relatively recently. These included the "marriage bar" (in which women had to resign from their jobs upon marriage), differential salary scales, lack of access to contraceptives and tax laws which acted as a strong deterrent (treating the wife's income as that of her husband and taxing it at his highest marginal rate). The period from 1973 to 1981 saw most of these deterrents removed and strong anti-discrimination legislation passed. Nevertheless, attitudes, although having undergone change, have tended to remain relatively traditional in the area of women's role and the family. They have, furthermore, been underpinned by a strong religious ethos and enshrined in the Constitution of the Irish State.

The purpose of the present study was to examine the cross-cultural generalisability of the previous findings concerning the psychological effects of employment for married women, as well as to see whether these effects occurred in both working-class and middle-class women. A second major purpose was to explore a variety of measures relating to the quality of women's working lives, both inside and outside the home, which might help to explain any obtained differences in reported well-being.

Methods

The Irish data presented here were collected in the context of a harmonised survey of the quality of working life which was carried out in eight member countries of the European Community under the auspices of the Statistical Office of the European Communities, Luxembourg, in the context of a new series of harmonised surveys of subjective social indicators designed to complement the more familiar objective social indicators (see Shanks, 1975; Fine-Davis and Davis, 1977). This was one of the first times that work in the home was treated as "work" and compared with employment outside the home. In the Irish survey a nationwide representative sample of 1,862 respondents aged 18 and over was selected using the Electoral Register as the sampling frame. The data were collected in the fall of 1978 by means of individual interviews in the respondents' homes. The present analysis compares 539 non-employed married women (i.e., housewives) and 76 employed married women, aged 18 to 65, who emerged in the nationwide sample. To the extent possible, the same questions were asked of both of these groups and it is these common questions that are focused upon here. Specifically, the two groups were asked about their satisfaction with eight different aspects of their work, the qualities required by their work, the demands made by their work and their degree of coping with work demands. Both groups were also compared on several measures of physical and psychological well-being: (1) two measures of health (number of sick days in the last 12 months and overall satisfaction with health); (2) overall satisfaction with work and (3) two measures of life satisfaction – one a single item, four-point satisfaction measure and the second a composite score of four factorially pure Likert items, rated on seven-point scales of agreement vs. disagreement (e.g., "Taking all things together, I would say I am very happy these days," "In general, I find that the way I am spending my life these days is not very satisfying," etc.). In the case of all of the comparisons, three-way analysis variance was used with a 2 x 2 x 2 factorial design, varying two levels each of employment status, socio-economic status and age.

Results

Satisfaction with aspects of work

Table 4.1 presents analysis of variance results for eight dependent measures of satisfaction with various aspects of work. In the case of the employed women, these questions referred to their employment; in the case of the housewives, they referred to their work in the home. Employed married women were found to be significantly more likely than housewives to be satisfied with the perceived importance of their work in the eyes of the general public ($F = 21.5$; $p < .001$). Employed married women were also significantly more likely than housewives to report satisfaction with the content and type of work they were doing ($F = 5.9$; $p < .05$). However, a significant three-way interaction between employment status, age and socio-economic status (SES) indicated that, whereas satisfaction with work content was greater for young, high-SES, employed women, this was not the case for young, low-SES, employed women ($F = 9.3$; $p < .01$). Among the latter group, there was little difference between housewives and those in paid

Table 4.1 Summary of analysis of variance results: source level means for main effects of three independent variables on satisfaction with various aspects of work (N = 578 married women)[a]

Satisfaction with:[b]	*Employment status*		*Age*		*SES*		*Significant interaction effects*
	Employed (n = 70)	*Non-employed (n = 508)*	*18–39 years (n = 261)*	*40–65 years (n = 317)*	*Low (n = 285)*	*High (n = 293)*	
Work environment	3.45	3.48	3.47	3.49	$F = 22.8^{***}$ 3.33	3.63	Age x employment status $F = 4.6^{*}$
Importance of respondent's work in the eyes of the public	$F = 21.5^{***}$ 3.52	2.97	$F = 11.9^{***}$ 2.89	3.16	3.02	3.06	None
Content and type of work	$F = 5.9^{*}$ 3.58	3.38	$F = 7.6^{**}$ 3.32	3.47	$F = 15.0^{***}$ 3.29	3.50	Age x SES x employment status $F = 9.3^{**}$
Stress due to nature of work	3.37	3.17	3.14	3.23	3.14	3.24	None
Opportunities for further training/vocational qualifications	3.03	2.87	2.81	2.94	$F = 15.7^{***}$ 2.71	3.06	None
Earnings/housekeeping money	3.19	3.23	3.30	3.17	$F = 26.6^{***}$ 3.03	3.45	Age x employment status $F = 7.9^{**}$
Provision of enough material, equipment and staff to complete work	3.33	3.33	$F = 4.0^{*}$ 3.40	3.26	$F = 13.4^{***}$ 3.19	3.48	Age x employment status $F = 5.1^{*}$
Autonomy	3.51	3.59	3.59	3.57	$F = 14.0^{***}$ 3.48	3.69	None

a In some cases the n drops to a lower figure due to non-applicable responses; however, in no case do such variations change the interpretations made.
b Satisfaction measured on 4-point scale: 1 = "very dissatisfied"; 4 = "very satisfied."

$^{***} = p < 0.001$
$^{**} = p < 0.01$
$^{*} = p < 0.05$

employment. These results suggest that the work available to young, lower-SES women is slightly less desirable or roughly equivalent to housework, whereas the work available to high-SES women in this age group (18–39) would appear to be more stimulating than housework.

In this context, it is interesting to consider that previous research conducted in Ireland showed that employment was related to higher self-esteem on the part of high-SES young women, whereas it was related to lower self-esteem on the part of low-SES employed women, which may reflect different social class norms concerning the sex-role appropriateness of employment on the part of married women of child-bearing age (Fine-Davis, 1979a – see also Chapter 3). Consistent with this interpretation, the present results showed that older, low-SES employed women (i.e., those 40 to 65) expressed much higher levels of satisfaction with their work content than did their younger counterparts. This may reflect a greater attachment to the work situation during the phase of the life cycle when family responsibilities have diminished, as well as the possibility of having attained more responsible or interesting jobs. However, other findings offer further insights into the discrepancy between older and younger low-SES women. First, lower-SES women were less satisfied generally with the amount of money they received, whether in employment or as housekeeping money ($F = 26.6$; $p < .001$). Second, younger employed women were less satisfied with their earnings than older employed women ($F = 7.9$; $p < .01$). Since the younger low-SES employed woman is less satisfied with her earnings than her older counterpart, a perception which probably reflects her lower wages, employment may thus be less attractive to her.

Work requirements and demands

In addition to assessing levels of satisfaction with various aspects of work, the study compared the skills and qualities employed married women and housewives perceived as required in their work.

As may be seen in Table 4.2, there were no differences between the two groups on any of the indices (i.e., [1] psychomotor, [2] manual/technical or [3] conceptual/verbal and interpersonal). However, a significant interaction effect occurred for the index of conceptual/verbal and interpersonal skills. This index (reliability = .82) included such qualities as leadership, decision making, creativity, planning, negotiating, expressing, etc. The interaction effect demonstrated that high-SES employed women were most likely to use such skills in their work, next most likely to use these skills were housewives of both social classes, and least likely to use them were low-SES employed women ($F = 12.3$; $p < .001$).

There were no differences between employed married women and housewives in the extent to which they perceived their work as "demanding", nor in their ability to cope with the demands of their work. Younger women (both housewives and employed), however, were more likely to perceive greater demands ($F = 4.0$; $p < .05$).

Table 4.2 Summary of analysis of variance results: source level means for main effects of three independent variables for various characteristics of work (N = 613 married women)

Work characteristics	*Employment status*		*Age*		*SES*		*Significant interaction effects*
	Employed (n = 76)	*Non-employed (n = 537)*	*18–39 years (n = 278)*	*40–65 years (n = 335)*	*Low (n = 303)*	*High (n = 310)*	
Index of psychomotor skills	3.09	2.95	$F = 15.5^{***}$ 3.19	2.79	2.96	2.98	None
Index of conceptual/verbal/interpersonal skills	4.28	4.20	4.32	4.12	$F = 9.0^{**}$ 4.00	4.41	SES x employment status $F = 12.3^{***}$
Index of manual/technical skills	1.45	1.61	1.60	1.59	1.56	1.62	SES x age x employment status $F = 12.1^{***}$
Assessment of demands made by daily work[a]	3.64	3.64	$F = 4.0^{*}$ 3.74	3.56	3.58	3.70	None
Degree of coping with work requirements[b]	2.90	2.76	$F = 11.3^{***}$ 2.88	2.70	2.77	2.79	None
Length of work week (hours)	$F = 150.9^{***}$ 36.13	66.23	62.43	62.46	62.36	62.54	None

a 5-point scale: 1 = "demands very small"; 5 = "demands very great"
b 4-point scale: 1 = "often requires too much"; 2 = "sometimes requires too much"; 3 = "generally able to cope"; 4 = "underemployed, could do more"

*** = $p < 0.001$
** = $p < 0.01$
* = $p < 0.05$

Women in this age group (18–39) are most likely to have increased family responsibilities, which constitute additional demands upon the basic workload, be it inside or outside the home. However, in spite of their greater work demands, younger women were not less able to cope; they were in fact more likely to report that they were able to cope than older women ($F = 11.3$; $p < .001$).

Subjective measures of well-being

To what extent is a married woman's employment status related to her feelings of well-being? The employed married women and housewives were compared on five different measures of physical and psychological well-being. These included a relatively "objective" measure of health (i.e., the number of sick days in the previous year), a subjective measure of health status, as well as measures of satisfaction with one's work and one's life in general. Table 4.3 presents analyses of variance for the two groups (employed vs. housewives) while simultaneously exploring the effects of age and socio-economic status. The results indicate that employment status is associated with greater perceived well-being on three measures: satisfaction with one's health ($F = 4.3$; $p < .05$), satisfaction with one's work ($F = 13.3$; $p < .001$), and life satisfaction ($F = 4.8$; $p < .05$).

It is interesting to note that the lesser satisfaction with health on the part of housewives was not associated with a significantly greater number of sick days, suggesting that the phenomenon we are seeing is primarily psychological in nature. Far more significant than employment status, however, was socio-economic status. Lower-SES respondents were worse off on all measures and all differences were highly significant. The lower-SES group was more likely to report a greater number of sick days, greater dissatisfaction with their health and greater dissatisfaction with their work as well as with life in general. Older respondents were also worse off in terms of three of the five measures. They reported a greater number of sick days, greater dissatisfaction with their health and a lesser degree of life satisfaction.

Discussion and implications

In summary, the findings have shown that employed married women in Ireland are significantly more likely than housewives to express overall satisfaction with their work and with two major aspects of it: its content and its perceived value in the community. One exception to this was the finding that younger, low-SES, employed women were not more likely than housewives of similar age and SES to express satisfaction with their work content. Several possible interpretations of this were put forth, including (1) that the work available to young, low-SES women may be less interesting than housework and (2) that social pressures and norms may be exerted on younger women from working-class backgrounds to exercise a more traditional role. Lower-SES women, regardless of age or employment status, reported less satisfaction with their work in several respects, i.e.,

Table 4.3 Summary of analysis of variance results: source level means for main effects of three independent variables for various aspects of health, work and life in general (N = 615 married women)

	Employment status		*Age*		*SES*		*Significant interaction effects*
	Employed (n = 76)	*Non-employed (n = 539)*	*18–39 years (n = 278)*	*40–65 years (n = 337)*	*Low (n = 304)*	*High (n = 311)*	
Number of sick days[a]			$F = 6.0^{*}$		$F = 7.3^{**}$		None
	1.87	2.09	1.91	2.19	2.21	1.91	
Satisfaction with health[b]	$F = 4.3^{*}$		$F = 23.1^{***}$		$F = 9.1^{**}$		None
	3.66	3.48	3.65	3.37	3.41	3.59	
Satisfaction with present work[b]	$F = 13.3^{***}$				$F = 14.8^{***}$		None
	3.77	3.52	3.53	3.56	3.46	3.64	
Life satisfaction I[b]	3.62	3.55	3.61	3.52	$F = 11.0^{***}$		None
					3.48	3.64	
Life satisfaction II[c]	$F = 4.8^{*}$		$F = 10.0^{**}$		$F = 13.0^{***}$		None
	5.77	5.44	5.65	5.34	5.30	5.66	

a 5-point scale: 1 = "no sick days"; 5 = "more than 28 sick days"
b 4-point scale: 1 = "very dissatisfied"; 4 = "very satisfied"
c Composite score ranging from 1 to 7, based on level of agreement (1 = "strongly disagree"; 7 = "strongly agree") with 4 factorially pure Likert items measuring life satisfaction

*** = $p < 0.001$
** = $p < 0.01$
* = $p < 0.05$

it did not offer as much autonomy, opportunities for further training, income, etc. as did the work of higher-SES women. It was also found that among lower-income women, paid employment drew upon fewer of their conceptual/verbal and interpersonal skills than did housework. Such findings clearly suggest that the skills of lower-SES women are not being fully utilised in the workplace, a factor which may in part be responsible for the lower work satisfaction of these women. However, in spite of this, the overall scores of employed women – regardless of social class – indicated that they were more satisfied generally with their work, their health and their life in general than were housewives. Thus, the data show that employment is related to greater satisfaction and sense of well-being among married women of both social classes, but it is related to even greater satisfaction for high-SES women.

The increased workload of a job outside the home, together with that of a housewife after working hours, did not seem to lead to such work overload that health problems ensued. No differences in sick days were reported and, as noted earlier, employed women reported significantly greater satisfaction with their health. One cannot impute causality here: we do not know if healthier women join the workforce or if holding a job outside the home in some way contributes to health. However, a plausible interpretation, based on the data, is that the satisfaction gained from the work itself may contribute in part to a feeling of health and well-being.

The fact that the single item four-point scale measure of life satisfaction did not pick up differences based on employment status and age, but that the four-item factor analytically derived measure using seven-point agree-disagree scales did, provides further support for the usefulness of more robust measures which are capable of picking up greater subtlety of response. The single item measure of life satisfaction may indeed be eliciting a social desirability response (Robinson and Shaver, 1973). As Shaver and Freedman (1976) also found, more specific measures, such as psychological symptoms of anxiety, feelings of worthlessness, etc. did yield significant differences between the employed and non-employed women in their sample. While employment status significantly predicted three of the five measures of well-being, socio-economic status predicted all five and at a highly significant level in each case ($p < .001$). These findings clearly show that the quality of life of lower-income women is inferior, regardless of whether they work inside or outside of the home. These findings were underpinned by many specific results documenting the ways in which the quality of their working life was inferior.

In view of previous research findings in Ireland concerning the attitudes and other characteristics of employed and non-employed married women, the relative dissatisfaction of housewives is somewhat surprising. For example, housewives were found to hold more traditional sex-role attitudes, to be less supportive of maternal employment, and to be less likely to perceive limitations in the housewife role (Fine-Davis, 1979a). Thus, their own behaviour (i.e., being housewives) is quite congruent with their attitudes about appropriate sex-role behavior. Furthermore, they were found to be more religious (Fine-Davis, 1979a) – and religiosity was found to be significantly related to traditional sex-role attitudes (Fine-Davis, 1979b). Housewives were also found to have a larger expected family size and to be less likely to use contraceptives than employed married women (Fine-Davis, 1979a). They also reported that their important others (i.e., husband, mother, and father) would be disapproving if they took up employment (Fine-Davis, 1979a). Thus, their entire lifestyle, values and attitudes are supportive of their current behavior. Why then, are they less satisfied than employed women with their health, their work and their life in general? It may be that they are not fully aware that they are relatively dissatisfied, or if so, why they are. If they were, it would generate a state of cognitive dissonance which would exert pressure towards a shift in either attitudes or behaviour. Apparently, precisely this must be happening to sizable numbers of Irish married women, since their rate of labour force participation has trebled in the last 20 years (Sexton, 1981) and all evidence points to its continuing.

Note

1 A previous version of this chapter was published in Fine-Davis, M. (1985) Housework vs. employment: Quality of working life and psychological well-being among Irish married women. In: M. Safir, M. Mednick, D. N. Israeli and J. Bernard (Eds.), *Women's Worlds: From the New Scholarship*. New York: Praeger, pp. 105–116.

References

Cochrane, R. and Stopes-Roe, M. (1981). Women, marriage, employment and mental health. *British Journal of Psychiatry*, 139, 373–381.

Cumming, E., Lazer, C. and Chisholm, L. (1975). Suicide as an index of role strain among employed and not employed married women in British Columbia. *Canadian Review of Sociology and Anthropology*, 12 (4), 462–470.

Ferree, M. M. (1976). Working class jobs: Housework and paid work as sources of satisfaction. *Social Problems*, 23 (4), 431–441.

Fine-Davis, M. (1979a). Social-psychological predictors of employment status of married women in Ireland. *Journal of Marriage and the Family*, 41 (1), 145–158.

Fine-Davis, M. (1979b). Personality correlates of attitudes toward the role and status of women in Ireland. *Journal of Personality*, 47 (3), 379–396.

Fine-Davis, M. and Davis, E. E. (1977). The continuing social survey: A nationwide study of subjective social indicators and related public attitudes. *Administration*, 25 (4), 503–518.

Komarovsky, M. (1962). *Blue Collar Marriage*. New York: Vintage Books.

Oakley, A. (1974). *The Sociology of Housework*. London: Martin Robertson & Co. Ltd.

Powell, B. (1977). The empty nest, employment, and psychiatric symptoms in college-educated women. *Psychology of Women Quarterly*, 2 (1), 35–43.

Robinson, J. P. and Shaver, P. R. (1973). *Measures of Social-Psychological Attitudes* (rev. ed.). Ann Arbor: Institute for Social Research, University of Michigan.

Sexton, J. J. (1981). The Changing Labour Force. Paper presented at Conference on "The Irish Economy and Society in the Eighties," The Economic and Social Research Institute, Dublin, 6 October.

Shanks, M. (1975). Multipurpose and Subjective Surveys – A User's View. Paper presented at the Seminar on Multipurpose Surveys and Subjective Questions, Statistical Office of the European Communities, Luxembourg, 25–28 November.

Shaver, P. and Freedman, J. (1976). Your pursuit of happiness. *Psychology Today*, (3), 26–33.

Spreitzer, E., Snyder, E. E. and Larson, D. (1975). Age, marital status, and labor force participation as related to life satisfaction. *Sex Roles*, 1 (3), 235–247.

Weaver, C. N. and Holmes, S. L. (1975). A comparative study of the work satisfaction of females with full-time employment and fulltime housekeeping. *Journal of Applied Psychology*, 60 (1), 117–118.

Chapter 5

Denial of discrimination? Attitudinal and other barriers to women's equal participation in the workplace

Introduction

The international and Irish context

Women's poorer position in the labour force has been shown to be an international phenomenon manifest in the OECD countries (OECD, 1980), the European Community (Eurostat, 1983), the Nordic countries (Haavio-Mannila and Skard, 1985) and Ireland (Commission on the Status of Women, 1972; McCarthy, 1978; Smyth, 1984; Blackwell, 1986; Second Commission on the Status of Women, 1993; Drew, 1996; O'Connor, 1998). Census data, as well as survey data, have indicated that the pattern of job structures in work organisations results in women being clustered at the lower end of the organisational hierarchy in all the occupations they occupy (McCarthy, 1978). This includes lower wages, reflected in a significant gender pay gap (Ruane and Sutherland, 1999). It also includes less inclusion of women at higher levels and in management (e.g., McCarthy, 1978; Russell et al., 2009; Eurofound, 2018). There has been extensive occupational segregation by gender, which is more pronounced in the case of women (Ruane and Sutherland, 1999). Women are often employed in traditionally female occupations (e.g., nursing, teaching, secretarial work, etc.) (Commission on the Status of Women, 1972) and these jobs traditionally do not attract high levels of pay or status. Moreover, as they are largely gender segregated, it is difficult to make comparisons with other comparable kinds of work. As Drew (1996) notes:

> In common with many other countries, Irish women are occupationally segregated: horizontally by "crowding" into a limited range of occupations most notably in the "caring" professions (nursing, teaching, social work), retailing and "personal services" (cleaning, catering, hairdressing etc.) and insurance, finance and business services; and vertically through the underrepresentation of women in skilled occupations and management. The limited sources of analysis on gender segregation cover the 1970s to 1980s and suggest a decline in horizontal segregation. However, data for vertical

> segregation showed that women were severely under-represented at executive/managerial level and other "high occupational status categories" (Blackwell, 1986). This segregation has also contributed to the earnings differential between men and women.
>
> (p. 7)

The latest figures from the European Union show that the uneven concentration of women and men in different sectors of the labour market is a persistent problem in the EU. More women work in education, health and social work (30% of women compared to 8% of men) while significantly more men are employed in science, technology, engineering and mathematics (7% of women compared to 33% of men) (European Institute for Gender Equality, 2019a). Individual country data shows that this gender segregation also holds true for Ireland, with 34% of women working in education, health and social work, compared with 8% of men. Similarly just 6% of women work in science, technology, engineering and mathematics (STEM) occupations compared with 26% of men (European Institute for Gender Equality, 2019b). As Hearn (2001) cogently points out: "A well-established mode of gendering is gender segregation in organisations (p. 12)."

Apart from gender segregation in terms of types of occupations, lack of equal pay has also been a key issue. Ireland's membership of the European Community from 1973 onwards directly led to enactment of equal pay legislation. This was due to the fact that all members of the then European Economic Community (EEC) were required to implement EEC directives agreed by the European Community, including equal pay legislation, which was passed in 1974 and implemented in Ireland in 1976 (see Second Commission on the Status of Women, 1993, p. 106). This led to an increase in women's earnings. Callender and Meenan (1994) noted that women's average hourly earnings in manufacturing had been just 58% of men's in 1967, but rose to 68% by 1987. The Second Commission on the Status of Women (1993) observed that over the previous decade women's hourly earnings, as a proportion of men's, had remained static at 68% (p. 102) and, as Drew (1996) noted, this was despite the equal pay legislation. By 1998 women's average hourly earnings had increased to 73% (Ruane and Sutherland, 1999; Hannon and Sinclair, 1999), reflecting a gender gap of 27%, and by 2005 were 86% of men's (CSO, 2007) – the gender gap was now 14%. Thus, the effects of the equal pay legislation, while not immediate, were incremental, resulting in major change since its enactment. The gender gap further narrowed to 12% in 2012, but by 2014 it had reverted back to 14% (Gartland, *Irish Times*, 2017). Nevertheless, in spite of these fluctuations, the overall trend has been upwards. Thus, the reasons for women's lower wages and lesser status in the labour force relative to men in part reflect the structural characteristics of women's employment, but also include other attitudinal and social factors.

The extent to which women's poor position in the organisational hierarchy is due to discriminatory attitudes and practices on the part of management and the extent to which it is a result of other factors has not been established. It has sometimes been suggested that women do not seek greater responsibility at work and that is why they are not better represented at the higher levels of management. It is argued that married women in particular already have too much to do balancing job and family responsibilities that they could not cope with more demanding jobs – or at least they cannot do so without more flexible hours and assistance with childcare and household tasks.

Some of these issues were explored in the present study in order to see how women perceived their own situation in relation to the workplace and in terms of their own career advancement. We explored these issues in several sequential studies over time to ascertain women's perceptions of whether they had experienced discrimination in employment, and we also compared these attitudes with those of other groups in Irish society.

Introduction to the studies and data collected – 1975, 1986, 2005

This chapter focuses on perceptions of discrimination against women in the workplace as well as barriers to their career advancement. Employed female respondents were asked about their own experience of discrimination in three separate studies over a thirty-year period, beginning with the first study in 1975, and subsequently in two follow-up studies in 1986 and 2005. Women were asked about the extent to which, if any, they had experienced discrimination in several areas of work: (1) getting a job, (2) training, (3) pay, (4) promotion and (5) kind of work or quality of work experience. They were also asked about (6) discrimination by the educational system. Initial comparisons were made in 1986 with the 1975 data, enabling us to compare the level of discrimination experienced by women in 1975 with that experienced in 1986. It was of particular interest to explore whether the anti-discrimination legislation, i.e., the Anti-Discrimination (Equal Pay) Act of 1974 and the Employment Equality Act (1977) had had any impact on women's perceived discrimination during this period. These items were then replicated in a study carried out in 2005, so that we are able to see how women's experience of discrimination has changed over a thirty-year period of time.

The data examined in this chapter are from three different studies. (Details on the methodology of each study, e.g., sampling, etc. are contained in Chapter 2.):

1 A study of attitudes towards the role and status of women was carried out in 1975 (Fine-Davis, 1976, 1977).
2 A study of changing gender roles in Ireland was carried out in 1986. The results comparing the data from the 1975 and 1986 studies were presented in Volume II of a series of three reports published by the Joint Oireachtas Committee on Women's Rights of the Irish Parliament in 1988 (Fine-Davis, 1988a, 1988b, 1988c). The 1986 study also asked respondents about barriers to career advancement.

3 A third study, carried out in 2005 (Fine-Davis et al., 2005), focused on work-life balance in the Irish population. In the course of this study we replicated the earlier measures of perceived discrimination and barriers to career advancement, thus enabling us to examine how attitudes had changed in these areas over three points in time – 1975, 1986 and 2005.

The 1986 and 2005 studies were designed in such a way as to explore attitudes from several perspectives. The first concerned women's *own* experience of discrimination in the workplace. The second was a comparison of women's own experience of discrimination with their perception of the extent of discrimination experienced by *women in general.* A third set of comparisons made was that between employed women, on the one hand, and other groups concerning estimates of the extent of discrimination experienced by employed women in general. These "other groups" included employed men and non-employed women. The purpose was to see if employed women were more aware of discrimination, since they could identify with the group in question, if they were less aware, or if there was a general consensus concerning levels of discrimination.

The extent to which women's relatively poor position in the organisational hierarchy is due to discriminatory attitudes and practices on the part of management and the extent to which it may be due to other factors (such as women not wanting more responsibility) has not been fully established. Thus, a second focus of the research was an examination of attitudes concerning barriers to women's career advancement. The purpose of this part of the study was (a) to ascertain which barriers, if any, employed women perceived were important in relation to their own career advancement and (b) to examine how these views compared with the perceptions of others, that is, employed men and non-employed women. By obtaining information on these questions from different vantage points, it was hoped that some light might be shed on these important questions.

Employed women's experience of discrimination: 1975–1986

In the 1975 study employed women were asked a series of questions concerning whether or not they had personally experienced discrimination in the area of employment because of being a woman, and, if so, to what extent. The questions concerned the possibility of discrimination:

1 in *getting a job*
2 in *job training*
3 in terms of *pay*
4 in terms of the *kind of work* or *quality of work experience* given to her (as opposed to that given to other workers)
5 in terms of *promotion*

In addition, women were asked if they felt they had in any way been discriminated against by the *educational system* because of being a woman.

Identical questions were put to the 1986 sample of employed women to see if there had been any changes in the intervening 11 years, during which several important developments had taken place. The most important of these were the passage of the Anti-Discrimination (Pay) Act of 1974, which legislated for equal pay, and the Employment Equality Act of 1977, which prohibited discrimination on the grounds of sex or marital status in recruitment for employment, in training, in conditions of employment or in the provision of opportunities for promotion. The latter act provided *inter alia* for the establishment in 1977 of the Employment Equality Agency, a statutory body with the role of enforcing this anti-discrimination legislation. The Equal Pay Act was not implemented until 1976, due to economic hardship in the country, so that the data from the 1975 study were collected after legislation was passed, but prior to its implementation (see Second Commission on the Status of Women, 1993).

Experience of discrimination in getting a job

Table 5.1 presents data showing the extent to which employed women experienced discrimination in relation to employment and by the educational system. Data are presented for 1975 for Dublin only and for 1986 with separate breakdowns for Dublin and rural areas. The data are also presented separately for married and single women.

In 1975, 27% of Dublin women had experienced some degree of discrimination in getting a job. Of these, about one-third, or 7.7% of the total sample, had experienced either "a fair amount" or "a great deal" of discrimination. By 1986 this had increased significantly. Of the Dublin women in the 1986 sample, 40% said they had experienced some degree of discrimination in getting a job, with 15.8% of the total sample reporting "a fair amount" or "a great deal" of discrimination. This difference was found to be statistically significant ($p < .01$) even when controlling for age, socio-economic status and marital status, as shown in Table 5.2.

Rural women reported less discrimination in getting a job than Dublin women did, with just 20% of rural women reporting any level of discrimination in getting a job. In contrast to Dublin, married rural women did not report the more extreme levels of discrimination at all, although 8.4% of single rural women did.

Experience of discrimination in job training

In 1975, 28% of employed women in Dublin reported having experienced some degree of discrimination in job training. However, this figure was much higher for single women (40%) than for married (22%). In 1986, the total percentage

Table 5.1 Employed women's experience of discrimination: 1975–1986

a) Experience of discrimination in getting a job

	1975			*1986*			*1986*		
	DUBLIN ONLY			DUBLIN			RURAL		
	Married (*n* = 120)	*Single* (*n* = 60)	*Total* (*n* = 180)	*Married* (*n* = 60)	*Single* (*n* = 60)	*Total* (*n* = 120)	*Married* (*n* = 60)	*Single* (*n* = 60)	*Total* (*n* = 120)
	%								
A great deal	5.0	-	3.3	8.3	8.3	8.3	-	1.7	0
A fair amount	4.2	5.0	4.4	5.0	10.0	7.5	-	6.7	3.3
To some extent	4.2	6.7	5.0	11.7	13.3	12.5	6.7	6.7	6.7
Very little	11.7	18.3	13.9	11.7	11.7	11.7	13.3	5.0	9.2
Not at all	75.0	70.0	73.3	63.3	56.7	60.0	80.0	80.0	80.0
	100.0%	100.0%	100.0%	100.0%	100.0%	100.0%	100.0%	100.0%	100.0%

b) Experience of discrimination in job training

	1975			*1986*			*1986*		
	DUBLIN ONLY			DUBLIN			RURAL		
	Married (*n* = 120)	*Single* (*n* = 60)	*Total* (*n* = 180)	*Married* (*n* = 60)	*Single* (*n* = 60)	*Total* (*n* = 120)	*Married* (*n* = 60)	*Single* (*n* = 60)	*Total* (*n* = 120)
	%								
A great deal	5.0	3.3	4.4	1.7	5.0	3.3	1.7	3.4	2.5
A fair amount	4.2	15.0	7.8	10.0	11.7	10.8	1.7	1.7	1.7
To some extent	3.3	10.0	5.6	10.0	13.3	11.7	6.7	6.8	6.7
Very little	9.2	11.7	10.0	23.3	15.0	19.2	5.0	11.9	8.4
Not at all	78.3	60.0	72.2	55.0	55.0	55.0	85.0	76.3	80.7
	100.0%	100.0%	100.0%	100.0%	100.0%	100.0%	100.0%	100.0%	100.0%

c) Experience of discrimination in terms of pay

	1975			1986			1986		
	DUBLIN ONLY			DUBLIN			RURAL		
	Married (n = 120)	*Single (n = 60)*	*Total (n = 180)*	*Married (n = 60)*	*Single (n = 60)*	*Total (n = 120)*	*Married (n = 60)*	*Single (n = 60)*	*Total (n = 120)*
	%								
A great deal	20.8	18.3	20.0	13.3	10.0	11.7	6.7	3.3	5.0
A fair amount	10.8	26.7	16.1	11.7	16.7	14.2	6.7	6.7	6.7
To some extent	10.8	11.7	11.1	28.3	11.7	20.0	21.7	11.7	16.7
Very little	15.0	11.7	13.9	10.0	15.0	12.5	6.7	5.0	5.8
Not at all	42.5	31.7	38.9	36.7	46.7	41.7	58.3	73.3	65.8
	100.0%	100.0%	100.0%	100.0%	100.0%	100.0%	100.0%	100.0%	100.0%

d) Experience of discrimination in terms of the kind of work or quality of work experience

	1975			1986			1986		
	DUBLIN ONLY			DUBLIN			RURAL		
	Married (n = 120)	*Single (n = 60)*	*Total (n = 180)*	*Married (n = 60)*	*Single (n = 60)*	*Total (n = 120)*	*Married (n = 60)*	*Single (n = 60)*	*Total (n = 120)*
	%								
A great deal	10.8	10.0	10.6	5.0	5.0	5.0	-	1.7	0.8
A fair amount	10.8	11.7	11.1	10.0	11.7	10.8	3.3	8.5	5.9
To some extent	4.2	8.3	5.6	16.7	18.3	17.5	16.7	6.8	11.8
Very little	15.0	15.0	15.0	11.7	11.7	11.7	13.3	8.5	10.9
Not at all	59.2	55.0	57.8	56.7	53.3	55.0	66.7	74.6	70.6
	100.0%	100.0%	100.0%	100.0%	100.0%	100.0%	100.0%	100.0%	100.0%

(Continued)

Table 5.1 (Continued)

e) Experience of discrimination in terms of promotion

	1975			*1986*			*1986*		
	DUBLIN ONLY			DUBLIN			RURAL		
	Married (n = 120)	*Single (n = 60)*	*Total (n = 180)*	*Married (n = 60)*	*Single (n = 60)*	*Total (n = 120)*	*Married (n = 60)*	*Single (n = 60)*	*Total (n = 120)*
	%								
A great deal	7.5	16.7	10.6	8.3	5.0	6.7	3.3	3.3	3.3
A fair amount	4.2	5.0	4.4	10.0	13.3	11.7	8.3	6.7	7.5
To some extent	3.3	5.0	3.9	16.7	8.3	12.5	6.7	6.7	6.7
Very little	13.3	20.0	15.6	11.7	15.0	13.3	13.3	8.3	10.8
Not at all	71.7	53.3	65.6	53.3	58.3	55.8	68.3	75.0	71.7
	100.0%	100.0%	100.0%	100.0%	100.0%	100.0%	100.0%	100.0%	100.0%

f) Experience of discrimination by the educational system

	1975			*1986*			*1986*		
	DUBLIN ONLY			DUBLIN			RURAL		
	Married (n = 120)	*Single (n = 60)*	*Total (n = 180)*	*Married (n = 60)*	*Single (n = 60)*	*Total (n = 120)*	*Married (n = 60)*	*Single (n = 60)*	*Total (n = 120)*
	%								
A great deal	5.0	5.0	5.0	11.7	11.7	11.7	-	3.4	1.7
A fair amount	5.0	5.0	5.0	15.0	5.0	10.0	5.0	5.1	5.0
To some extent	5.8	1.7	4.4	16.7	10.0	13.3	16.7	15.3	16.0
Very little	4.2	3.3	3.9	11.7	11.7	11.7	13.3	6.8	10.1
Not at all	80.0	85.0	81.7	45.0	61.7	53.3	65.0	69.5	67.2
	100.0%	100.0%	100.0%	100.0%	100.0%	100.0%	100.0%	100.0%	100.0%

Table 5.2 A comparison of employed women's experience of discrimination: 1975–1986 (Dublin only), controlling for age, marital status and socio-economic status (N=300)

Mean scores and significant F-ratios for main effects of 4-way analysis of variance

Discrimination:	*Year*		*Age*		*Marital status*		*Socio-economic status*	
	1975 (n = 180)	*1986 (n = 120)*	*18–34 (n = 150)*	*35–65 (n = 150)*	*Married (n = 180)*	*Single (n = 120)*	*Low (n = 150)*	*High (n = 150)*
1 In getting a job	F = 8.79**							
	1.51	1.92	1.78	1.56	1.65	1.70	1.6	1.67
2 In job training					F = 4.87*			
	1.65	1.86	1.84	1.62	1.61	1.92	1.74	1.72
3 In terms of pay			(F = 3.54; p = .061)					
	2.65	2.40	2.72	2.38	2.51	2.60	2.59	2.51
4 In terms of kind of work or quality of work experience							F = 4.43*	
	2.03	1.99	2.11	1.90	1.98	2.06	2.18	1.84
5 In terms of promotion	1.80	1.98	1.97	1.77	1.79	2.00	1.93	1.81
6 By the educational system	F = 22.19***							
	1.47	2.15	1.84	1.66	1.85	1.61	1.75	1.75

*P < .05
**P < .01
***P < .001

All items presented on 5-point scale:
1 "Not at all"
2 "Very little"
3 "To some extent"
4 "A fair amount"
5 "A great deal"

of employed women in Dublin reporting some degree of discrimination in job training rose to 45% and the discrepancy between married and single women disappeared. As in the case of "getting a job," rural women were less likely to report discrimination in job training than were urban women, with just under 20% of rural women reporting any discrimination in job training. The figure was higher for single women (24%) than for married (15%), as was also the case in Dublin in 1975.

Experience of discrimination in terms of pay

With regard to pay, much higher proportions of women reported discrimination than had done so in the case of getting a job or job training. In 1975, 61% of Dublin women reported some degree of pay discrimination, with 36% reporting either "a fair amount" or "a great deal."

While there was no overall significant shift in perceived pay discrimination from 1975 to 1986, there was however a trend among single women in the direction of *less* pay discrimination in 1986 than in 1975 ($p = .093$), even when other key demographic variables were controlled. In percentage terms, 68% of single women from Dublin reported some degree of pay discrimination in 1975, whereas in 1986 only 53% did so. This indicates that some shift in a positive direction took place during the decade following the implementation of the Anti-Discrimination (Pay) Act; however, much discrimination in this area was still felt.

In both 1975 and 1986 there was a trend which revealed that younger women (18–34) were more likely to report pay discrimination than older women (35–65) ($p = .06$) – see Table 5.2.

Rural women were less likely than urban women to report pay discrimination, yet greater proportions reported discrimination in this area than in the other areas. Thirty-four per cent of rural women reported some degree of pay discrimination (as compared with 58% of urban women). Among rural women, married women were more likely to report pay discrimination (42%) than single women were (27%).

Discrimination in terms of kind of work or quality of work experience

In 1975, 42% of employed Dublin women reported some degree of discrimination in terms of the kind of work or quality of work experience given to them (as women), as opposed to that given to other workers. This proportion remained fairly stable from 1975 to 1986 and married and single women did not differ appreciably from each other (Table 5.1d).

There was a significant effect of social class in both 1975 and 1986 indicating that employed Dublin women of lower socio-economic background experienced more discrimination in terms of the kind of work or quality of work experience given to them than women of higher socio-economic background (see Table 5.2).

Rural women in 1986 reported somewhat less discrimination in this area than did Dublin women, with just 29% reporting some degree of discrimination in terms of kind of work or quality of work given to them. Married rural women were somewhat more likely to report discrimination (33%) than single women (25%); however those single women who reported it were more likely to report "a fair amount" or "a great deal," rather than "some extent" or "very little" (see Table 5.1d).

Discrimination in terms of promotion

A fairly sizeable proportion of employed Dublin women (34%) reported discrimination in the area of promotion in 1975. Twenty-eight per cent of married women did so and 47% of single women. By 1986 the proportion of married women reporting discrimination in this area increased to 47% whereas the proportion of single women decreased somewhat to 42% (Table 5.1e). This interaction effect between marital status and year was statistically significant ($F = 4.18$; $p < .05$).

As in the case of the previous variables, rural women in 1986 reported somewhat less discrimination in the area of promotion than did urban women. The overall percentage reporting any discrimination in this area was 28%, with the proportion of married women being somewhat higher (32%) than that of single women (25%) (Table 5.1e).

Discrimination by the educational system

Apart from examining discrimination in the workplace itself, women were also asked whether they thought they had been discriminated against as women by the educational system. In its commentary on and recommendations concerning the report *Schooling and Sex Roles* (Hannan et al., 1983), the Employment Equality Agency noted that the statutory responsibility of the agency "has to take account of those factors which determine access to and achievement in employment" (Employment Equality Agency, 1983, p. 10). The recognition of the vital importance of education in this regard was an impetus for initiating the Hannan et al. study, which documented the existence of unequal opportunity for girls in the educational system. In the commentary on the report, Tansey points out:

> The extent of sex differentiation is deeply institutionalised in the ideological and cultural presumptions underlying the education system. Provision, allocation and choice are influenced by the "hidden curriculum" which reflects the attitudes and values which are dominant in society, and clearly reflected in the schools.
>
> (Tansey, 1983, p. 34)

It is in this sense that the question concerning discrimination by the educational system was put to respondents in both the 1975 and 1986 studies. In 1975 relatively few of the employed Dublin women were aware of having been discriminated against by the educational system, with only 18% expressing any degree of discrimination in this area, and differences between married and single women were slight. However, by 1986 this level rose rather dramatically. Overall, 47% reported some level of discrimination by the educational system (Table 5.1f). This figure reflected a higher proportion of married women (55%) than single women (38%). As may be seen in Table 5.2, this increase in perceived discrimination from 1975 to 1986 was the most significant trend observed concerning women's perceptions of discrimination over this period ($F = 22.19$; $p < .001$).

While we do not have rural data for 1975, the 1986 data revealed a rather high level of perceived discrimination by the educational system on the part of rural women (with 33% reporting some level of discrimination – 35% of married and 30.5% of single women – see Table 5.1e).

Summary and discussion

The data have revealed that in each of the areas studied, proportions ranging from 15% to 58% of employed women reported experiencing some level of discrimination in 1986. The extent of discrimination varied from "very little" to "a great deal" and the reader is invited to examine Table 5.1 in detail concerning these variations. As Table 5.2 revealed, there were no significant shifts in the direction of *less* discrimination from 1975 to 1986, overall; however, there was a tendency for single women to experience less discrimination in the area of pay in 1986 than in 1975, which may indicate some initial positive effects of the Equal Pay legislation. There was also a reduction in single women's experienced discrimination in the area of promotion, though this was counterbalanced by an increase in perceived discrimination by married women.

Two of the areas examined showed an overall *increase* in perceived discrimination from 1975 to 1986: (1) that of getting a job and (2) that experienced in the educational system.

It is unlikely that discriminatory practices increased during this period, particularly in view of the equality legislation introduced in 1975 and 1977. Therefore, the findings suggest that women's *awareness* of discrimination was undoubtedly heightened during this period. This was probably due to discussion in the media of the equality legislation and related issues associated with the U.N. Decade for Women (1975–1985). Coverage in the media of the report on *Schooling and Sex Roles* by Hannan et al. (1983) may also have had an effect on women's awareness of discrimination by the educational system. Further, the then Minister for Education, Gemma Hussey, who held office from 1983 to 1986, addressed the problem of sex-role stereotyping in textbooks, which also obtained media coverage. This too may have affected public awareness of discrimination in schools.

These results should, therefore, not be disturbing in and of themselves, since it may be necessary to achieve an awareness of a problem before one can do something to remedy it.

Employed women's experience of discrimination – an update in 2005: did attitudes change two decades later?

Some twenty years later, we once again posed the same questions to employed women in Ireland to see if the intervening years had had any effect on women's perceived experience of discrimination in the workplace and the educational system. We are now able to compare attitudes of employed Dublin women from 1975, 1986 and 2005, employed rural women from 1986 and 2005, and women from Dublin, rural Ireland and the whole country in 2005. The "whole country" sample includes women from larger towns and also the cities of Cork, Limerick and Galway and thus these data give the best picture of the country as a whole. Table 5.3 presents these comparisons.

In relation to the first variable, "Getting a Job," Dublin women in 2005 were most likely to say they were not discriminated against at all. Just under three quarters (72.9%) said they had not been discriminated against at all. This figure is very similar to the proportion who said this in 1975 (73.3%), whereas in 1986 a smaller proportion of Dublin women (60%) felt this way, indicating that there

Table 5.3 Employed women's experience of discrimination: 1975, 1986, 2005

a. Experience of discrimination in getting a job

	1975	*1986*	*1986*	*2005*	*2005*	*2005*
	Dublin (N = 180)	*Dublin (N = 120)*	*Rural (N = 120)*	*Dublin (N = 85)*	*Rural (N = 108)*	*Whole country (N = 275)*
A great deal	3.3	8.3	0.8	1.2	0.9	1.1
A fair amount	4.4	7.5	3.3	2.4	1.9	2.2
To some extent	5.0	12.5	5.7	11.8	7.4	11.3
Very little	13.9	11.7	9.2	11.8	7.4	8.4
Not at all	73.3	60.0	80.0	72.9	82.4	77.1
Total	100.0%	100.0%	100.0%	100.0%	100.0%	100.0%

b. Experience of discrimination in job training

	1975	*1986*	*1986*	*2005*	*2005*	*2005*
	Dublin (N = 180)	*Dublin (N = 120)*	*Rural (N = 120)*	*Dublin (N = 85)*	*Rural (N = 108)*	*Whole country (N = 275)*
A great deal	4.4	3.3	2.5	0.0	0.0	0.0
A fair amount	7.8	10.8	1.7	7.1	0.9	1.2
To some extent	5.6	11.7	6.7	13.1	5.5	9.8
Very little	10.0	19.2	8.4	10.7	8.3	7.3
Not at all	72.2	55.0	80.7	69.0	85.3	81.7
Total	100.0%	100.0%	100.0%	100.0%	100.0%	100.0%

(Continued)

Table 5.3 (Continued)

c. Experience of discrimination in terms of pay

	1975	*1986*	*1986*	*2005*	*2005*	*2005*
	Dublin (N = 180)	*Dublin (N = 120)*	*Rural (N = 120)*	*Dublin (N = 85)*	*Rural (N = 108)*	*Whole country (N = 275)*
A great deal	20.0	11.7	5.0	0.0	2.7	1.8
A fair amount	16.1	14.2	6.7	11.9	2.7	5.8
To some extent	11.1	20.0	16.7	26.2	11.8	17.0
Very little	13.9	12.5	5.8	3.6	9.1	6.9
Not at all	38.9	41.7	65.8	58.3	73.6	68.5
Total	100.0%	100.0%	100.0%	100.0%	100.0%	100.0%

d. Experience of discrimination in terms of the kind of work or quality of work experience

	1975	*1986*	*1986*	*2005*	*2005*	*2005*
	Dublin (N = 180)	*Dublin (N = 120)*	*Rural (N = 120)*	*Dublin (N = 85)*	*Rural (N = 108)*	*Whole country (N = 275)*
A great deal	10.6	5.0	0.8	1.2	1.8	1.1
A fair amount	11.1	10.8	5.9	4.7	0.0	2.5
To some extent	5.6	17.5	11.8	14.1	10.1	12.7
Very little	15.0	11.7	10.9	18.8	7.3	11.6
Not at all	57.8	55.0	70.6	61.2	80.7	72.1
Total	100.0%	100.0%	100.0%	100.0%	100.0%	100.0%

e. Experience of discrimination in terms of promotion

	1975	*1986*	*1986*	*2005*	*2005*	*2005*
	Dublin (N = 180)	*Dublin (N = 120)*	*Rural (N = 120)*	*Dublin (N = 85)*	*Rural (N = 108)*	*Whole country (N = 275)*
A great deal	10.6	6.7	3.3	1.2	0.0	0.4
A fair amount	4.4	11.7	7.5	5.9	3.7	5.1
To some extent	3.9	12.5	6.7	15.3	8.3	10.9
Very little	15.6	13.3	10.8	7.1	8.3	8.0
Not at all	65.6	55.8	71.7	70.6	79.8	75.7
Total	100.0%	100.0%	100.0%	100.0%	100.0%	100.0%

f. Experience of discrimination by the educational system

	1975	*1986*	*1986*	*2005*	*2005*	*2005*
	Dublin (N = 180)	*Dublin (N = 120)*	*Rural (N = 120)*	*Dublin (N = 85)*	*Rural (N = 108)*	*Whole country (N = 275)*
A great deal	5.0	11.7	1.7	0.0	0.9	1.4
A fair amount	5.0	10.0	5.0	2.4	1.8	2.2
To some extent	4.4	13.3	16.0	7.1	6.4	6.9
Very little	3.9	11.7	10.1	20.0	2.8	9.1
Not at all	81.7	53.3	67.2	70.6	88.1	80.4
Total	100.0%	100.0%	100.0%	100.0%	100.0%	100.0%

was an increase in perceived discrimination from 1975 to 1986 which may have resulted from heightened awareness of the issue. The subsequent decrease in perceived discrimination from 1986 to 2005, and reversion to earlier levels, suggests that things may actually have changed for the better and fewer women were reporting discrimination in getting a job.

The attitudes of rural women did not change perceptibly from 1986 to 2005. In 1986 80% said they had not experienced any discrimination in getting a job and in 2005 this figure stood at 82.4%.

In relation to job training, as we have already noted, there was more awareness of discrimination in 1986 than in 1975: 72.2% of Dublin women reported no discrimination in 1975 and fewer did so (55%) in 1986. This figure went up again in 2005 to 69%, reflecting the fact that 31% of Dublin women reported some level of discrimination in job training. In the case of rural women, 80.7% said they had not experienced any discrimination in job training in 1986 and this figure went up to 85.3% in 2005. Thus, Dublin women were about twice as likely as rural women to say they had experienced discrimination in job training in 2005 (31% vs. 14.7%).

In relation to pay, there was a greater level of reported discrimination. In 1975 20% of Dublin women said they experienced "a great deal of discrimination," with a further 16.1% saying they experienced "a fair amount." This level decreased by 1986. Just 11.7% said they experienced "a great deal" and 14.2% said "a fair amount." When aggregating these two categories, it is evident that the level of discrimination decreased from 36.1% to 25.9%. This pattern is in contrast to some of the other areas in which perceived discrimination went up, most likely reflecting increasing awareness. These results reflect the fact that the equal pay legislation had an effect on actual pay and also on attitudes from 1975 to 1986. These data attitudinally confirm the effect of the decrease in the gender pay gap from 1975 to 1986 (Callender and Meenan, 1994; Ruane and Sutherland, 1999). By 2005 no Dublin women reported "a great deal" of pay discrimination, although 11.9% reported "a fair amount." This continuing trend strongly points to the fact that the equal pay legislation had a continuing positive effect on Dublin women's actual wages and their attitudes towards their wages. Fewer rural women reported pay discrimination in 1986 than did Dublin women – just 5% reported "a great deal" and 6.7% "a fair amount." By 2005 this had dropped to just 2.7% saying "a great deal" and the same proportion saying "a fair amount."

Further positive trends were seen over time in relation to women's perception of the kind of work or quality of work given to them. As may be seen in Table 5.3d, 21.7% of Dublin women said they experienced either a fair amount or a great deal of discrimination in this area in 1975; this dropped to 15.8% by 1986 and to 5.9% by 2005. This trend also obtained for rural women, but it was of much lesser magnitude: in 1986 6.7% said they experienced a fair amount or a great deal and by 2005 this dropped to 1.8%.

In relation to promotion, Dublin women were somewhat more likely to report discrimination in getting promoted in 1986 than they had been in 1975, but were much less likely to do so in 2005, suggesting that things had improved in this area from 1986 to 2005. While 15% had reported a fair amount or a great deal of discrimination in relation to promotion in 1975 and 18.4% had done so in 1986, just 7.1% did so in 2005. As we have seen before, rural women were less likely to report discrimination in promotion in 1986 than Dublin women were (just 10.8% said "a fair amount" or "a great deal") and even fewer reported it in 2005, with just 3.7% reporting "a fair amount" and none reporting "a great deal."

We saw previously that perceived discrimination by the educational system significantly increased from 1975 to 1986 (Table 5.2: $F = 22.19$; $p < .001$). However, the 2005 data show that these attitudes reverted to a large extent to the earlier levels present in 1975. For example, among Dublin women, 81.7% said they had experienced no discrimination by the educational system in 1975. However, by 1986 just 53.3% said they had experienced none, whereas 46.7% had experienced some degree of discrimination. By 2005, 70.6% said they had experienced no discrimination, while 29.4% had experienced some. Among rural women 32.8% had experienced some degree of discrimination in 1986, but by 2005, this had dropped to 11.9%. Thus, it is clear that the period from 1975 to 1986 was a period of increasing awareness among women of how they were being discriminated against in the workplace and by the educational system. However, the following period, reflecting greater awareness in society and increasing implementation of equality legislation, led to decreasing levels of perceived discrimination by 2005.

Perceptions of own discrimination vs. discrimination against "women in general"

In addition to being asked whether they had ever personally experienced discrimination, employed women were also asked how much, if at all, they thought "women in general" were discriminated against in employment. We shall begin with the 1986 data and then examine this in 2005.

Comparisons between perceived discrimination against oneself vs. women in general: the 1986 data

Table 5.4 presents a comparison of these two sets of perceptions in terms of mean scores – one regarding the respondent herself and the other regarding "women in general." It may be seen that highly significant differences were obtained in all cases (all at the $p < .001$ level of significance). In every case, employed women felt that "women in general" had experienced more discrimination than they themselves had. This discrepancy was particularly great with regard to hiring and promotion, but was also highly significant for the other areas, including job training, pay and kind of work or quality of work experience. It also held with regard to perceived discrimination by the educational system.

Table 5.4 Employed women's perception of extent of own experience of discrimination in employment in comparison with their perception of the extent of discrimination experienced by women in general: 1986 (N = 240)

Discrimination:	*Own experience of discrimination*		*Perceived discrimination against women in general*		
	Mean	*S.D.*	*Mean*	*S.D.*	*t-Value*
1 In hiring	1.64	1.14	2.97	1.15	−14.92***
2 In job training	1.63	1.07	2.68	1.18	−12.00***
3 In terms of pay	2.10	1.37	3.01	1.27	−9.97***
4 In terms of kind of work or quality of work experience	1.77	1.15	2.86	1.22	−11.97***
5 In terms of promotion	1.80	1.24	3.24	1.26	−14.26***
6 By the educational system	1.89	1.28	2.25	1.25	−4.91***

***$p < .001$

Mean scores were based on 5-point response scales:
1 = "Not at all"
2 = "Very little"
3 = "To some extent"
4 = "A fair amount"
5 = "A great deal"

We can examine these findings in greater detail by looking at Table 5.5, which shows percentage responses to all five response categories, as well as separate data for married and single women. This more graphically illustrates what was summarised previously. For example, in relation to "getting a job," whereas 70% of employed women said they personally had not experienced any discrimination in this area, only 12.9% of them thought that "women in general" had not experienced any discrimination in this area. Conversely, whereas only 30% of employed women had experienced some discrimination in this area, 87% thought women in general had. Looking at the more extreme categories, it may be seen that whereas only 10% of employed women reported having experienced discrimination in getting a job, 68% of them thought that women in general experienced either a great deal or a fair amount of discrimination in getting a job. Similar trends held for the other areas of discrimination. Whilst 18.7% of employed women reported personally having experienced "a great deal" or "a fair amount" of pay discrimination, 39% felt that women in general experienced this level of pay discrimination. With regard to promotion, 14.6% reported experiencing either a great deal or a fair amount of discrimination, yet 43.3% thought women in general experienced either a fair amount or a great deal of discrimination in terms of promotion.

Table 5.5 A comparison of employed women's own experience of discrimination with their and others' perceptions of the extent of discrimination experienced by women in general: 1986 (N = 600)

	Own experience of discrimination			*Perceived extent of discrimination experienced by women in general*						
	Employed women			*Employed women*			*Other groups*			
	Married (n = 120)	*Single (n = 120)*	*Total (n = 240)*	*Married (n = 120)*	*Single (n = 120)*	*Total (n = 240)*	*Non-employed married women (n = 120)*	*Married men (n = 120)*	*Single men (n = 120)*	*Total (n = 360)*
a In getting a job										
A great deal	4.2	5.0	4.6	10.0	9.2	9.6	8.4	6.7	6.7	7.2
A fair amount	2.5	8.3	5.4	24.2	20.8	22.5	18.5	25.8	18.3	20.9
To some extent	9.2	10.0	9.6	32.5	40.0	36.3	29.4	38.3	34.2	34.0
Very little	12.5	8.3	10.4	21.7	15.8	18.8	26.9	20.0	20.8	22.6
Not at all	71.7	68.3	70.0	11.7	14.2	12.9	16.8	9.2	20.0	15.3
	100.0%	100.0%	100.0%	100.0%	100.0%	100.0%	100.0%	100.0%	100.0%	100.0%
b In job training										
A great deal	1.7	4.2	2.9	7.5	7.5	7.5	5.9	6.7	5.2	5.9
A fair amount	5.8	6.7	6.3	15.0	13.3	14.2	14.3	20.0	14.7	16.3
To some extent	8.3	10.1	9.2	37.5	39.2	38.3	26.9	30.0	25.0	27.3
Very little	14.2	13.4	13.8	20.0	15.8	17.9	29.4	20.0	34.5	27.9
Not at all	70.0	65.5	67.8	20.0	24.2	22.1	23.5	23.3	20.7	22.5
	100.0%	100.0%	100.0%	100.0%	100.0%	100.0%	100.0%	100.0%	100.0%	100.0%
c In terms of pay										
A great deal	10.0	6.7	8.3	14.2	11.7	12.9	11.7	18.6	11.0	13.8
A fair amount	9.2	11.7	10.4	25.0	26.7	25.8	16.7	22.9	24.6	21.3
To some extent	25.0	11.7	18.3	30.8	23.3	27.1	35.8	28.0	23.7	29.2
Very little	8.3	10.0	9.2	15.8	20.0	17.9	17.5	16.1	16.9	16.9
Not at all	47.5	60.0	53.8	14.2	18.3	16.3	18.3	14.4	23.7	18.8
	100.0%	100.0%	100.0%	100.0%	100.0%	100.0%	100.0%	100.0%	100.0%	100.0%

d In terms of kind of work or quality of work experience										
A great deal	2.5	3.4	2.9	10.0	8.3	9.2	4.2	10.1	6.8	7.0
A fair amount	6.7	10.1	8.4	24.2	19.2	21.7	25.8	21.8	16.1	21.3
To some extent	16.7	12.6	14.6	33.3	32.5	32.9	25.8	28.6	33.1	29.1
Very little	12.5	10.1	11.3	15.8	19.2	17.5	25.8	21.0	25.4	24.1
Not at all	61.7	63.9	62.8	16.7	20.8	18.8	18.3	18.5	18.6	18.5
	100.0%	100.0%	100.0%	100.0%	100.0%	100.0%	100.0%	100.0%	100.0%	100.0%
e *In terms of promotion*										
A great deal	5.8	4.2	5.0	20.0	16.7	18.3	16.7	21.2	13.7	17.2
A fair amount	9.2	10.0	9.6	25.8	24.2	25.0	20.8	18.6	19.7	19.7
To some extent	11.7	7.5	9.6	32.5	31.7	32.1	28.3	32.2	30.8	30.4
Very little	12.5	11.7	12.1	11.7	10.8	11.3	20.8	16.9	20.5	19.4
Not at all	60.8	66.7	63.8	10.0	16.7	13.3	13.3	11.0	15.4	13.2
	100.0%	100.0%	100.0%	100.0%	100.0%	100.0%	100.0%	100.0%	100.0%	100.0%
f By the educational system										
A great deal	5.8	7.6	6.7	5.0	5.8	5.4	5.0	6.7	5.9	5.9
A fair amount	10.0	5.0	7.5	16.7	10.8	13.8	9.2	6.7	2.5	6.1
To some extent	16.7	12.6	14.6	16.7	22.5	19.6	17.5	16.8	12.6	15.6
Very little	12.5	9.2	10.9	25.8	20.0	22.9	25.0	26.9	29.4	27.1
Not at all	55.0	65.5	60.3	35.8	40.8	38.3	43.3	42.9	49.6	45.3
	100.0%	100.0%	100.0%	100.0%	100.0%	100.0%	100.0%	100.0%	100.0%	100.0%

These large discrepancies in personal experience vs. perceptions concerning women in general may be due to at least three factors. First, not all of the employed women have actually experienced discrimination themselves; nevertheless they would be aware of its existence generally. Secondly, even if women have experienced discrimination, it may have been in only one or two areas, rather than in all five. Thirdly, and perhaps most importantly, women may not *recognise* that they are personally being discriminated against for several reasons. Among these is the fact that much of women's employment is largely sex-segregated and since all of one's co-workers are female, one is not aware of discrimination against oneself *per se* because one is actually being discriminated against as a woman *en bloc*. This would certainly be relevant with regard to the issues of pay and kind of work or quality of work experience. This phenomenon is graphically illustrated in some quotations from qualitative research.

In order to explore these hypotheses concerning the underlying reasons for these discrepant attitudes, qualitative data was obtained subsequent to the main 1986 study from four groups of women attending adult education courses.[1] The groups were asked to respond to the two parallel sets of questions concerning own experience of discrimination and extent of discrimination experienced by women in general. They were then asked to write down any comments concerning their own experiences. Several comments made by nurses in one of the groups lent support to the hypothesis concerning the effects on one's perceptions of working in sex-segregated occupations. For example:

> "I'm not discriminated against because I'm in a woman's profession (but others are)."
>
> "Because I am part of a predominantly female profession I think I have side stepped the bulk of discrimination from an employment point of view."
>
> "Being in nursing, it is largely female workers, so discrimination is not very evident to me."

Comparisons between perceived discrimination against oneself vs. women in general: the 2005 data

We examined these same issues in the 2005 study to explore whether the discrepant attitudes between one's own experience of discrimination in the workplace and discrimination against "women in general" still obtained almost twenty years later (see Table 5.6). A comparison of Table 5.4 with Table 5.6 shows that the same trend observed in 1986 held in 2005, that is to say, women were more likely to think "women in general" experienced more discrimination in relation to work than they themselves experienced. This was true with respect to hiring, job training, pay, kind of work or quality of work experience and promotion. It also held in relation to perceived discrimination by

Table 5.6 Employed women's perception of extent of own experience of discrimination compared with their perception of the extent of discrimination experienced by women in general: 2005 data (N = 283)

	Own experience of discrimination		*Perceived discrimination against women in general*		
	Mean	*S.D.*	*Mean*	*S.D.*	*t-value*
In hiring	1.41	0.838	2.62	0.973	−18.279***
In job training	1.36	0.772	2.3	1.019	−15.147***
In terms of pay	1.65	1.06	2.93	1.251	−16.157***
In terms of kind of work or quality of work experience	1.49	0.876	2.59	1.072	−16.187***
In terms of promotion	1.47	0.916	2.97	1.144	−19.934***
By the educational system	1.33	0.795	1.7	0.991	−7.975***

***p < .001

Mean scores were based on 5-point response scale:
1 = "Not at all"
2 = "Very little"
3 = "To some extent"
4 = "A fair amount"
5 = "A great deal"

the educational system. In all cases the differences were highly significant (p < .001), as they had been in 1986.

A comparison of the means for 2005 with those from 1986 reveals that employed women were somewhat *less likely* to report having experienced discrimination in 2005 than employed women had been in 1986. Similarly, less discrimination was thought to be experienced by "women in general" in 2005 than it was in 1986. Nevertheless, the means concerning discrimination against "women in general" were still higher than those which women gave for themselves. They were in the range 2.3 to 2.97 in 2005, indicating "very little" discrimination or discrimination "to some extent," whereas the means concerning discrimination against oneself ranged from 1.33 to 1.65 (reflecting perceived discrimination ranging from "not at all" to "very little"). The area in which women themselves reported most discrimination was in relation to pay (mean = 1.65). This area elicited an even higher mean score for "women in general" (mean = 2.93). The area of greatest perceived discrimination against "women in general" was in relation to promotion (mean = 2.97).

With regard to hiring, many women would be unaware if their sex had played a role in whether or not they had got a *particular* job, since such information is confidential. Yet women know that questions related to one's gender, such as marriage plans, plans to have children, etc., are often brought up in job interviews (even though such questions are now illegal).

Finally, women may be denying the extent to which they themselves have been discriminated against. This may be for psychologically protective reasons. If one actually felt like a victim of discrimination, this should logically lead to anger and perhaps seeking legal redress. Yet such behaviour would be unwelcome by management, would cause disruption in one's life and would be inconsistent with expected norms of feminine behaviour, which is supposed to be friendly, cooperative and generally passive. Thus, in order to avoid problems and rocking the boat – and to avoid risks – it has probably been easier for women to deny, even to themselves, that they have suffered discrimination as women. Yet the fact that they are so aware of discrimination against women generally raises questions about their perceptions concerning their own experience.

Perceptions of discrimination: a comparison of employed women and other groups, 1986–2005

The perceptions of employed women concerning the extent of discrimination against women did not differ significantly – except in one case – from those of other groups in the sample, namely men and non-employed women, as may be seen from Table 5.7. Percentage data comparing employed women with other groups on these items are contained in Table 5.5. Concerning hiring, job training, pay, kind of work/quality of work experience and promotion, there were

Table 5.7 Perceptions of extent of discrimination experienced by women in general: a comparison of employed women and other groups, 1986 (N = 599)

	Employed women (n = 240)		*Others (men and non-employed women) (n = 359)*		
	Mean	*S.D.*	*Mean*	*S.D.*	*t-value*
In hiring	2.97	1.15	2.82	1.44	1.56 N.S.
In job training	2.67	1.18	2.55	1.18	1.20 N.S.
In terms of pay	3.01	1.27	2.94	1.30	0.64 N.S.
In terms of kind of work or quality of work experience	2.85	1.22	2.74	1.19	1.07 N.S.
In terms of promotion	3.24	1.26	3.08	1.27	1.48 N.S.
By the educational system	2.25	1.25	2.00	1.18	2.46*

*p < .05; N.S. = Non-significant

Mean scores were based on 5-point response scales:
1 = "Not at all"
2 = "Very little"
3 = "To some extent"
4 = "A fair amount"
5 = "A great deal"

no significant differences between employed women's perceptions and those of other groups in society regarding the extent of discrimination which women experienced. However, with regard to discrimination by the educational system, employed women were more likely than other groups to believe that women experienced this.

The fact that other groups (i.e., males and non-employed females) essentially concurred with the employed females' estimates of the extent of discrimination in general would tend to lend support to the veracity of the employed women's perceptions. One then must ask again, why are the employed women so significantly under-reporting their *own* experience of discrimination? The evidence would tend to support the hypothesis that substantial denial may be taking place and this must in some way be an adaptive mechanism. Apparently acknowledging one's *own* experience of discrimination and, of necessity, acting on that knowledge, is apparently not an attractive option for most women. It is more comfortable for them to accept the situation and choose to deny it.

We carried out the same analysis some 20 years later – in 2005 – to see if these findings would hold, and we found some surprising findings. Table 5.8 compares employed women's perceptions of the extent of discrimination against women in general with the attitudes of others, namely men and non-employed women.

It may be seen that in four out of the six cases, employed women were significantly *more* likely to think women were discriminated against in the workplace than others thought they were. This included in relation to hiring, job training,

Table 5.8 Perceptions of extent of discrimination experienced by women in general: a comparison of employed women and other groups, 2005 data (N = 909)

	Employed women (n = 275)		*Others (men and non-employed women) (n = 634)*		
	Mean	*S.D.*	*Mean*	*S.D.*	*t-value*
In hiring	2.62	0.97	2.46	1.06	2.26*
In job training	2.30	1.00	2.12	1.03	2.5*
In terms of pay	2.94	1.25	2.61	1.21	3.74*
In terms of kind of work or quality of work experience	2.59	1.08	2.53	1.14	0.75 N.S
In terms of promotion	2.96	1.16	2.73	1.24	2.78*
By the educational system	1.71	0.99	1.67	1.05	0.54 N.S.

*p < .05; N.S. = Non-significant

Mean scores were based on 5-point response scales:
1 = "Not at all"
2 = "Very little"
3 = "To some extent"
4 = "A fair amount"
5 = "A great deal"

pay and promotion. This differs from the findings in 1986 which showed that there were no significant differences in perceptions between these two groups (as shown in Table 5.7). This suggests that employed women have become more attuned to discrimination in the workplace over this period. Although the differences are significant at just the $p < .05$ level, they reflect a consistent shift from the previous results of 1986.

Barriers to women's career advancement: 1986–2005

Barriers to women's career advancement: a comparison of employed women and other groups: the 1986 study

The previous data have shown that employed women tend to think that they have experienced less job discrimination than other women have, although the data also showed that employed women shared views similar to those of the rest of the community concerning the prevalence of discrimination against women in general. Among all groups it was perceived to be fairly widespread. This awareness would seem to be consistent with findings of numerous other studies over roughly the same time period which documented women's poorer position in the labour force (e.g., McCarthy, 1978; Eurostat, 1983; Smyth, 1984; Haavio-Mannila and Skard, 1985; Blackwell, 1986; Ruane and Sutherland, 1999). Census data, as well as survey data have indicated that "the pattern of job structures in work organisations . . . shows that women are clustered at the lower end of the organisational hierarchy, in all the occupations they occupy" (McCarthy, 1978, p. 109). Russell et al. (2009) concluded, following their 10-year comparison of female participation in the Irish labour market over the period 1997 to 2007, that while women had made "significant inroads into traditionally male areas, and also into jobs with a higher skills profile," vertical and horizontal segregation had not been significantly eroded and that these two indices of segregation showed "very little change over the 10 years observed" (p. 75).

However, the extent to which women's poor position in the organisational hierarchy is due to discriminatory attitudes and practices on the part of management and the extent to which it is a result of other factors has not been established. It has sometimes been suggested that women do not *seek* greater responsibility on the job and that is why they are not more represented at the higher levels of management. It is argued that married women in particular already have too much to do balancing job and family responsibilities that they could not cope with more demanding jobs – or at least they cannot do so without more flexible hours and assistance with childcare and household tasks.

These issues were explored both in the 1986 study and later in 2005 in order to see how women perceived their own career advancement. Specifically, women were asked to what extent nine potential barriers to career advancement were relevant for them. In order to see to what extent other groups, and in particular, men, had similar or dissimilar perceptions concerning the barriers to women's career advancement, comparable questions were asked of the other groups in the study, i.e., married men, single men and non-employed married women. Table 5.9 presents levels of agreement concerning nine potential barriers to women's career advancement from the original 1986 study.

Table 5.9 Perceived barriers to women's career advancement: a comparison of employed women and other groups, percentage responses (N = 600)

	Employed Women		*Non-Employed Married Women*	*Married Men*	*Single Men*
	Married	*Single*			
	(n = 120) %	*(n = 120)* %	*(n = 120)* %	*(n = 120)* %	*(n = 120)* %
1 "There are no avenues for advancement in my work".			**1 "There are no avenues for advancement in their work".**		
Slightly Agree	16.0	19.2	22.5	14.2	20.2
Moderately Agree	14.3	21.7	14.2	9.2	12.6
Strongly Agree	21.8	15.0	7.5	2.5	2.5
TOTAL AGREE	52.1	55.9	44.2	25.9	35.3
2 "I would need more training or educational qualifications in order to get ahead".			**2 "They would need more training or educational qualifications in order to get ahead".**		
Slightly Agree	15.1	10.8	19.2	24.2	19.3
Moderately Agree	18.5	18.3	22.5	25.0	17.6
Strongly Agree	21.0	25.8	16.7	6.7	5.0
TOTAL AGREE	54.6	54.9	58.4	55.9	41.9
3 "I have too much to do already balancing job and family responsibilities".			**3 "They have too much to do already balancing job and family responsibilities".**		
Slightly Agree	16.0	1.8	26.7	30.8	31.1
Moderately Agree	10.9	1.8	23.3	10.0	18.5
Strongly Agree	5.9	6.2	10.0	7.5	5.9
TOTAL AGREE	32.8	9.8	60.0	48.3	55.5
4 "The attitudes of management at my workplace tend to favour promoting men rather than women".			**4 "The attitudes of management tend to favour promotion of men rather than women".**		
Slightly Agree	9.3	7.0	20.8	29.4	19.3
Moderately Agree	5.1	9.6	30.0	38.7	39.5
Strongly Agree	14.4	11.3	34.2	22.7	20.2
TOTAL AGREE	28.8	27.9	85.0	90.8	79.0

(Continued)

Table 5.9 (Continued)

	Employed Women		*Non-Employed Married Women*	*Married Men*	*Single Men*
	Married (*n* = *120*) %	*Single* (*n* = *120*) %	(*n* = *120*) %	(*n* = *120*) %	(*n* = *120*) %
5 "I lack self-confidence".			**5 "They lack self-confidence".**		
Slightly Agree	11.8	9.2	7.6	10.8	17.8
Moderately Agree	3.4	7.5	14.3	11.7	3.4
Strongly Agree	3.4	6.7	4.2	2.5	3.4
TOTAL AGREE	18.6	23.4	26.1	25.0	24.6
6 "I don't want more responsibility".			**6 "They don't want more responsibility".**		
Slightly Agree	12.6	6.7	11.7	15.0	16.0
Moderately Agree	14.3	11.7	9.2	8.3	12.6
Strongly Agree	10.1	11.7	1.7	1.7	4.2
TOTAL AGREE	37.0	30.1	22.6	25.0	32.8
7 "If I had more flexible working hours, I could manage better and probably would be better able to advance in my career".			**7 "If they had more flexible working hours, they could manage better and probably would be better able to advance in their career".**		
Slightly Agree	11.9	8.8	21.7	30.0	33.6
Moderately Agree	7.6	7.1	25.8	30.0	31.9
Strongly Agree	10.2	13.3	40.0	27.5	21.8
TOTAL AGREE	29.7	29.2	87.5	87.5	87.3
8 "My husband would disapprove if I were too successful".			**8 "Their husband would disapprove if they were too successful".**		
Slightly Agree	1.7		10.8	17.5	16.8
Moderately Agree	2.5		15.8	9.2	10.1
Strongly Agree	7.6		9.2	5.0	8.4
TOTAL AGREE	11.8		35.8	31.7	35.3
9 "If I had more help with housework and childcare I could put more into my job".			**9 "If they had more help with housework and childcare they could put more into their job".**		
Slightly Agree	8.5		29.2	37.5	35.3
Moderately Agree	7.6		25.8	24.2	26.9
Strongly Agree	9.3		31.7	21.7	18.5
TOTAL AGREE	25.4		86.7	83.4	80.7

It may be seen in Table 5.9 that the barriers which employed women themselves saw as the greatest to their career advancement in 1986 were

1 the fact that there were simply no avenues for advancement in their jobs (52% of married women and 56% of single women stated that this was true for them) and
2 that they would need more training or educational qualifications in order to get ahead (55% of both married and single women agreed with this).

However, an examination of the effects of other variables showed that socio-economic status played a very significant role in determining these responses. In both cases, women of lower socio-economic background were more likely to perceive a lack of avenues for advancement in their jobs as well as a need for further training in order to get ahead. Women of lower socio-economic status were also more likely to say that they lacked self-confidence and they saw this as a barrier to their advancement. Women from rural areas were also more likely to perceive a lack of opportunity for career advancement, whereas women from urban areas were more likely to think they would need more training in order to get ahead (see Table 5.10). More detailed analysis showed that, while rural women in general were less likely than urban women to feel a need for training, among rural women, married women were more likely than single women to do so. Among urban women, while there was a generally strong belief in the need for further training in order to get ahead, this was particularly strong among young single women (18–34) ($F = 4.49$; $p = .035$).

Among the other seven potential barriers, none elicited an agreement higher than 37% on the part of employed women. Not surprisingly, certain problems were more salient for some groups than for others. For example, married women were significantly more likely to cite the fact that they already had too much to do balancing job and family responsibilities. However, it will be noted that only 33% of married women cited this as a barrier; the majority of married working women did not.

Similar proportions of married and single women (about 28%) expressed the view that attitudes of management tended to favour promotion of men rather than women. It was found that younger women (18–34) were significantly more likely than older workers to see management attitudes as a barrier to their advancement, and this held particularly for young women of lower socio-economic (SES) background ($F = 9.43$; $p = .002$). In rural areas, this attitude on the part of lower-SES women was particularly pronounced among *married* women, whereas in urban areas, it was more prevalent among single women ($F = 6.71$; $p < .01$).

It is sometimes said that women do not go forward for promotion because they lack self-confidence. Contrary to any such stereotypes, only 18.6% of the married women workers and 23.4% of the single ones felt that a lack of self-confidence was a barrier to their advancement.

Table 5.10 Employed women's perceptions of barriers to career advancement: 1986 (N = 240)

		Marital Status		*Age*		*Socio-economic Status*		*Background*	
		Married (n = 120)	*Single (n = 120)*	*18–34 (n = 120)*	*35–65 (n = 120)*	*Low (n = 120)*	*High (n = 120)*	*Rural (n = 120)*	*Urban (n = 120)*
1	There are no avenues for advancement in my work.					$F = 11.05^{***}$		$F = 3.58; p = .06$	
		4.08	4.00	4.06	4.02	4.53	3.55	4.32	3.77
2	I would need more training or educational qualifications in order to get ahead.					$F = 15.06^{***}$		$F = 5.34^{*}$	
		4.16	4.06	4.21	4.02	4.69	3.53	3.76	4.45
3	I have too much to do already balancing job and family responsibilities.	$F = 18.28^{***}$							
		3.22	2.19	2.51	2.92	2.83	2.61	2.77	2.67
4	The attitudes of management at my workplace tend to favour promotion of men rather than women.			$F = 8.63^{**}$					
		3.11	2.81	3.39	2.57	3.21	2.73	2.94	3.00
5	I lack self-confidence.					$F = 7.01^{***}$			
		2.39	2.71	2.50	2.60	2.86	2.24	2.48	2.62
6	I don't want more responsibility.			$F = 3.82; p = .052$					
		3.39	3.12	2.98	3.52	3.38	3.12	3.39	3.09
7	If I had more flexible working hours, I could manage better and probably would be better able to advance in my career.			$F = 7.42^{**}$					
		3.14	3.21	3.55	2.80	3.27	3.07	2.9	3.39

$^{*}p < .05$ $^{**}p < .01$ $^{***}p < .001$ Mean scores are presented. Responses were on 7-point scale: 1 = "strongly disagree"; 7 = "strongly agree"

Interestingly enough, in rural areas *older* women were more likely to express a lack of self-confidence, whereas in urban areas, this applied more to *younger* women, as shown in a significant interaction effect ($F = 5.52$; $p = .02$).

Another view that is sometimes put forth is that women do not *want* more responsibility on the job. This would appear to be true for a certain proportion of women (30% of single and 37% of married). However, it did *not* apply to the other 63–70% of women workers. It also applied far less to women aged 18 to 49 than to women aged 50 and over.

Concerning the lack of availability of flexible hours, about 29% of employed women felt that if they were more available they would be able to manage better and would therefore be better able to advance in their careers. Younger women were significantly more likely to feel that the lack of flexible hours were a barrier to their career advancement.

Among married women, 25% felt that if they had more help with housework and childcare they would be able to put more into their jobs and therefore be more likely to get ahead, and an examination of demographic effects on this were not significant, i.e., women aged 18–34 and 35–65 equally agreed with this, as did women in lower and higher socio-economic groups and those living in rural and urban areas (see Table 5.11). We also asked employed married women if they

Table 5.11 Employed married women's perceptions of barriers to career advancement: 1986 (N = 120)

	Age		*Socio-economic status*		*Background*	
	18–34 (n = 60)	*35–65 (n = 60)*	*Low (n = 60)*	*High (n = 60)*	*Rural (n = 60)*	*Urban (n = 60)*
1. My husband would disapprove if I were too successful.	2.12	1.92	2.20	1.84	$F = .74^{**}$ 1.56	2.47
2. If I had more help with housework and childcare I could put more into my job.	3.17	2.90	3.03	3.03	2.96	3.09

$^{*}p < .05$
$^{**}p < .01$
$^{***}p < .001$

Mean scores are presented. Responses were on 7-point scales:
1 = "strongly disagree"
2 = "moderately disagree"
3 = "slightly disagree"
4 = midpoint
5 = "slightly agree"
6 = "moderately agree"
7 = "strongly agree"

thought their husbands would disapprove if they were too successful. While only a small proportion (11.8%) agreed with this, of which the largest proportion said they "strongly agreed," there were no age or social class differences; however, there was a significant effect of rural/urban location indicating that urban women were more likely to say this was the case ($F = 7.74$; $p < .01$).

Employed women's attitudes concerning barriers to their career advancement were compared with the attitudes of other groups in the community (Table 5.12). There are striking and, in many cases, unexpected findings throughout. The most striking difference is that *other groups* (i.e., men and non-employed women) were far more likely to see the nine items as barriers to women's career advancement than the employed women did themselves. They also saw different things as barriers than the employed women did.

For example, whereas the employed women felt that for them the biggest barriers were (a) a lack of avenues for career advancement and (b) a need for more training and education, these reasons were only ranked seventh and fifth respectively among men and non-employed women. These latter groups were far more likely to see management attitudes, a lack of flexible hours and a lack of household help and childcare as significant barriers to employed women's career advancement. The percentage discrepancies here are extremely large (shown in Table 5.9) and the statistical comparisons of the means (contained in Table 5.12) are highly significant. For example, whereas only 28% of employed women cited management attitudes as a barrier to their advancement, they were cited as important by 90.8% of employed married men, by 79% of employed single men and by 85% of non-employed married women. With regard to a lack of flexible hours, just 29% of employed women cited this as a barrier to their advancement, whereas 87% of all other groups thought it was. Regarding lack of household help and childcare, only 25% of employed married women cited this as a barrier to their advancement in the workplace, yet over 80% of employed men and non-employed married women saw it as a barrier which employed married women faced.

Discussion and interpretation of the 1986 data

Why do we see such large discrepancies in perceptions between employed women and others in society? In contemplating this question it may be useful to refer back to the previous findings which indicated that employed women were less likely to think that they had been discriminated against in the workplace than others thought they were. This was interpreted in terms of a possible *denial* of one's own discrimination as an adaptive mechanism because it would be too uncomfortable, and indeed dissonance producing, to acknowledge to oneself that one was a victim of discrimination. One does not like to see oneself as a victim. This would mean one would have to see oneself as a second-class citizen, someone who was being mistreated, and this would be uncomfortable.

Table 5.12 Perceived barriers to women's career advancement: a comparison of employed women and other groups, 1986 (N = 600)

Potential barriers to career advancement	*Employed women (n = 240)*		*Others (n = 360)*		*t-Value*
	Mean	*S.D.*	*Mean*	*S.D.*	
1 No avenues for advancement	4.08	2.25	3.30	1.83	4.63***
2 Would need more training/ education to get ahead	4.20	2.34	4.05	1.95	0.81 N.S.
3 Too much to do already balancing job and family	2.70	1.86	4.11	1.81	−9.12***
4 Attitudes of management favour promotion of men	2.98	2.20	5.50	1.47	−16.67***
5 Lack of self-confidence	2.55	1.83	2.76	1.84	−1.41 N.S.
6 Don't want more responsibility	3.25	2.14	2.98	1.74	1.70 N.S.
7 If had flexible hours could manage better and be better able to advance	3.17	2.08	5.55	1.47	−16.24***
8 Husband would disapprove if too successful	2.02+	1.80	3.18	2.05	−5.50***
9 If had more help with housework and childcare could put more into job	3.03+	1.96	5.34	1.46	−11.72***

+Data presented on these two items for married women only in the employed group
*$p < .05$ **$p < .01$ ***$p < .001$
N.S. = Non-significant

The data concerning perceived barriers to career advancement are, on the surface, surprising. Yet if one looks deeper, the data are actually quite consistent with the previous findings.

Women did not admit even to themselves that they were being discriminated against: they were just like all other workers – in fact they saw themselves as less discriminated against than "women in general." Therefore, they did not *deserve* any special considerations such as flexible hours or help with housework or childcare facilities. They should be able to do it all. What is very interesting, and revealing, is that *other* groups whom one might not have expected to be sympathetic to the needs of employed married women, on the contrary, appeared to be particularly sensitised to their needs. They seemed to realise quite clearly that employed married women needed flexible hours, household help and childcare facilities. They had no hesitation in citing these as major obstacles to women's career advancement. They too saw very clearly that management attitudes contributed to women's poorer position in the organisational hierarchy. The fact that most managers are married men and the fact that 90% of the married men in the sample agreed that management attitudes were a key barrier to women's advancement is something which should be taken seriously. These men know what they're talking about.

The fact that there was not more pressure from employed women for supports such as flexible working hours and childcare facilities prior to the data collection in the 1986 study may be explained, at least in part, on the basis of the attitudes which we have just examined. Women did not acknowledge – even to themselves – that they deserved certain working conditions that others clearly acknowledged without hesitation.

On the other hand, the data also showed that other groups in the population did not fully appreciate the extent to which many women felt trapped in jobs which had no channels for upward mobility – no career ladders. While 54% of employed women cited this as a major barrier to their career advancement, this reality was appreciated by only 35% of single men and 26% of married men.

Barriers to women's career advancement: a comparison of employed women and other groups: an update in 2005

Some 20 years later a similar comparison was made between employed women and others in society concerning perceived barriers to women's career advancement. This comparison allows us to compare attitudes from 1986 with those almost 20 years later in 2005 to see if attitudes had remained the same or had changed.

This comparison, made in 2005, is shown in Table 5.13. As was the case in 1986, in six out of nine cases there were significant differences in perceived barriers to women's career advancement between employed women and others in society. However, in 2005 these perceptions were different in several cases to what they were in 1986. There was still a highly significant difference concerning attitudes of management favouring promotion of men. In 2005, as in 1986, men and non-employed women were significantly more likely than employed women to say that management attitudes favouring men was a barrier to women's advancement ($p < .001$). Similarly, these other groups were also more likely than employed women to say that if women had more help with housework and childcare they could put more into their job ($p < .001$). This view was true in 1986 and it was also true in 2005, indicating that others were more aware of women's need for help than working women themselves were.

However, while working women were *less likely* to say that they had too much to do already balancing job and family in 1986, by 2005 they were *more likely* to acknowledge this. Similarly in relation to flexible hours, employed women were *more likely* than other groups to think that they would be able to manage better and be better able to advance in their career if they had flexible hours. The reverse had been the case in 1986, with others being more likely to think that lack of flexible hours was a barrier to women's career advancement.

Table 5.13 Perceived barriers to women's career advancement: a comparison of employed women and other groups, 2005 (N = 915)

Potential barriers to career advancement	*Employed women (n = 263)*		*Others (men and non-employed women) (n = 652)*		
	Mean	*S.D.*	*Mean*	*S.D.*	*t-value*
No avenues for advancement	3.09	2.37	3.11	1.95	−0.10 N.S
Would need more training/education to get ahead	4.01	2.45	3.87	2.10	0.82 N.S
Too much to do already balancing job and family	3.37	2.26	3.68	2.03	−1.94 N.S
Attitudes of management favour promotion of men	2.32	1.91	4.83	1.90	−18.23***
Lack of self-confidence	2.04	1.63	2.28	1.62	−2.01*
Don't want more responsibility	3.14	3.08	2.39	1.69	3.71***
If had flexible hours could manage better and be better able to advance	3.55	2.40	2.53	1.69	6.32***
Husband would disapprove if too successful	2.82	2.10	5.09	1.80	−15.53***
If had more help with housework and childcare could put more into job	3.12	2.12	5.49	1.57	−16.49***

*$p < .05$; **$p < .01$; ***$p < .001$

Interestingly enough, employed married women were more likely to say their husband would disapprove if they were too successful in 2005 (mean = 2.82) than they were in 1986 (mean = 2.02), and others (men and non-employed women) also endorsed this view and in fact were even more likely in 2005 to think this would be the case (mean = 5.09) than they did in 1986 (mean = 3.18). This finding in the 2005 data may well reflect an indirect measure of a "backlash" against women's increasing success in the labour market, which was much less apparent in 1986. This notion of a backlash, which entails attempts to reverse women's gains in the workplace, is a phenomenon which Faludi (1991) and others have observed. We have also seen some evidence of this in more recent research in Ireland which identified a perceived threat of women's career success on the part of men and women's acute awareness of it (Fine-Davis, 2016).

Summary and discussion of the findings: 1975–2005

Perceived discrimination

Because of the anti-discrimination legislation which became operative in 1976 (Equal Pay) and 1977 (Equal Opportunity), one might have expected less experience of discrimination in 1986 than in 1975; however, this was not the case. There was no difference in the level of perceived discrimination over this period in the areas of training or in the kind of work or quality of work experience which women had. Concerning promotion, single women reported slightly less discrimination over this period, but married women reported a good deal more discrimination. There was a trend (which did not quite reach statistical significance) in the direction of single women experiencing less discrimination in the area of pay in 1986 than they had in 1975. This trend did not occur for married women. Furthermore, there was an increase in perceived discrimination in getting a job and as a result of the educational system. The increase in perceived discrimination by the educational system was the most significant finding obtained.

Thus, the only positive effects which appear to have occurred in this initial period between 1975 and 1986 were the very slight improvements for single women in the areas of pay and promotion. However, this was accompanied by a significant worsening of the promotional situation experienced by married women. It is unlikely that discriminatory practices increased during this period, particularly in view of the equality legislation implemented in 1976 and 1977. Furthermore, attitudes towards equal opportunity and gender roles had shifted in a more egalitarian direction over this same time period (Fine-Davis, 1988a, 2015). What the results do suggest is that women's *awareness* of discrimination became heightened during the eleven years from 1975 to 1986. This may have occurred as a result of discussion in the media of equality issues, relating to the U.N. Decade for Women (1975–1985), and as a result of the equality legislation. In particular, media attention concerning discrimination in the educational system in terms of access to higher maths and science, as well as sex-role stereotyping in textbooks, may have contributed to employed women's increased awareness of discrimination by the educational system. These results need not necessarily be seen as disturbing, since it may be necessary to first achieve an awareness of a problem before one can begin to remedy it. Nevertheless, the fact that women's perceptions of discrimination did not decrease gave some cause for concern. It suggested that continued efforts had to be made to see to it that actual discrimination decreased.

During the period 1975 to 1986 women became increasingly aware of their own discrimination by the educational system and in getting a job. This was also true on the part of married women in the area of promotion. Nevertheless employed women tended to underestimate their own experience of discrimination compared with that experienced by "women in general."

Several interpretations of this discrepancy were put forth. Firstly, not all employed women had experienced discrimination themselves, yet they would have been aware of its existence. Secondly, even if they had experienced discrimination, they may have only done so in one or two areas, not in all five (getting a job, job training, pay, kind of work and promotion). Thirdly, and perhaps most importantly, many women may not have recognised that they were being discriminated against because they were working in largely sex-segregated employment (e.g., nursing, teaching, contract cleaning, etc.). Where all of one's co-workers were female, one may not be aware of discrimination against oneself *per se* because there is no basis for comparison. Women were actually being discriminated against *en masse*. Qualitative data obtained from nurses in an exploratory follow-up tended to support this hypothesis. While it has long been recognised that this is a structural mechanism for keeping women's wages lower than those of men, it would now appear that sex-segregated employment has an even more insidious outcome, i.e., it blinds women to the fact of their own discrimination because they experience no direct comparisons with men.

Finally, the obtained discrepancies may have been due in part to the fact that women may have been denying the extent to which they were being discriminated against. Since an acknowledgement of such discrimination might have led to the necessity of taking action to rectify the situation and since such action as seeking legal redress is inconvenient, risky and inconsistent with expected norms of female behaviour, most women may have preferred "not to see" that they were in fact victims of discrimination.

The perceptions of employed women concerning the extent of discrimination against women in general by and large did not differ from those of other groups (i.e., employed men and non-employed married women). This basic consensus about the level of discrimination against women in general would further tend to put a question mark over the reasons for the discrepancies in the employed women's responses and lead one to ask why employed women are under-reporting their *own* experience of discrimination. This evidence lends further support to the hypotheses that women were denying their own experience of discrimination because the psychological and practical consequences of fully acknowledging their own discrimination would be too uncomfortable and too costly. The phenomenon of denial of discrimination has been found by other researchers in other countries, notably Crosby (1984) in the United States. This kind of denial is consistent with the notion of *avoidance* that has been put forth concerning racial and other minority groups:

> If a member of a minority group cannot abolish the status restrictions under which he lives, he can, at least under many circumstances, avoid situations where he must experience prejudice, or he can avoid some aspects of situations and thus reduce their painful and disagreeable impact. . . . Many motives encourage avoidance: the desire to preserve self-respect, to escape the need for conforming to the role of an inferior.
>
> (Simpson and Yinger, 1958, p. 231)

In addition to *avoidance*, another strategy often employed by racial and other minorities is that of *acceptance*. As Simpson and Yinger point out,

> It has frequently been said that Gandhi's biggest task was to persuade the outcasts of India to protest against their status.
>
> (p. 251)

Perceived discrimination: update in 2005

By 2005 attitudes had changed. In four out of six cases, employed women were significantly *more* likely to think women were discriminated against in the workplace than others thought they were. This included in relation to hiring, job training, pay and promotion. This differs from the findings from 1986 which showed that there were no significant differences in perceptions between these two groups. This is a clear indicator that employed women had become more attuned to discrimination in the workplace over this period. Although the differences are significant at just the $p < .05$ level, they reflect a consistent shift from the previous results of 1986.

Barriers to career advancement: 1986–2005

In 1986 the findings concerning barriers to women's career advancement showed that employed women were significantly *less likely* to perceive as barriers several factors which others (i.e., employed men and non-employed married women) saw as obstacles to women's career advancement. These included: (a) attitudes of management favouring promotion of men, (b) the lack of flexible hours and (c) the lack of household help or childcare.

While these results appear, on the surface, surprising, they are actually quite consistent with the results concerning women's denial of discrimination of which they were the object. Since women did not acknowledge this discrimination, they did not see it as a barrier to their advancement. Since they did not admit even to themselves that they were being discriminated against, they had to then see themselves as just like all other workers, i.e., not deserving of special consideration, particularly in a time of recession and high unemployment in which anyone with a job may have felt fortunate and particularly disinclined to rock the boat. The result of this is that married women workers did not demand the policies and supports which they required in order to effectively carry out the dual roles of worker and wife/mother, such as flexible working hours and childcare facilities.

What is very interesting and revealing is that other groups whom one might not have expected to be sympathetic to the needs of employed married women, on the contrary, appeared to be sensitive to their needs. They appeared to realise that employed married women needed flexible hours, household help and childcare facilities. They apparently had no hesitation in citing these as major obstacles to women's career advancement. They too seemed to see that management attitudes contributed to women's poorer position in the organisational hierarchy.

The fact that there has not been more pressure from employed women for things such as flexible hours and childcare facilities may be explained, at least in part, on the basis of the attitudes revealed by the study. Women did not acknowledge – even to themselves – that they deserved certain working conditions that others clearly acknowledged without hesitation.

On the other hand, the data also showed that other groups in the population did not fully appreciate the extent to which many women felt trapped in jobs which had no channels for upward mobility – no career ladders. This obstacle was particularly important for women working in jobs of lower occupational status. Such women were also particularly aware of the need for further training and education in order to get ahead. The fact that employed women were significantly more likely to perceive "no avenues for advancement" as a more significant barrier than others did suggested the need to educate and raise the awareness of employers about the demoralising and iniquitous situation of dead-end jobs, which many women found themselves in.

As was the case in relation to perceived discrimination, employed women's attitudes towards the barriers to their career advancement also changed to some extent by 2005, though in some areas they remained the same. There was still a highly significant difference concerning attitudes of management favouring promotion of men. In 2005, as in 1986, men and non-employed women were significantly more likely than employed women to say that management attitudes favouring men was a barrier to women's advancement ($p < .001$). Similarly, these other groups were also more likely than employed women to say that if women had more help with housework and childcare they could put more into their job ($p < .001$). This view was true in 1986 and it was also true in 2005, indicating that others were more aware of women's need for help than working women themselves were.

However, while working women were *less likely* than others to say that they had too much to do already balancing job and family in 1986, by 2005 they were *more likely* to acknowledge this. Similarly in relation to flexible hours, employed women were *more likely* than other groups to think that they would be able to manage better and be better able to advance in their career if they had flexible hours. The reverse had been the case in 1986, with others being more likely to think that lack of flexible hours was a barrier to women's career advancement. Thus, we can say on the basis of the empirical data over time that women have become more aware of discrimination, are less likely to experience it in some ways and are more aware of the actual barriers to their own advancement.

Note

1 We are grateful to Muireann Conaty, who collected this qualitative follow-up data in the context of counselling courses which she taught at Maynooth College.

References

Blackwell, J. (1986). *Woman in the Labour Force*. Dublin: Employment Equality Agency.

Callender, R. and Meenan, F. (1994). *Equality in Law Between Men and Women in the European Community – Ireland*. Dordrecht, Boston and London: Martin Nijhoff and Luxembourg: Office for Official Publications of the European Communities.

Central Statistics Office. (2007). *Census 2006: Principal Demographic Results*. Dublin: Stationery Office.
Commission on the Status of Women (1972). *Report to Minister for Finance*. Dublin: The Stationery Office.
Crosby, F. (1984). The denial of personal discrimination. *American Behavioral Scientist*, 27, 371–386.
Drew, E. (1996). *Key Concepts Employed to Understand Gender in Relation to the Labour Market*. Paper No. 37. Aalborg, Denmark: FREIA, Feminist Research Centre in Aalborg, Department of Development and Planning, Aalborg University.
Employment Equality Agency (1983). *Schooling and Sex Roles: Agency Commentary. Recommendations and Summary Findings of Report*. Dublin: Employment Equality Agency.
Eurofound (2018). *Women in Management: Underrepresented and Overstretched?* Luxembourg: Publications Office of the European Union.
European Institute for Gender Equality (2019a). *Gender Equality Index 2019: Work-Life Balance*. Vilnius: European Institute for Gender Equality.
European Institute for Gender Equality (2019b). *Gender Equality Index 2019: Ireland*. Vilnius: European Institute for Gender Equality.
Eurostat (1983). *EEC Labour Force Sample Survey 1981*. Luxembourg: Statistical Office of the European Communities.
Faludi, S. (1991). *Backlash: The Undeclared War Against Women*. London: Chato & Windus.
Fine-Davis, M. (1976). *Structure, Determinants and Correlates of Attitudes Toward the Role and Status of Women in Ireland, with Particular Reference to Employment Status of Married Women*. Unpublished doctoral dissertation, Department of Psychology, Trinity College, University of Dublin.
Fine-Davis, M. (1977). *Attitudes Toward the Status of Women: Implications for Equal Employment Opportunity*. Report to the Department of Labour. Dublin: Department of Psychology, Trinity College Dublin.
Fine-Davis, M. (1988a). Changing gender role attitudes in Ireland: 1975–1986. In: *First Report of the Second Joint Committee on Women's Rights* (P1. 5609). Vol. I: Attitudes Towards the Role and Status of Women 1975–1986. Dublin: The Stationery Office, May.
Fine-Davis, M. (1988b). Changing gender role attitudes in Ireland: 1975–1986. In: *Second Report of the Second Joint Committee on Women's Rights* (P1. 5673). Vol. II: Issues Related to Equal Employment Opportunity. Dublin: The Stationery Office, June.
Fine-Davis, M. (1988c). Changing gender role attitudes in Ireland: 1975–1986. In: *Third Report of the Second Joint Committee on Women's Rights* (P1. 5796). Vol. III: Attitudes Towards Moral Issues in Relation to Voting Behaviour in Recent Referenda. Dublin: The Stationery Office, July.
Fine-Davis, M. (2015). *Gender Roles in Ireland: Three Decades of Attitude Change*. London: Routledge.
Fine-Davis, M. (2016). *Changing Gender Roles and Attitudes to Family Formation in Ireland*. Manchester: Manchester University Press.
Fine-Davis, M., McCarthy, M., Edge, G. and O'Dwyer, C. (2005). *Work-Life Balance and Social Inclusion in Ireland: Results of a Nationwide Survey*. Dublin: National Flexi-Work Partnership (Centre for Gender and Women's Studies, Trinity College Dublin; IBEC; ICTU; FÁS, Age Action Ireland and Aware).

Gartland, F. (2017). Gender pay gap is widening in Ireland, CSO figures show. *Irish Times*, 19 October.

Haavio-Mannila, E. and Skard, T. (1985). The arena for political activity: The position of women in Nordic societies today In E. Haavio-Mannila et al. (Eds.), *Unfinished Democracy: Women in Nordic Politics*. Oxford: Pergamon Press, pp. 1–5.

Hannan, D., Breen, R., Murray, B., Watson, D., Hardiman, N. and O'Higgins, K. (1983). *Schooling and Sex-Roles: Sex Differences in Subject Provision and Student Choice in Irish Post-Primary Schools*. Paper No. 113. Dublin: Economic and Social Research Institute.

Hannon, E. and Sinclair, J. (1999). *The Implications of the Employment Equality Act 1998*. Dublin: European Foundation for the Improvement of Living and Working Conditions.

Hearn, J. (2001). *Men and Gender Equality: Resistance, Responsibilities and Reaching Out*. Keynote Paper, Men and Gender Equality, Örebro, Sweden, 15–16 March.

McCarthy, E. (1978). Women and work in Ireland: The present and preparing for the future. In: M. MacCurtain and D. O'Corrain (Eds.), *Women in Irish Society: The Historical Dimension*. Dublin: Arlen House, pp. 103–117.

O'Connor, P. (1998). *Emerging Voices: Women in Contemporary Irish Society*. Dublin: Institute of Public Administration.

OECD (1980). *Women and Employment*. Paris: OECD.

Ruane, F. P. and Sutherland, J. M. (1999). *Women in the Labour Force*. Dublin: Employment Equality Agency.

Russell, H., McGinnity, F., Callan, T. and Keane, C. (2009). *A Woman's Place: Female Participation in the Irish Labour Market*. Dublin: The Equality Authority and the Economic and Social Research Institute.

Second Commission on the Status of Women (1993). *Report to Government*. Dublin: The Stationery Office.

Simpson, G. E. and Yinger, J. M. (1958). *Racial and Cultural Minorities: An Analysis of Prejudice and Discrimination*. New York: Harper and Row.

Smyth, A. (1984). *Breaking the Circle: The Position of Women Academics in Third Level Education Ireland*. EEC Action Programme on the Promotion of Equal Opportunities for Women: Action B11 Vocational Choices National Advisory Group.

Tansey, J. (1983). The main findings of the report. In: Employment Equality Agency, *Schooling and Sex-Roles: Agency Commentary, Recommendations and Summary Findings of Report*. Dublin: Employment Equality Agency, pp. 21–37.

Chapter 6

Attitudes to childcare and the evolution of childcare policy

Background

Because so few married women were in the workforce until the early 1970s, and even then the proportion was quite small, childcare was not on the policy agenda. Perhaps the first time childcare was raised as a policy issue was in the *Report of the First Commission on the Status of Women* in 1972, and it has been the subject of national discussion in Ireland since the early 1980s as mothers increasingly entered the labour force. A series of Government reports focused on the issue in the 1980s and 1990s and international bodies also focused on it in comparative perspective in the early 2000s (e.g., OECD, 2003, 2004) and still do (e.g., European Commission/EACEA/Eurydice, 2019; OECD, 2019). Childcare as a policy issue has increasingly become the subject of political and social debate as well as academic research and analysis in Ireland (e.g., Collins and Wickham, 2001; Horgan, 2001; Hayes, 2002; Fine-Davis, 2004, 2007, 2015, 2016; Bradley, 2011; Hynes, 2012; McGinnity et al., 2013; Mahon and Bailey, 2015; Russell et al., 2018; Russell et al., 2019).

Increasing labour force participation of married women

Married female labour force participation in Ireland had, by Western standards, been exceptionally low in the 1960s and '70s. Only 5.2% of married women were employed in 1961 and though this rate increased by 50% in the next 10 years, it merely raised the participation rate to 7.5% by 1971 (Table 6.1). However, from 1971 to 1981 married women's participation more than doubled to 16.7% and continued to increase over the next two decades, almost trebling from 16.7% in 1981 to 45.3% in 1999. While all women's participation also increased over this period, the overall increase was largely due to the increase in married women's employment (Callan and Farrell, 1991). Participation increased to an even higher level (66.3%) by 1999 among women in the prime childbearing age group (25–34 years old), as illustrated in Table 6.1. In the following 10 years from 1999 to 2009 married women's participation increased even further to 54% overall and to 72.6% among women in the prime childbearing age group. The increase

Table 6.1 Married women's labour force participation in Ireland: 1961–2009 (%)

	1961	*1971*	*1977*	*1981*	*1989*	*1994*	*1999*	*2001*	*2009*
All ages	5.2	7.5	14.4	16.7	23.7	32.4	45.3	46.4	54.0
Age 25–34	4.8	8.8	16.7	21.6	39.0	54.5	66.3	64.7	72.6

Sources: CSO: *Labour Force Surveys* (1971–97); CSO: *Quarterly National Household Surveys* (1999–2009); Callan and Farrell (1991).

in the participation rate of married women in the prime childbearing age group may seem counter-intuitive, since it is more difficult for a woman with children to work, yet, as we found in our 1975 study of employed and non-employed married women, those with dependent children were significantly more likely to be positive to maternal employment than women with no dependent children (Fine-Davis, 1979) – see Chapter 3 for these findings. This was true both of women who were employed and women who were non-employed. This finding is in line with Bailyn's earlier theory (1964) which postulated that women who do not have children idealise motherhood, but after they achieve it they are more likely to want to work.

Thus, women with young children were now in the labour force "in force" and these children had to be looked after. It finally became apparent that women's labour force participation not only was *not* taking away jobs from men and school leavers, as had been feared in the 1970s and '80s (Fine-Davis, 1988a),[1] but it was in fact significantly contributing to Ireland's boom in the 1990s known as the "Celtic Tiger" (Fahey and FitzGerald, 1997).

In the early period of the 1970s to 1980 the increase in women's labour force participation was due to the spate of administrative and legal changes in the area of gender equality (the removal of the marriage bar in 1973, the enactment of equal pay and equal opportunity legislation in 1975 and 1977, changes in the tax code in 1980) and the removal of other deterrents to married women working, e.g., the lack of contraception, which was finally legalised in 1979. In the later period the increase was associated with economic growth and indeed was seen to contribute to the Celtic Tiger (Fahey and FitzGerald, 1997). At all points, from the 1970s onwards, the participation of women in the prime childbearing age group (25–34) increased at an even more rapid rate than that of other groups of married women.

Reports of the First and Second Commissions on the Status of Women: 1972 and 1993

The social changes taking place in Ireland concerning the role and status of women in the late 1960s and early 1970s – which reflected changes also taking place in the United States and Western Europe – led to the establishment by the

Government of the Commission on the Status of Women on 31 March 1970. Its terms of reference were

> to examine and report on the status of women in Irish society, to make recommendations on the steps necessary to ensure the participation of women on equal terms and conditions with men in the political, social, cultural and economic life of the country and to indicate the implications generally – including the estimated cost – of such recommendations.
>
> (Commission on the Status of Women, 1972, p. 7)

The commission addressed a wide range of areas with implications for the status of women, including employment, equal pay, social welfare, taxation, legal issues, politics and participation in public life, education and cultural affairs, and women in the home. At the very outset of its Report, the Commission referred to "underlying factors which limit women's participation even in the absence of formal discrimination." These included attitudes and stereotyped gender roles:

> ". . . the removal of these actual discriminations leaves untouched a larger and more subtle area of discrimination consisting of those factors which limit women's participation even in the absence of formal discrimination, that is, the stereotyped role that is assigned to women, the inculcation of attitudes in both boys and girls in their formative years that there are definite and separate roles for the sexes and that a woman's life pattern must be predominantly home-centred while the man's life pattern will be predominantly centred on employment. It is from this type of cultural mould that formal discrimination arises and it is only by the removal of such traditional attitudes that women can hope to achieve complete self-fulfilment and equal participation in all aspects of the life of the community."
>
> (Commission on the Status of Women, 1972, p. 12)

The Commission further noted that:

> Apart from attitudes of managements to the recruitment and training of women in employment there is a broader question of traditional male attitudes to women's role in society and male reluctance to accept women as an equal partner on either a social or domestic level. The full-time housewife devoting all her time and energy to looking after her husband and children is often pictured as the ideal woman. Many women may be afraid of not conforming to this role and this can lead to a reluctance on their part to involve themselves in matters outside the home and in questions affecting women in general or the community as a whole, whether they be social, political or other pursuits.
>
> (Ibid., p. 13)

Given the prevalence of women working in the home, which was the norm at the time, it is interesting to note that the Commission's Report was very sensitive to this:

> We would emphasise here, as we have elsewhere in this report, that it is not our intention nor our wish that women with family responsibilities should be forced into employment, but we do consider that if such women choose to work outside the home they should be reasonably free to do so and that barriers in the way of such choice should, as far as possible, be removed.
>
> (Ibid., pp. 13–14)

The notion of "family responsibilities" echoes the article in the Irish Constitution which states that

> 2.1 In particular, the State recognises that by her life within the home, woman gives to the State a support without which the common good cannot be achieved.
>
> 2.2 The State shall, therefore, endeavour to ensure that mothers should not be obliged by economic necessity to engage in labour to neglect of their duties in the home.
>
> (Article 41.2, Constitution of Ireland, 1937)

These articles of the Constitution reflect the ethos of the State of Ireland at that time and for much of the time following. Bradley (2011) observes that

> Specifically, Article 41, grounded in the Catholic principle of subsidiarity supports a highly privatised autonomous model of family life in which the woman cares for home and children while husband acts as breadwinner with state intervention confined to exceptional circumstances where parents fail in their duty to their children (Article 42) (All Party Oireachtas Committee on the Constitution, 2006). While the intention of Article 41 and Article 42 may have been to defend the family against unwarranted interference by the state, analysts have argued that the emphasis on the rights of the family and the clear subjugation of children within that institution resulted in the granting of higher value to the rights of parents over those of children. . . . The principle of subsidiarity and the privatised model of family life it espoused . . . enabled the state to occupy a distant and non-interventionist role thus situating the church, the voluntary sector and the family as the main and in certain instances sole supplier of social services (Fanning, 2003; Chubb, 1992; Kiely, 1999).
>
> (Bradley, 2011, p. 46)

However, the Commission on the Status of Women, while acknowledging this role, also acknowledged women's right not only to work outside the home if they so chose, but also to be free of barriers to this employment. The Commission's report recommended changes in various areas to make this possible, including taxation and childcare. Childcare was referred to as a sub-category under "Women and Employment" and it was referred to as "Day-Care for Children." This section was introduced thus:

> Many married women who find that they must re-enter employment, or mothers who are ill or hospitalised for any length of time, are faced with the task of finding suitable care facilities for young children. The most satisfactory solution to this problem is where arrangements can be made for parents or other relations to undertake responsibility for them while the mother is working or incapacitated. Frequently, it is not possible for the mother to make this kind of arrangement and she must either try to avail of professional child-minding facilities or else depend on older children to look after the younger ones outside school hours.
>
> (Commission on the Status of Women, 1972, p. 129)

It is clear from this that maternal employment was very much not the norm and when it did take place it was women's responsibility to sort out childcare arrangements, preferably within the family. The State was not seen to have a responsibility in this regard.

A Second Commission on the Status of Women (1993) was established in 1990, twenty years after the First Commission, in order to review the implementation of the recommendations of the first Commission and to consider and make recommendations on the means, administrative and legislative, by which women could be able to participate on equal terms and conditions with men in economic, social, political and cultural life and to this end, to consider the efficacy and feasibility of positive action measures. This was followed by three Progress Reports on the implementation of the recommendations of the Second Commission on the Status of Women (Government of Ireland, 1994, 1996, 1999).

Government Working Party Reports on Childcare Facilities for Working Parents: 1983 and 1994

In the interim between the two Commissions on the Status of Women, which addressed the issue of childcare in the context of many issues affecting the status of women, the increase in the number of married women and in particular, mothers, in the workforce continued unabated, and it became increasingly clear that it would be necessary to address the childcare needs of these women. The initial concern with the issue of childcare manifested itself in a succession of Government Working Party reports and reports of other Governmental and non-Governmental bodies beginning in the early 1980s. There were no fewer than seven reports on this topic during the period 1983 to 1999 (Working Party on Child Care Facilities for Working Parents, 1983; Working Group on Childcare

Facilities for Working Parents, 1994; Commission on the Family, 1998; Goodbody Economic Consultants, 1998; National Forum for Early Childhood Education, 1998; Expert Working Group on Childcare, 1999; Department of Education and Science, 1999).

The first Working Party on Child Care Facilities for Working Parents was convened by the Irish Minister for Labour in 1981 and it reported to the Government in 1983 (Working Party on Child Care Facilities for Working Parents, 1983). This report recommended that there should be a national programme of community-based childcare facilities for working parents:

> Day care needs of working parents should be regarded as an aspect of the totality of local community needs and, as such, any measures designed to meet these needs should also form part of the total network to community-based services which are intended to cater for community needs on a co-ordinated, integrated basis.
>
> (R. 11, Chapter III, paragraph 3.30)

The Report also recommended the establishment of a National Statutory Child Care Authority whose functions should include "the power to prescribe standards and minimum requirements, subject to the approval of the Minister for Health, governing the operation of day care services" as well as "the power to ensure the provision of adequate training for personnel involved in providing child care services and to give formal recognition to such training courses" (R. 21, paragraph 3.48). It further recommended that "as a general rule working parents should be charged according to their capacity to pay for day care services provided by public authorities for their children" (R. 22, 3.54). The report also addressed the issue of alternative working arrangements and in this regard recommended that "consultations should be arranged among interested parties with a view to examining how services provided by both statutory and private bodies should be better adjusted to facilitate working parents." Trade unions and employers were encouraged "to adopt a more positive attitude to part-time and temporary employment and to the position and status of those workers as an integral part of the established labour force" Chapter IV, R. 24).

In retrospect, this report was ahead of its time and many of its recommendations are still aspirations in current childcare policy discussions, as will be elaborated upon later in this chapter.

A second Working Group on Child Care Facilities for Working Parents was convened approximately 10 years later and it also issued a report with recommendations (Working Group on Childcare Facilities for Working Parents, 1994), this time reporting to the Minister for Equality and Law Reform.

However, no significant Government initiatives were forthcoming during the period 1981 to 1999, in spite of the plethora of Government reports on childcare, all of which made similar recommendations, as well as projections that the demand for childcare would be likely to increase by 25% to 50% over the period 1998 to 2011 (Goodbody, 1998).

Workplace childcare

In light of the Government's lack of a response to the first *Report of the Working Party on Child Care Facilities for Working Parents (1983)*, the Irish Congress of Trade Unions, which itself had been represented on this Working Party, decided to take its own initiative by focusing on childcare in the workplace. It devoted its Annual Women's Congress to this topic in 1989 and produced a pack for delegates on how to set up a workplace childcare centre. It further commissioned a review of the international research literature which demonstrated the economic and social benefits of childcare in the workplace (Fine-Davis, 1989).

During this time several workplace childcare centres were established in places such as Radio Telefis Eireann (RTE), the Electricity Supply Board (ESB), Eircom, etc. (Coughlan, 2000). As Horgan (2001) pointed out "workplace nurseries are a developing concept in Ireland. The provision, however, currently takes place mainly in the public sector" (p. 107). Referring to Family Friendly Initiatives in the Workplace (Employment Equality Agency, 1996), Horgan noted that there were 16 work-based nurseries established by organisations such as the universities, Aer Rianta, ESB, etc. (Horgan, 2001, p. 107).

Importance of early childhood care and education

All of the Government commissions and working parties which reported in the years 1983 to 1999, as well as subsequent ones, emphasised the importance of the educational component of childcare.

International research had shown that high-quality preschool education led to immediate measurable gains in cognitive and social development, which persisted through adolescence and adulthood and could have a significant role in combating later educational and social disadvantage (Expert Working Group on Childcare, 1999). The Goodbody Report (1998), summarising extensive international psychological evidence, concluded that

> Quality childcare has a beneficial impact on the development of children and especially on disadvantaged children. This impact is enhanced when the childcare provision includes an element of early education. The benefits to children persist through to adulthood and are garnered by the child, the State and society as a whole.
>
> Provision of *high quality* childcare is crucial to obtaining these benefits – they are unlikely to be obtained if provision is of low quality. High quality childcare is characterised in part by several observable factors – high adult-child ratios, small group sizes, well remunerated and trained caregivers.
>
> (Ibid., p. iv)

Longitudinal research, following children over more than 20 years, had shown that investment in high-quality early education paid off in terms of later social benefits and economic savings to society – a conclusion underscored both by the Report of the Expert Working Group on Childcare (1999) and the White Paper on Early Childhood Education (Department of Education and Science, 1999).

Successive Government working parties and commissioned reports emphasised the value of high quality educational childcare and, in many cases, recommended that there be a national programme of childcare facilities (see Fine-Davis, 2004). Research on public attitudes in Ireland had also indicated a consistently high level of support for state-supported preschool education for more than 35 years (Fine-Davis, 1983a, 1983b; Fine-Davis et al., 2005).

However, it was not until 1999, almost 20 years after the first Government Working Party on Child Care was convened in 1981 that the Government began to implement a childcare policy, known as the Equal Opportunities Childcare Policy (EOCP). The two decades from 1981 to 1999 were spent largely on analysis of the problem and discussion of how to cope with it. Following the development of the EOCP there continued to be an outpouring of reports on childcare from various sources, including the National Economic and Social Forum (NESF, 2005), the National Women's Council of Ireland (2001, 2005), the Irish Congress of Trade Unions (ICTU, 2002a) and the "Social Partners" (the Irish Business and Employers Confederation and the Irish Congress of Trade Unions) combined (IBEC/ICTU, 2005). The OECD was also an important player in this discussion from an international perspective and its reports commented *inter alia* on the Irish situation in comparison with other countries (e.g., OECD, 2003, 2004, 2006).

During this time, Hayes (2002) pointed out that one of the difficulties in relation to recent Government childcare policy, was that of overlap of responsibility by several Government departments. Referring to the White Paper prepared by the Department of Education and Science, *Ready to Learn* (1999) and the *National Childcare Strategy* (Expert Working Group on Childcare, 1999), prepared by the Department of Justice, Equality and Law Reform, Hayes pointed out that

> the fact that two Government departments would produce two separate strategies for childcare/early childhood education in the same year is an example of the difficulty policy-makers seem to have when addressing policy issues that concern in the main, the same-population [*sic*] children. The PPF (Programme for Prosperity and Fairness) continues this trend by locating co-ordination of responsibility for childcare within the Department of Justice, Equality and Law Reform, while identifying the Department of Education and Science as responsible for developing early childhood education. Where there is no clear lead department in the sector, the likelihood of inefficiency and overlap is increased. Contradictory departmental strategies impacting on the same population, lead to confusion in terms of policy responsibility. This, in turn, leads to a fragmented policy response in relation to the same

> policy issue, in this case the development and support of early childhood services for children.
>
> (Hayes, 2002, p. 70)

Since Hayes wrote in 2002, the Office of the Minister for Children was established, originally in the Department of Health, and since 2011 there has been a new Government Department of Children and Youth Affairs. This has helped to increase coordination which previously had been under no fewer than seven Government departments (OECD, 2006). However, it still remains the case that early childhood care and education is in the Minister's Office, whereas preschool education for four- and five-year-olds (the "infant classes") are in the Department of Education and Science, so there is still a lack of full coordination for preschool-age children.

The difference between the period from 1981 to 1999 and the period from 2000 to the present is that childcare is now firmly on the Irish political agenda (e.g., Horgan, 2001; Hayes, 2002; Fine-Davis, 2004, 2007; IBEC/ICTU, 2005; NESF, 2005; Mahon and Bailey, 2015; Russell et al., 2018).

Provision of childcare in Ireland: an historical perspective with international comparisons

Extent and type of care

Forty years ago most young children in Ireland were cared for in their own homes when their mothers went out to work. Data from a nationwide survey of employed and non-employed mothers carried out in 1981 for the first Government Working Party on Child Care for Working Parents (Fine-Davis, 1983b) shows that infants and preschool children of working mothers were most likely to be looked after in their own homes (55.6%) or in another home (40.2%); only a very small proportion were taken care of in a childcare centre, crèche or preschool (3.1%) (Table 6.2b). These children were most often looked after by relatives, either the father (18%) or other relative (over 35%), and the kind of training or experience childcare providers possessed was most often "practical experience," such as raising one's own children (66%). Having training and qualifications in childcare was the exception rather than the rule (see Table 6.2c).

Yet when mothers, both employed and non-employed, were asked in 1981 about their preferences regarding childcare for infants and preschool children, in terms of *where* this should ideally be carried out and *by whom*, the first choice was in the child's own home and the second choice was in a childcare centre. This is illustrated in Table 6.3. While 57.9% of employed mothers and 54.7% of non-employed mothers preferred childcare arrangements for their preschoolers in their own home, only 5.5% and 3.2% respectively wanted care in someone else's home. Between 20 and 22% of all mothers wanted this care in a preschool centre near home and a further 16–20% wanted it in a childcare

Table 6.2 Childcare arrangements of employed mothers with infants and pre-school-age children: 1981

	No. of Children	%
a. Who cares for infant/preschooler(s) while mother at work		
Father	60	18.6
Child's brother/sister	3	1.0
Other relative (residing in home)	41	12.7
Other relative (non-resident)	73	22.7
Non-relative (residing in home)	15	4.6
Non-relative (non-resident)	122	37.9
Mother	8	2.5
Total	**322**	**100.0**
b. Location where infant/ preschooler(s) cared for while mother at work		
In the home	174	55.6
In another home	126	40.2
In a childcare centre, crèche or preschool at workplace	2	0.6
In a childcare centre, crèche or preschool other than at workplace	8	2.5
Other	3	1.0
Total	**313**	**100.0**
c. Qualifications of childminder		
Teacher	8	2.5
Cert. in childcare	2	0.6
Nurse	16	5.1
Practical experience (e.g., has raised own children)	209	66.8
No special qualification	64	20.4
Other	14	4.4
Total	**313**	**100.0**

Source: Fine-Davis (1983b), Table 12, pp. 102–103 in *Working Party on Child Care Facilities for Working Parents* (1983).

centre in the workplace, for a total of 36–40% saying a childcare centre was their first choice.

The preferred caregiver for preschool children was a relative (49.9% of employed and 45.9% of non-employed mothers gave this preference). Almost as many said their first choice would be a person trained in childcare (43% of employed mothers and 47.7% of non-employed). Another adult was much less preferred (7.1% and 6.4% respectively) (see Table 6.4).

Thus while over 40% of preschool children were cared for by another adult (other than a relative) and over 40% were cared for in another home (as shown in Table 6.2), these were not the first preferences of mothers. The actual situation

Table 6.3 Preferred childcare arrangements for preschool children (age 2–5): 1981

1st Preference	*Employed*		*Non-employed*	
	n	%	*n*	%
(a) In own home	336	57.9	241	54.7
(b) In another home	32	5.5	14	3.2
(c) Childcare centre / preschool near home	117	20.2	98	22.3
(d) Childcare centre / preschool at workplace	95	16.4	87	19.8
Total	**580**	**100.0**	**440**	**100.0**

2nd Preference	*Employed*		*Non-employed*	
	n	%	*n*	%
(a) In own home	77	13.3	53	12.1
(b) In another home	172	29.8	109	25.0
(c) Childcare centre / preschool near home	177	30.6	139	31.9
(d) Childcare centre / preschool at workplace	152	26.3	135	31.0
Total	**578**	**100.0**	**436**	**100.0**

Source: Fine-Davis (1983b), Table 48, p. 128 in *Report of Working Party on Child Care Facilities for Working Parents (1983)*.

Table 6.4 Preferred caregiver for preschool children (age 2–5): 1981

1st Preference	*Employed*		*Non-employed*	
	n	%	*n*	%
(a) Relative	289	49.9	202	45.9
(b) Person trained in childcare	249	43.0	210	47.7
(c) Other adult	41	7.1	28	6.4
Total	**579**	**100.0**	**440**	**100.0**

2nd Preference	*Employed*		*Non-employed*	
	n	%	*n*	%
(a) Relative	175	31.2	151	35.0
(b) Person trained in childcare	248	44.3	177	41.1
(c) Other adult	137	24.5	103	23.9
Total	**560**	**100.0**	**431**	**100.0**

Source: Fine-Davis (1983b), Table 49, p. 129 in *Working Party on Child Care Facilities for Working Parents* (1983).

reflects the need of a large proportion of mothers to use childminders given that preschool centres and trained staff were scarce and relatives were also not always available.

Some twenty years later reliance on relatives and childminders for childcare was still very common, although the usage of childcare centres had increased. Data based on a survey module on childcare included in the National Household Survey in late 2002 (CSO, 2003) illustrates the patterns of childcare use in Ireland at that time. Over 73,000 families, or 42.5% of all families with preschool children, relied on childcare provided by someone other than the parents during working hours. Not surprisingly, couples where both partners were employed had the greatest need for childcare. Over three-quarters (55,300) of these families had some form of childcare arrangements for their preschool children (Ibid.). In 2005 the number of families with preschool children who relied on non-parental childcare arrangements during the normal working day had increased to 82,600 (CSO, 2006).

Table 6.5 shows the types of non-parental childcare used by preschool children in 2002, 2005 and 2016 when both parents were employed. It may be seen that a third were cared for by a paid carer, generally a childminder, both in 2002 and 2005 (CSO, 2003, 2006). A high proportion in both time periods was also cared for by a relative (41.4% in 2002 and 39.6% in 2005) who was generally unpaid (28.5% in 2002 and 27.7% in 2005).

What is striking is that only 22.1% of children in 2002 and 23.3% of children in 2005 were cared for in crèches or childcare centres. This suggests either that there were not enough childcare facilities available or that their cost was too high or both. The high level of care provided by relatives (both paid and unpaid) shows how family members – often grandparents – were drafted in to help with childcare.

The 2002 survey found that just under 20% of families with preschool children would welcome the availability of alternative childcare arrangements. Around half of these would like a crèche or Montessori, preferably work-based. Over 45%

Table 6.5 Non-parental childcare arrangements for preschool children of employed couples: 2002, 2005 and 2016

Childcare arrangement	*2002* %	*2005* %	*2016* %
Unpaid relative	28.5	27.7	28.1
Paid relative	12.6	11.9	[6.8]
Paid carer	33.2	33.6	29.7
Créche/Montessori	22.1	23.3	28.6
Other	3.5	3.6	[6.6]
Total	**100.0**	**100.0**	**100.0**

Source: My calculations based on CSO (2003, Table 3); CSO (2006, Table 2a); and (CSO, 2016a) based on special run by the CSO. Please note: Figures in brackets indicate percentages based on small numbers and are, therefore, subject to a wide margin of error.

said they were not availing of their desired option due to the cost and 33.5% said the option was not available (CSO, 2003).

By 2016 the figures had changed somewhat, with slightly fewer preschool children using paid carers (29.7%) and more using childcare centres and crèches (28.6%). There continued to be a high level of reliance on unpaid relatives (28.1%), who can usually be assumed to be grandparents.

International comparisons

An international comparison in four European countries (France, Denmark, Italy and Ireland) of types of childcare used by working parents with at least one child under six showed that Irish parents were more likely to rely on relatives for childcare and less likely to utilise childcare centres than parents in France or Denmark (Fine-Davis et al., 2004) (Table 6.6). This trend was also apparent in Italy, where grandparents were often providers of childcare. In France the most common childcare option was the école maternelle. In the other three countries the most common was the childcare centre, nursery or non-workplace crèche. Grandparents and partners were also a common first option in Italy and Ireland, as were unregistered child minders in Ireland. The total using a workplace or other crèche / childcare centre or nursery was 82% in Denmark, 57% in Italy, and taken together with the école maternelle the total in France was 79%, whereas in Ireland the total was 40.4%, which included 12.1% in "school," which refers to the "infant classes" for four- and five-year-olds which take place in the national schools (Ibid.).

Table 6.6 Childcare arrangements for youngest child when parent is at work (most often): percentage distributions for four European countries, 2004 (N = 400)

	France %	*Italy* %	*Denmark* %	*Ireland* %	*All countries* %
Self	2.0	0.0	0.0	0.0	0.5
Partner	1.0	13.0	3.0	15.2	8.0
Grandparent	5.0	21.0	2.0	17.2	11.5
Other relative	1.0	2.0	1.0	1.0	1.3
Work crèche / childcare ctr / nursery	6.0	1.0	3.0	11.1	5.3
Other crèche / childcare ctr / nursery	18.0	56.0	79.0	28.3	45.0
School / école maternelle	46.0	0.0	1.0	12.1	14.8
Childminder (registered)	13.0	1.0	9.0	3.0	6.5
Childminder (unreg)/ babysitter/neighbour	6.0	2.0	2.0	12.1	5.8
Other/N.A.	2.0	4.0	0.0	0.0	1.6
Total	**100.0**	**100.0**	**100.0**	**100.0**	**100.0**

Source: Fine-Davis et al. (2004), Table 8.19, p. 118.

Cost of childcare in Ireland

The average weekly cost of childcare for families with preschool children only was €105.36 nationally in Q4, 2002 and €120 in Q1, 2005; the comparable cost in Dublin was over €131 in Q4, 2002 and €145 in Q1, 2005. The increase in the cost of childcare nationally was 23% in the two-year period between the two surveys – an increase of 20.1% for school-going children and 27.3% for preschool children (CSO, 2006). The increase in the cost of childcare was significantly higher than the rate of inflation, which ranged from about 1.8 to 3.8% in 2003–2004 (Department of Finance, 2003, 2004). Assuming the rate of increase in the cost of preschool childcare was 13.6% per annum (27.3% divided by two), this reflects almost five times the average rate of inflation in 2003–4.

The CSO (2006) reported that when parents required more than 40 hours of childcare, the average cost was €184 per week. One preschool child could easily require 40 or more hours of childcare if their parents worked full time. If there were two preschool children in the family the cost would be €368 per week. With a Government subsidy of €50 per week per child (from Child Benefit and the Childcare Allowance of €1,000 for children five and under available at that time) this would come to a net cost to parents of €268 per week or over €1,000 per month for childcare. Should those two full-time working parents live in Dublin, the cost would have been even higher. At €5.15 per hour, 40 hours of child-care for preschool children would have cost €206 per week and full-time childcare for two preschoolers €412 per week. Subtracting the Government subsidy of €50 per child per week, the parents still had a net childcare bill of €312 per week or over €1250 per month. Childcare costs in Ireland consumed a higher proportion of working parents' earnings than in any other EU member state in 1999–2001 (Langford, 1999; *Irish Times*, 17 May 2001, p. 3). Childcare costs were so high that people, especially those on lower wages, had to spend a very significant proportion of their take-home pay on childcare. According to the Irish Congress of Trade Unions, childcare costs for working parents more than doubled from 1998 to 2001 (Yeates, *Irish Times*, 6 August 2001, p. 7). Moreover, tax relief for childcare expenses was and is still not available. As time has moved on from these estimates, the cost of childcare in Ireland has remained among the most expensive in Europe (Kelleher, 2019; European Commission/EACEA/Eurydice, 2019).

When one considers these childcare costs in relation to the falling birth rate, it is understandable that people were having fewer children. Parents simply could not afford to have more children when childcare costs were so high. This issue is still relevant today. A recent study of attitudes to family formation in Ireland found that 78% of Irish men and women in the child-bearing age group agreed that "these days most couples simply can't afford to have more than two children." Similarly, 68% said that "the cost of living is restricting the number of children I will have/did have" (Fine-Davis, 2016, Table 5.2, p. 101).

Views of the social partners and other national and international bodies

Views of the Social Partners

The trade unions and employers, collectively referred to as "the Social Partners," have consistently expressed concern about childcare supply, quality and cost over many years.

Launching the results of the Irish Congress of Trade Union's (ICTU) Survey on Members' Childcare Needs in April 2002, Joan Carmichael, then assistant general secretary, stressed that "action on childcare must be seen as a priority area for Government. Government must address the cost of childcare to ensure its affordability for parents. . . . What is needed now is the identification and implementation of an appropriate mix of measures to increase childcare supply and make the cost affordable for parents" (ICTU, 2002b).

David Begg, then general secretary of the Irish Congress of Trade Unions, in his address to ambassadors of EU and accession countries (Begg, 2004), stressed the need to build social infrastructure particularly relevant to care of children. He drew attention to the "currently huge differences in the quality and availability of childcare in different European countries." "Ireland, for example," he said, "could not be remotely compared to Denmark because we have no effective public policy on childcare."

Two years later in 2006, Begg said that "the market has failed to deliver on care. In fact, all it has delivered are higher prices, poor access and uneven quality." He further advocated that "care had to be approached in a strategic and holistic fashion with the creation of a national 'infrastructure of care' now an urgent priority. In policy terms, care must assume the status of a 'public good,' similar to that enjoyed by education" (ICTU, 2006).

He predicted that "the consequences of failing to do so will be severe and do long-term social and economic damage" and that "faced with such costs people will either leave the workforce or choose to limit their families, leaving the future Irish economy wholly dependent on migrant workers to meet labour supply" (Ibid.). This prediction proved to be prescient, with the birth rate continuing to fall (OECD, 2003; Fine-Davis, 2016) and migrant labour playing an increasingly important role in the economy.

The Irish Business and Employers Confederation (IBEC) has also expressed concern about the lack of childcare provision in relation to needs of the labour force for some time (e.g., IBEC, 1998). In 2004 its then director general, Turlough O'Sullivan, in the *Foreword* to an IBEC (2004) Education Policy document, *Education for Life – The Challenge of the Third Millennium*, pointed out that "there is universal agreement that investment in education has been one of the key contributors to the economic success of recent years" (p. 1). The Policy Document further states that "a properly resourced and co-ordinated pre-school programme is an essential precursor to the primary school system and would benefit all families – regardless of whether one, both or neither parents are working" (p. 10).

Views of other national and international bodies

Various other national and international bodies have issued reports and submissions on childcare. These have included, among others, the National Women's Council of Ireland, the National Economic and Social Forum (NESF), the Chambers of Commerce of Ireland and the OECD.

The OECD has pointed out that "maternal labour force withdrawal, even if not permanent, involves considerable (opportunity) costs for the society as a whole" (2003, p. 119). As demographic trends are showing a decline in birth rates, the OECD advocates policies that reduce the "indirect costs for mothers to work by offering affordable quality childcare, regular part-time employment opportunities and, generally, making the labour market more inclusive" (Ibid., p. 120).

In a comparative study of childcare in Ireland, Japan and Austria, the OECD (2003) confirmed that childcare was more costly in Ireland than in either of the other two countries, in fact it was twice as high (p. 181). Not only that, but Irish childcare costs were found not to be income related, as they were in Austria and Japan. Even more worrying was the fact that for a lone parent with average earnings living in Dublin "the cost of childcare for one child was equivalent to 30% of after-tax net income, and it would be another 30% for a second child" (OECD, 2003, p. 148). Thus they pointed out that "childcare costs can be a barrier to work in Ireland" (Ibid.).

This has particular implications for women, as the National Women's Council of Ireland (2001) pointed out, citing the Expert Working Group on Childcare (1999): "the availability and cost of childcare and the difficulties around reconciling employment and family lives are the most significant barriers to women accessing and participating in the labour force" (NWCI, 2001, p. 15).

The situation described earlier has particular implications for single parents since a very high proportion of single parents in Ireland are not employed (OECD, 2003, p. 188). Lone parents have particular constraints because they have less time available due to lack of support from a partner. They are also at relatively high risk of poverty because of low educational levels together with low employment rates (Ibid., p. 192). For most lone parents, social welfare is their principal or only source of income. For those who work part-time, there is a risk that beneficiaries "become content with an intermediate position, combining some benefit and some earnings on a long term basis" (Ibid., p. 196). Unless such women are helped out of this poverty trap, the cycle of poverty is likely to be perpetuated into the next generation. Unemployment is still high in this group, with just 58% working, the lowest in the eurozone (Irish Times, 2019).

The OECD concluded that "there is a need for earlier intervention in Ireland of a more active nature towards OPFP (One Parent Family Payment) – clients with very young children, including childcare support, while for the existing long-term clientele comprehensive measures to upgrade skills are likely to be necessary" (OECD, 2003, p. 199). They further pointed out that "while the Irish tax/benefit system largely supports the work/care choice, this is countered by expensive childcare for those without access to other arrangements, to the extent that it may not be financially worthwhile for second earners to work" (Ibid., p. 200). This will act as a deterrent to further maternal employment, as informal modes of childcare become less and less available. Thus, women with young children, both lone parents and those in relationships, are vulnerable to social exclusion from the labour market because of the lack of affordable childcare.

This also has implications for businesses. According to Tom Clarke, president of Chambers of Commerce of Ireland (2003),

> A glaring anomaly currently exists in the economy. On the one hand, businesses, particularly SMEs, are coming under increased pressure to source suitable staff from a rapidly vanishing pool of available labour. Yet, on the other hand, women in particular are being blocked from entering the labour force due to the lack of accessible and affordable quality childcare.

While this quote was from some time ago, the analysis is still relevant since the accessibility and affordability of childcare are still important current issues, as will be further discussed later.

Another national body, the National Economic and Social Forum, added its voice to this national social debate in its report entitled *Early Childhood Care and Education* (NESF, 2005). It began by asking why there should be a need for another report on childcare, given that a sequence of major reports preceded it. Their answer was: "the very inadequate implementation of policy which has occurred and the very insufficient financial investment in the education and care of our younger citizens" (p. ix).

In spite of the concern expressed by numerous national and international bodies, the National Women's Strategy, issued by the Department of Justice, Equality and Law Reform (2007) two years after the publication of the NESF report, was rather vague about childcare. It stated that "the availability of quality and affordable childcare . . . has long been cited as a key element to support working mothers and those mothers who wish to undertake retraining to enable them to re-enter the labour market." It also listed as Objective 5-A: "To ensure that childcare services are optimal to meet the needs of parent and child alike." However, there was no mention of *provision* of childcare in the entire strategy.

Public attitudes to childcare over time

Public attitudes to childcare are also highly germane to this issue. These have been studied over time in attitudinal surveys.

Irish attitudes to social policies that would support working parents, such as attitudes to public provision of childcare, tax relief for childcare expenses and attitudes to flexible working, were very progressive, even four decades ago (Fine-Davis, 1983a, 1983b, 1988b) and continue to be so in more recent times (Fine-Davis et al., 2005; Fine-Davis, 2016).

A high level of support was expressed for a national programme of childcare facilities for preschool children in a 1981 nationwide survey of mothers' attitudes towards childcare and employment (Fine-Davis, 1983b). Over 90% of the sample favoured such a policy. A comparable level of support was expressed by married women in a 1986 survey (Fine-Davis, 1988b). Ninety per cent of employed married women said they would favour such a policy: 54% were strongly in favour and 44% said such a programme could apply to them. Support was also quite strong on the part of non-employed married women, with 88% favouring such a policy (42% strongly) and 48% seeing it as applicable to them. Married men were also quite supportive: 81% favoured such a policy (40% strongly) and 50% said it applied to them (Ibid.).

In the 1981 survey 88% of married women favoured tax concessions for childcare costs (Fine-Davis, 1983b) A similar degree of support was expressed in the 1986 study (Fine-Davis, 1988b). Again, there was also strong support from non-employed married women (81% favoured this policy) and from married men, of whom 83% supported the policy. The latter group were most likely to see this as applicable to them (57% did so).

These data, which are more than 30 years old, show how patient Irish people have been in waiting for public childcare facilities. The data also reveal a strong consensus among employed and non-employed married women as well as married men. There is no dissent between employed and non-employed married women on these issues, as is sometimes made out to be the case. This myth was often used as a rationale for not providing public services out of fear that this would offend non-employed married women or "women in the home." Such a fear is not reality based. Research not only shows that these groups share similar attitudes on these matters, but also shows that these are not two distinct groups. Women move in and out of the labour force depending on their circumstances.

A nationwide survey carried out in 2004/5, almost 25 years after the first study cited earlier, found that 92% of the sample agreed that "there should be a national programme of childcare facilities for pre-school age children." Of these, 54.6% strongly agreed. Strongest support was from those in the age group 35–49 (Fine-Davis et al., 2005). This high level of support (91%) was also seen in a more recent survey, carried out in 2010 on a nationwide sample of 1,404 Irish men and women in the childbearing age group. This study also showed 91% agreement with the statement "free preschool education should be available to all children in the same way that primary education is" and 91% agreement with a policy of tax concessions for childcare costs (Fine-Davis, 2016).

In comparing attitudes in the late 1970s with attitudes more recently, it is also possible to compare public views on who should bear the responsibility for

Table 6.7 Perceived responsibility for financing of childcare centres: comparison of nationwide, representative samples, 1978 and 2004/5

	1978 (*N = 1,852*) %	*2004/5* (*N = 1,204*) %
The Government	28.6	23.0
Employers	2.1	1.5
Parents	13.2	4.7
Combination of Government and employers	7.4	18.7
Combination of Government and parents	11.3	11.8
Combination of employers and parents	5.6	4.3
Combination of Government, employers and parents	19.3	31.5
Not sure	7.4	4.3
Shouldn't be supported at all	5.1	0.2
Total	**100.0**	**100.0**

Sources: Fine-Davis (1983a) and Fine-Davis et al. (2005).

funding childcare over time. The same question was posed to a nationwide representative sample in 1978 (Fine-Davis, 1983a) and again in 2004 (Fine-Davis et al., 2005) concerning who should assume primary responsibility for financing childcare facilities: the Government, employers, parents or a combination of these. As can be seen in Table 6.7, perceptions changed only slightly in the 26 years since the initial data were collected.

In both 1978 and 2004/5 the largest proportion felt childcare centres should be financed by a combination of (1) Government and employers, (2) Government and parents, (3) employers and parents or (4) Government, employers and parents. Over one-third of the sample (43.6%) in 1978 favoured one of these combinations. By 2004/5, the support for a combination had increased to 66.3%. The strongest support in both years was for a combination of Government, employers and parents: 19.3% favoured this option in 1978 and 31.5% favoured it in 2004/5. The next highest level of support was for Government alone to support childcare facilities. This was supported by 28.6% in 1978 and 23% in 2004/5. It is notable that whereas in 1978 12.5% were either not sure who should fund childcare or felt that it should not be supported at all, this figure dropped to just 4.5% in 2004/5, indicating that in the intervening years people had clearer ideas about childcare policy and were more likely to see it as legitimate.

The same question was posed to a nationwide representative sample of 1,021 mothers with at least one child aged between 0–15 in 1981, and these responses are compared in Table 6.8 with all women in the 2004/5 study who had a child aged between 0–12. Over 40% of mothers with dependent children surveyed in 2004/5 felt that the Government, employers and parents together should finance childcare centres, while only 24.0% of those in 1981 recommended this option. A similar proportion of respondents (26%) in both studies felt that the Government alone should pay for childcare centres. The proportion

Table 6.8 Perceived responsibility for financing of childcare centres: comparison of sample of mothers with at least one child aged 0–15 (1978) and 0–12 (2004/5)

	1981 (N = 1,020)	*2004/5 (N = 136)*
The Government	26.4	26.5
Employers	1.6	0.0
Parents	9.7	2.2
Combination of Government and employers	8.7	13.2
Combination of Government and parents	19.7	12.5
Combination of employers and parents	7.5	2.9
Combination of Government, employers and parents	24.0	42.6
Not sure	2.0	0.0
Shouldn't be supported at all	0.5	0.0
Total	**100.0**	**100.0**

Sources: Fine-Davis (1983b) and Fine-Davis et al. (2005).

of respondents who felt that parents alone should pay for childcare centres dropped substantially between 1981 and 2004/5. While 9.7% of respondents in 1981 felt parents alone should pay for childcare centres, just 2.2% in 2004 felt this way.

The attitudes of mothers do not appear to differ a great deal from those of the whole population. Funding by a combination of the Government, employers and parents was the option most supported by all respondents in 2004 (31.5%) and the same option was given the most support by all mothers with children aged 0–12, although by a larger margin – 42.6%.

It is thus clear that there has been strong support among the public for Government to take a major lead in funding childcare centres, but there has also been the view that employers and parents should also contribute to funding. An analysis of all responses suggests that the public sees parents' role in contributing to funding as second to that of Government, with the employers' role coming third.

The current demographic situation with regard to working mothers

Employment rates of mothers

By 2009 72.6 % of married women in the childbearing age group were employed, compared with only 54% of married women overall (CSO, 2009) – see Table 6.1. The labour force participation rate for all women (married or single, etc.) was also 54% at this time and again the participation rate of those in the childbearing age group was much higher at 77.9% (Ibid.). Given the increasing patterns of cohabitation and single motherhood, it is apparent that many young mothers of various family statuses (married, single, cohabiting, etc.) fell into this category. Since the early 2000s it has been less usual to look at women's marital status in relation to their employment status, since mothers were no longer necessarily married. Thus, official statistics and other research in this area began to focus on employment status of women, mothers or even parents, rather than on married women. For example, Russell et al. (2009) in their examination of labour force participation of parents found that 60.2% of women with children under five years of age were employed, as were 65% of women with children in the age group 5–15 (Table 2.2a, p. 18).

Thus it is clear that employment among women with very young children is keeping pace with the employment rate of Irish women in general, which in recent years has been approximately 60%, very close to the European average (CSO, 2016b). In 2016 the rate for Irish women was 59.5% compared with the EU rate of 61.4%, while the rate for Irish men was 69.9% compared with the EU rate of 71.8%.

A very recent examination of the employment rates of Irish mothers of young children found that they continue to remain high and increased as the child got older. Russell et al. (2018), examining data from the "Growing Up in Ireland" study – the national longitudinal study of children – found that when the "Study Child" was nine months old, a surprisingly high 46% of mothers were in paid employment. These mothers were somewhat more likely to work full-time (30 hours or more per week) than part-time. When the Study Child was three years old, over half (54%) of their mothers were in employment, with the proportion working full-time increasing slightly. By the time the child was five, 60% of mothers were in employment. These figures are very similar to those of the 2016 Census which found that the employment rate for women whose youngest child was aged between four and five was 60%. In contrast, the overall employment rate for women with no children was significantly higher at 85.7% (CSO, 2016b).

Effects of third-level education and female labour force participation on fertility rates

Since 1991 there has been a dramatic increase in the proportion of people attending university. In 1991 just 14% of males and 13.2% of females were educated to third level, but between 1991 and 2016 the percentage gradually increased and by 2016, 43.2% of women and 40.7% of men were graduates of university. The Central Statistics Office points out that the 1991 Census was the last to indicate a higher proportion of third-level qualifications among men compared with women (CSO, 2016c).

Economists predicted that this would have a dynamic effect on the workforce of the future, when employers would have to make accommodations to retain these highly educated female graduates. As FitzGerald predicted in 2004 on the basis of current demographic trends showing a majority of women now going on to third-level education: "If employers want the 'best and the brightest' they will find that a majority of them are women. If they don't adjust to the changing expectations of these skilled employees they will fail in business terms" (2004, p. 8). The Social Partners acknowledged this in 2005, noting that

> labour force participation by women is likely to increase even more significantly in the future, particularly in the area of highly skilled employment, given the now very high female participation rates in third level education. This suggests that a major issue for employers in the future will be the retention of highly skilled women employees, many of whom will have childcare requirements.
>
> (IBEC/ICTU, 2005, p. 6)

This issue was still relevant in 2018 when FitzGerald pointed out that in a tightening labour market "the large number of women who are not in the labour force represents a huge reserve of possible employees. However, the high cost of childcare and inflexible working conditions has made labour force participation unattractive for many women" (2018, p. 1).

The high educational level of women in Ireland also impinges on the birth rate, as women are postponing getting married and postponing having children (e.g., Punch, 2007; Lunn et al., 2009; Fine-Davis, 2016) in order to pursue careers.

Former Taoiseach (Prime Minister) Garret FitzGerald addressed the importance of this issue in the *Irish Times* of 9 June 2007, pointing out that "this is a sub-optimal situation, and public policy should, I believe, be directed towards easing the tensions that women experience so often having to choose between work and child-bearing, for example, by facilitating childcare for working mothers – the inadequate provision of which is clearly one of the causes of late marriages and late childbirths" (FitzGerald, 2007).

In most European countries the trend has been for decreasing fertility as female labour force participation increases. Ireland has followed this pattern. In line with increasing female labour force participation, the crude birth rate fell from 21.8 in 1980 to 15.0 in 2001 and the total fertility rate also fell, from 3.3 children in 1980 to 1.98 children in 2001 (Eurostat, 2002). However, paradoxically, those countries with the highest female labour force participation also showed the highest fertility (Villa, 2002; Fagnani, 2000, 2002, 2007). For example, while the total fertility in Denmark is and has been among the highest in the EU (currently 1.76), the Danish female participation rate is also among the highest at 76.6%. This trend is apparent in other Scandinavian countries. France has an even higher total fertility rate (1.92) than Denmark, together with high labour force participation of women with young children. Villa (Ibid.) points out that "among other factors, the increasing burden on women, having to continue paid work with family responsibilities, has played a major role in lowering fertility" (p. 16). Yet "those countries which have been able to develop the supply of social services (all personal services, in particular childcare services) and to move towards a more equal sharing of family responsibilities (between men and

Table 6.9 Total fertility rate, 1960–2016, for selected high- and low-fertility EU countries

	1960	*1970*	*1980*	*1990*	*2000*	*2004*	*2016*
HIGH							
Ireland	3.76	3.93	3.25	2.11	1.90	1.99	1.81
France	2.73	2.47	1.95	1.78	1.88	1.90	1.92
Denmark	2.57	1.95	1.55	1.67	1.77	1.78	1.79
LOW							
Poland	2.98	2.20	2.28	2.04	1.34	1.23	1.39
Hungary	2.02	1.98	1.92	1.87	1.32	1.28	1.45
Italy	2.41	2.42	1.64	1.33	1.24	1.33	1.34
EU – 15	2.59	2.38	1.82	1.57	1.50	1.54	
EU – 25	2.59	2.34	1.88	1.64	1.48	1.49	
EU – 28	-	-	-	-	-	-	1.59

Sources: Eurostat (2006), *Population Statistics*, Luxembourg: Office for Official Publications of the European Communities, from Table D-4, p. 76; and Eurostat News Release 52/2018 (28 March 2018) Births and fertility in 2016 Women in EU have first child on average at 29; and World Bank.

women) have not only successfully expanded female employment, but they also managed to halt the declining trend in fertility" (Ibid., pp. 16–17).

While Ireland had the highest total fertility rate in Europe (1.99) in 2004, this still reflected a significant decrease of almost 50% over the last three decades, compared to the rate of 3.93 in 1970 (see Table 6.9). Given these trends, Ireland's birth rate is likely to continue to fall to be in line with European norms unless policies intervene to change this trend. Ireland's current level of 1.81 is already below replacement level (2.1), and if it reaches the current European average of 1.59, as would be expected, this will be even further below replacement levels. While fertility levels in France and Denmark have remained stable from 2000 to 2016, Irish rates have dipped from 1.99 in 2004 to 1.81 in 2016.

A low birth rate means that there will be fewer young people to enter the labour force and hence a smaller base of workers to support the increasing numbers of older people in the population. This phenomenon has affected many countries and is referred to as the "demographic time bomb." In 2006 there were four people of working age for every person over 65. Falling birth rates, rising life expectancy, and the retirement of the baby boom generation mean that, by 2050, this ratio will have dropped to two workers paying for one pensioner (European Commission, 2006).

Thus, childcare facilities not only impinge on working parents' ability to reconcile work and family life, but they also have significant implications for the nation's birth rate and hence future population. This is another important reason why childcare policy is important for the well-being of the country as a whole. As Ireland currently has one of the highest birth rates in Europe, it is in a position to benefit from the experience of other countries before the birth rate falls further, as it has in many Eastern European and Mediterranean countries, where total fertility rates are now 1.2 or 1.3 – a phenomenon referred to as "lowest low" fertility (Kohler et al., 2002). In this regard, it should be borne in mind that the Scandinavian countries and France, all of which have a strong record of provision of childcare facilities and other social supports to working parents, have managed to retain a high level of female labour force participation as well as to maintain a relatively high birth rate.

Government childcare strategy: 2000 to the present

The initial major Government initiative in the childcare area was the Equal Opportunities Child Care Programme. Funded by the Irish Government and the European Union, this programme made available €436.7m to increase the supply and quality of childcare throughout Ireland as part of the National Development Plan 2000–2006 (Department of Justice, Equality and Law Reform, 2003). The main objectives of the programme were "to improve the quality of childcare; to maintain and increase the number of childcare facilities and places and to introduce a co-ordinated approach to the delivery of childcare services" (Ibid.). The programme provided grant assistance for capital developments to private childcare providers, self-employed providers and community-based childcare facilities. It also provided for staffing support in disadvantaged areas. In addition the programme established 33 county and city childcare committees throughout the country "to develop and implement co-ordinated strategic plans for childcare provision within their local area" (Ibid.).

In this context, elements of the Social Partnership Agreement 2003–2005, *Sustaining Progress* (Department of the Taoiseach, 2003), stated that as part of the broader strategy for development of childcare provision, the current National Childcare Strategy "will be augmented to achieve the objective of making childcare affordable for working parents in low-paid employment by increasing the provision of good quality childcare" (p. 27). The partnership also agreed that a partnership sub-committee, with representatives of Government, ICTU and IBEC, be established under the Equal Opportunities Childcare Programme (EOCP), with a secretariat provided under the programme. This sub-committee would consider recommendations on how to improve the availability of quality childcare for working parents and how the supply of pre- and after-school care could be accelerated (Ibid., pp. 89–90). This partnership issued a report in 2005 (IBEC/ICTU Subcommittee, 2005).

According to the National Employment Action Plan Ireland, 2003–2005 (Department of Enterprise, Trade and Employment, 2003), there was still much that needed to be done, as illustrated by this statement:

> Government funding for affordable childcare has yet to yield any significant gains for women returning to the workforce and remains one of the biggest obstacles to attaining the EU targets of 57% of women in the labour force by

> 2005 and 60% by 2010. A flexible childcare system needs to be established that would facilitate parents working outside 9–5 [*sic*] working day and those participating in adult education or mainstreaming education and training. It should be provided in a range of formats not just crèche based, but also increased emphasis on provision at community level and within the workplace.

In spite of the arguments put forward in numerous commissioned reports for a coherent, high quality childcare programme, the main thrust of childcare strategy in Ireland has been to subsidise existing childcare services in the community and to only directly provide services to the disadvantaged. Child Benefit Allowance was also increased substantially in several budgets which, it was argued, gave parents choice in terms of childcare, as it applied to all income groups and to both employed and non-employed mothers. Russell et al. (2018) pointed out that "during the economic boom years, sustained demand for financial support towards the cost of childcare intensified and between 2000 and 2005, the Child Benefit payment increased by more than two and a half times" (CPA, 2005). However, it has been pointed out that Child Benefit is also a measure to reduce child poverty and hence it could be used for other life necessities rather than targeted at childcare costs.

By reducing taxes in the 1999 and 2000 budgets, and to a lesser extent in the 2001 budget, the Government increased the take-home pay of workers so that they would be better able to afford to pay for childcare. Individualisation in the tax system also increased the relative take-home pay of working parents.

In December 2005, the minister for finance introduced a Five-Year National Childcare Investment Programme, costing €575m to run from 2006–2010. This programme was to support the creation of an additional 50,000 childcare places. This was to be achieved through capital grant aid to private providers and to community groups, building upon the previous Equal Opportunities Childcare Programme. In addition there was to be training of 17,000 childcare workers who were due to be employed in the sector over the next five years (O'Brien, 2006). Additional initiatives included a €1,000 per annum childcare payment for each child under six, introduced in 2006. Thus, Russell et al. (2018) observed that

> Until 2010, the Irish Government had resisted direct investment in universal childcare, preferring instead a focus on targeted funding for disadvantaged families using childcare services in the community and voluntary sector . . . and market based policies of cash payments such as child benefit, which is paid to all parents, irrespective of childcare use (McGinnity et al., 2013; Hayes, 2006).
>
> (Russell et al., 2018, p. 4)

Introduction of the Free Pre-School Year in Early Childhood Care and Education (ECCE) in 2010

In 2010 a notable development in childcare policy in Ireland took place with the initiation of the free preschool year for three-year-olds in January of that year, called the Pre-School Year in Early Childhood Care and Education

(ECCE) (Department of Children and Youth Affairs, 2011). This programme provides three hours of care per day in a childcare centre of the parent's choice to children between three years three months and four years six months on 1 September each year. This initiative was the first time that the Government facilitated access to free childcare on a universal scale, other than its provision of primary school for four- and five-year-olds (the "infant classes"), which are not mandatory, as the school starting age is six. The new free preschool year is not specifically designed to promote labour force participation of women; rather it is focused on the educational development of children (Department of Children and Youth Affairs, 2011; Monks, 2015) and is seen as a bridge to the infant classes. Hence, it has extended the available Government supported programmes for the 3–5 year age group. There is an emphasis on quality of the experience for the child. This is through a national curriculum called "Aistear," which is child centred, emphasising learning through play (National Council for Curriculum and Assessment and Early Childhood Ireland, 2009). The take up has been very high with over 90% participation and 95% of the eligible age cohort expected to avail of the programme in 2015 (Department of Children and Youth Affairs, 2015). This reflected a considerable increase in participation of children in this age group, since in 2011 only 27% of three-year-olds were in centre-based care (Williams et al., 2013). While the Government provides a capitation fee to cover costs for three hours per day, it is possible for parents to top this up and pay for additional time. In this way full-time childcare is subsidised by the Government and part-time childcare for three-year-olds is fully covered. The Early Childhood Care and Education programme (ECCE) was extended in 2016 to provide for a second year of preschool for children aged three to five. Thus preschool children in the 3–5 year age group are now able to avail of free preschool for three hours per day or 15 hours per week. This programme is the most significant policy development in the State's provision of childcare. It is significant because it recognises the State's responsibility in providing childcare to this age cohort. This is important both in terms of supporting women to participate in the labour force and in terms of providing age-appropriate education for young children.

Current childcare provision in comparative perspective

Expenditure on preschool education

Prior to the introduction of the ECCE programme in 2010, international assessments of Ireland's performance in the childcare sphere were less than wholeheartedly positive. According to a major report by the OECD (2004), *Education at a Glance*, spending on education in Ireland had failed to keep pace with recent economic growth in Ireland.

The 2004 OECD Report showed that we had the greatest increase in GDP of 26 countries compared – however our change in total expenditure on education did not match this. In examining expenditure on pre-primary education (for children age three and older), Ireland's expenditure was negligible and the lowest of all of the EU countries which the OECD examined. For example, in Denmark expenditure on pre-primary education was 0.8% of GDP, in France it was 0.7%, in Germany and Belgium it was 0.6%, in Italy and the U.K. 0.5%. Even the accession countries spent more of their GDP on pre-primary education than we did in 2004: Hungary spent 0.7% of their GDP, the Czech and Slovak Republics each spent 0.5%. and Poland, 0.4%.

More recent data from the OECD (2019) show that OECD countries spend on average just over 0.7% of GDP on early childhood education and care, with large variations across countries. While public expenditure on early childhood education and care is now higher than 1.0% of GDP in France and the Nordic countries – with total spending reaching as high as 1.6% in Sweden and 1.8% in Iceland – it is less than 0.5% of GDP in the Czech Republic, Ireland, Japan, Portugal, Turkey and the United States. Ireland has the next to lowest expenditure after the United States, with Turkey having the lowest (Ibid.). This is in spite of the introduction of the two free years of part-time preschool (ECCE) for the 3–5 year age group.

Cost

While there have been many positive developments in the area of childcare in Ireland since the OECD report (2004) cited earlier, many deficiencies still remain, especially when Ireland is compared with other countries in Europe. A notable deficiency is the high cost of childcare. It has recently been reported that while "Ireland has one of the largest proportions of under-fives in Europe . . . it is among the costliest nations when it comes to childcare" (Kelleher, 2019). This is the conclusion of the Eurydice Report which compares childcare provision in all 28 EU countries (European Commission/EACEA/Eurydice, 2019). Ireland is one of the countries with the highest fees for under threes and the report notes that those countries with the highest fees are those which rely on market-driven mechanisms to supply early childhood education and care to children under three, although some subsidies for the most disadvantaged may be available. It is noteworthy that in several countries, including several of the Scandinavian countries, costs for childcare are capped at a proportion of family income. For example, in Denmark, parents' fees must not make up more than 25% of a setting's estimated gross operating costs. In Hungary, fees and meals cannot exceed 25% of net family income per person in centre-based settings and 50% in home-based ones. In Finland, fees cannot exceed €289. In Norway, fees for a place in kindergarten are limited to 6% of the household income (Ibid., p. 57).

Analysis of recent Government policy

Consistent quality

While the budget measures and other policies from 1999 onwards may have been helpful in the short term in terms of stimulating the provision of childcare places and helping to subsidise childcare costs, they did not move Ireland closer to having the kind of comprehensive, integrated national programme of childcare facilities evident in some other European countries. The funding allocated to provide capital grants and staffing grants went primarily to private sector childcare and to community-based groups. Moreover the type and quality of childcare varies by each centre and this raises the question of how consistent the quality of such a diversity of childcare provision can be.

This is of particular concern given the findings of inspections of childcare centres. In a report of health inspections of childcare centres throughout the country in 2006 numerous worrying things emerged, from the risk posed to children in a Co. Tipperary preschool from "an electric fence on either side of an outdoor play area," as well as "foul odours coming from a fridge." An inspection of a facility in Kilkenny found "three children sleeping in cars seats rather than cots, prompting concerns about hanging." In the freezer "raw meats were being stored beside ready to eat ice cream." Children were also observed "playing with uncovered electric sockets." Children in a Co. Donegal crèche were "being left in front of television without verbal communication from an adult." These examples were identified from more than 100 inspections released by the Health Services Executive in response to a request under the Freedom of Information Act (*Irish Times*, 28 November 2006). The identification of risks through the inspections of childcare centres continued and in the 2017 Annual Report of the Child and Family Agency (Tusla, 2018a), a Variety of Problems were Identified by the Early Years Inspector, including "deficits" "in supporting the health, welfare and development of the child," which included:

> The playroom was sparsely equipped; Toys available were stored in a locked press or on a shelving unit which was turned in against the wall and inaccessible to the pre-school children; There was no evidence of a specific routine or plan on the day of inspection; Transitions were chaotic; The activities observed on the day were all adult led rather than enabling the pre-school children to initiate or take the lead with a chosen activity.
>
> (p. 42)

A perusal of the Annual Report (Ibid.) paints a picture of an array of thousands childcare centres throughout the country with varying standards. When the inspectorate notes "non-compliance" with regulations, it follows these up and in most cases the centres rectify the problem. However, only 2,033 inspections were carried out in 2017 on 4,484 registered services. At this rate, with fewer than half of centres receiving an inspection in a given year, it will be a slow process for childcare providers to reach compliance with all regulations. Moreover, is this the best way to ensure quality childcare – with a prime focus on the extent of "compliance" or "noncompliance" with a set of regulations?

Smith (2019), commenting on the Annual Report of the Early Years Inspectorate (Tusla, 2018a), observed that "the privatised model of childcare adopted in the Irish context means that there exist ongoing tensions between the imperative to turn a profit and the needs and rights of children." Referring to a broadcast by the national broadcaster, RTE, on childcare in Ireland and "further revelations in the media," Smith (2019) said that these "should give us serious pause for thought about the policy choices which have resulted in the commodification of care in Ireland."

Qualifications of staff

The 2019 Eurydice Report, which presents key data on early education and care in Europe (European Commission/EACEA/Eurydice, 2019) notes that in May 2019, "European education ministers stressed the importance of increasing the level of professionalisation among the ECEC[2] workforce. This investment in the workforce is crucial since there is a positive correlation between better-trained staff and a better quality service. Furthermore, the availability of highly qualified staff leads to higher quality staff-child interactions and therefore better developmental outcomes for children" (p. 71). As of at least 2006 it was not necessary to have any formal qualifications to own, manage or work in childcare in Ireland. It was estimated in 2006 by the OECD that 30% of childcare staff in Ireland were without any qualifications (OECD, 2006, p. 355). This issue was one which was also addressed by the Social Partners at around the same time (IBEC/ICTU Subcommittee, 2005). Emphasis has been placed both by the OECD and the Irish Social Partners on the need for more training of childcare personnel and also of childminders.

There is a wide variety of standards concerning training levels of core staff working with a group of younger children (usually under age three). According to the EU Eurydice report (European Commission/EACEA/Eurydice, 2019), 13 European countries require as a minimum qualification a bachelor's degree (Bulgaria, Germany, Estonia, Greece, France, Croatia, Cyprus, Lithuania, Slovenia, Finland, Bosnia and Herzegovina, Montenegro and Norway). In two other countries (Portugal and Iceland) a master's degree is required. The proportion of countries requiring core practitioners to have a bachelor's degree or higher level of qualification in ECEC (or in education) is much higher for those working with older children. In 29 of these countries, a bachelor's degree is required. In four others, a master's degree is the minimum requirement (France, Italy, Portugal and Iceland). In eight countries (Czechia, Ireland, Latvia, Malta, Austria, Romania, Slovakia and the United Kingdom – Scotland) – a group which includes Ireland – the minimum qualification level required to work as a core practitioner in any centre-based ECEC provision, for either age group, is below bachelor's level (Ibid., p. 73).

Staff-child ratios

The Eurydice report (Ibid.) also focuses attention on staff-child ratios:

> Child/staff ratios and group sizes appropriate to children's ages are generally seen as essential if children's care and education is to be delivered effectively.

> However, they are also key factors in successfully managing and retaining staff and, consequently, crucial to the process quality in ECEC. Workload, in terms of the number of children per staff member, is particularly important. Moreover, low ratios and small group sizes help to ensure that every child gets enough one-to-one attention, which is important for children's social and emotional development, their physical well-being, and their overall learning. Individual interactions with adults help children feel safe and reduce the feeling of being overwhelmed – both for children and adults. However, employing more staff, and especially highly qualified staff, implies higher costs. Therefore, the regulations regarding ratios and group sizes are a compromise between these competing priorities.
>
> (p. 87)

The actual staff-child ratios in Irish preschool childcare centres are higher than what is recommended by best international standards. The recent rules issued by the Department of Children and Youth Affairs, which oversees the ECCE programme of early childhood care and education, say that staff-child ratios should be one staff member per 11 children aged 2.5 to six. This is less than optimal for this age group and in apparent conflict with the guidelines of the Child and Family Agency in Ireland (Tusla, 2018b) for optimal staff-child ratios. The latter are in line with international best practice, but they are not adhered to in the case of the ECCE Programme, the programme which 90% of three- to five-year-old Irish children attend. These guidelines, depending on the child's age are as follows:

- (0–1 years) 1 staff member to 3 children
- (1–2 years) 1 staff member to 5 children
- (2–3 years) 1 staff member to 6 children
- (3–6 years) 1 staff member to 8 children

However the Tusla *Quality and Regulatory Framework: Full Day Care Service and Part-Time Day Care Service* specifies that

> The adult:child ratios are 1:11 for any child availing of the Early Childhood Care and Education (ECCE) scheme and attending a Sessional Pre-School Service (up to 3.5 hours). A child attending on a full day care basis avails of an ECCE scheme once a day only. The adult:child ratio of 1:8 or 1:6 is effective after 3.5 hours (when the ECCE Sessional Pre-School Service has finished) and the child is staying on in the Full Day Care Service for the rest of the day.
>
> (Tusla, 2018b, p. 10)

Thus, the ECCE programme, the major programme of childcare which 90% of Irish preschoolers now attend, does not operate optimal staff-child ratios for this group during the three hours per day that are provided free of charge. The staff-child ratio is 1:11, rather than 1:8 or 1:6.

In addition to the more recent ECCE programme, Ireland has also had for many years the "junior and senior infant classes" in the national schools (primary schools), which cater for children aged four and five. These are optional, as the school starting age is six. It has been noted that the class sizes and adult-child ratios in the infant classes also "compare very unfavourably with the optimum group sizes identified by research for early years settings" (Hayes and O'Flaherty, 1997, p. 37). The average adult-child ratios in these classes are even worse than those in the ECCE preschools at 1:25 or 1:26, whereas the optimum is 1:8 with class sizes of 15. This concern was reiterated by the General Secretary of the Irish National Teachers Organisation (INTO), John Carr, in 2003. Pointing out that the average class size is 29 children to one teacher, he said: "The fact that there are more than 20 children in an infants' class is scandalous. . . . Every class must be smaller, with the priority given to infant classes" (Holmquist, 2003, p. 4). As noted earlier, concerns about the class sizes and staff-child ratios have also been raised by the OECD (2006). Moreover, the curriculum is not play based and is more like "school" than preschool. The teachers are primary teachers with little or no training in preschool education (OECD, 2006).

A review of the international literature which examined optimal staff-child ratios concluded that

> evidence shows quite clearly that across the range of early years services, good things go together. In provision with high staff:child ratios, staff are more likely to be well qualified, have access to training, be better paid, and be less likely to leave their jobs. In high quality settings, staff spend more time planning how to deliver the curriculum, keep more effective records on the children in their care, and communicate more effectively with parents.
>
> (Munton et al., 2002, p. 105)

Conclusions

In most other European countries, children aged three to five (the "preschool" group) are usually catered for in preschool centres, écoles maternelles, etc. They are at an ideal age to respond favourably to an educational programme which is imbedded in play and are also ready for interaction with groups of similar-aged children.

The provision of "two free preschool years" recently introduced in Ireland provides for 15 hours a week of free childcare for three-to-five-year-olds. This is an advancement on the previous situation, though difficulties still remain. As is the case of the "infant classes," the ECCE programme is only available for part of the day and this dictates that alternative childcare must be found – and paid for – for children of mothers who wish to work more than part-time. One could argue that such policies reflect ambivalence to maternal employment, which is inconsistent with expressed Government aspirations in terms of gender equality.

The childcare needs of parents with children aged 0–2 are also not adequately being met. As the OECD (2006) points out, "services for children under 3 have often been seen as an adjunct to labour market policies, with infants and toddlers assigned to services with weak developmental agendas. . . . A challenge exists in many countries to focus more on the child, and to show greater understanding of the specific developmental tasks and learning strategies of young children" (p. 16). As Russell et al. (2018) point out: "Although the introduction of the ECCE scheme represented a significant policy shift in Ireland, care for children under the age of three continued to be seen as the sole responsibility of parents and remained costly" (p. 6). However, it should be noted that in most European countries the demand for ECCE (or ECEC) is not met for children under age three (Eurydice Report, European Commission, 2019, p. 43). A comparison of European countries in terms of the age at which a place in ECCE is guaranteed shows that children are guaranteed a place in most EU countries, although the age varies. For example, a child is guaranteed a place at the age of six months in Denmark, at nine months in Finland, age one in Sweden, Norway and Germany and at the age of three years in Spain, France, Hungary and the United Kingdom (England, Scotland and Wales). In just six countries a place in ECCE is not guaranteed. Ireland is one of these six; the others are Italy, Malta, Northern Ireland (U.K.), Slovakia and Romania (European Commission/EACEA/Eurydice, 2019, Figure B1, p. 44). However, the Eurydice report acknowledges that

> however, in Ireland, Italy and Iceland, the childcare gap[3] is *de facto* shorter as publicly subsidised ECEC is universally available without a legal entitlement *de jure*. In Ireland, while there is no legal entitlement to ECEC, there is universal provision available to parents and children from the age of 2 years and 8 months, reducing the childcare gap *de facto* to 2.7 years.
>
> (Ibid., p. 53)

Apart from the need to design and organise childcare in a way that is optimal for children, there is also a need to do so in a way that is optimal for parents. A model childcare facility would, for example, synchronise with parents' working hours and provide after-school care where necessary. IBEC (2004) in a policy document on education advocated "the more effective use of the national school network for the provision of pre-school, after-school and Montessori services" (Ibid.); it did not advocate further development of private sector childcare.

In this context, there are many examples of innovative approaches to childcare in other EU countries with a view to possible replication. These include good models of integrated or "wraparound" services linking community-based early educational services (or childcare) to preschool services and back into afterschool services – such as the Surestart initiatives in the U.K. The Dutch have been notably successful in designing model facilities which help parents to combine work and family life by providing one-stop centres where not just childcare but other services are available, such as after-school care (Mol, 2002). The Netherlands is also one of the few countries where part-time employment is common for men as well as women. There is much to learn from their experience in facilitating work-life balance of working parents here.

Both IBEC (2004) and ICTU (2006) – the Social Partners – have supported the notion of national infrastructural changes and investment in childcare. As Begg has pointed out, care has to be approached in a "strategic and holistic fashion with the creation of a national 'infrastructure of care' now an urgent priority." In policy terms, "care must assume the status of a 'public good' similar to that enjoyed by education" (ICTU, 2006). Were there a national programme of public childcare facilities, consistent high quality could be guaranteed. Given the benefits of quality early childhood education, the lack of a centralised high quality programme is a serious social policy deficit with implications for children and their development, for working parents in meeting their childcare needs and for society in preventing later social problems.

Notes

1 In a 1975 study in Dublin, 51.3% agreed that "if equal job opportunities are opened to women, this will just take away jobs from men who need them more" and 65% agreed that "when there is high unemployment, married women should be discouraged from working." In a nationwide survey in 1978 70.6% agreed with the latter statement.
2 ECEC refers to early childhood education and care; the term ECCE refers to early childhood care and education. The former is more often used in Europe and the latter in Ireland.
3 The "childcare gap" referred to earlier is the difference between the maximum length of adequately compensated postnatal childcare leave and the earliest start of a universal place guarantee in ECEC (legal entitlement or compulsory ECEC) (European Commission/EACEA/Eurydice, 2019, p. 53).

References

Bailyn, L. (1964). Notes on the role of choice in the psychology of women. *Daedalus*, 93, 700–710.

Begg, D. (2004). *Time to Get Serious About the Lisbon Strategy*. Address by David Begg, General Secretary of Congress to Ambassadors of EU and Accession Countries. www.ictu.ie/html/news/briefcase/s190204.htm.

Bradley, S. (2011). *Inside the Black Box an Exploration of the Impact of Action and Activity in the Inner Spheres of Policy Making on Early Childhood Education and Care Policy*. Doctoral thesis, Dublin Institute of Technology.

Callan, T. and Farrell, B. (1991). *Women's Participation in the Irish Labour Market*. Dublin: National Economic and Social Council.

Chambers of Commerce of Ireland (2003). *Labour Force Shortages Exacerbated by Childcare Crisis*. Press Release. www.chambersireland.ie/index.asp?docID=398.

Chubb, B. (1992). *The Government and Politics of Ireland*. London: Longman.

Collins, G. and Wickham, J. (2001). *What Childcare Crisis? Irish Mothers Entering the Labour Force*. Dublin: Employment Research Centre, Trinity College Dublin.

Commission on the Family (1998). *Strengthening Families for Life: Final Report of the Commission on the Family to the Minister for Social, Community and Family Affairs*. Dublin: Stationery Office.

Commission on the Status of Women (1972). *Report to Minister for Finance*. Dublin: The Stationery Office.

Coughlan, A. (2000). *Family-Friendly/Work-Life Balance Policies*. Dublin: Irish Business and Employer's Confederation.

CPA (2005). *Ending Child Poverty: Combat Poverty Agency Policy Statement*. Dublin: Combat Poverty Agency.

CSO (various). *Labour Force Surveys*. Dublin: Central Statistics Office.

CSO (1999–2009). *Quarterly National Household Surveys*. Dublin: Central Statistics Office.

CSO (2003). *Quarterly National Household Survey – Childcare Fourth Quarter 2002*. Dublin: Central Statistics Office.

CSO (2006). *Quarterly National Household Survey Childcare Quarter 1, 2005*. Dublin: Central Statistics Office.

CSO (2009). *Quarterly National Household Survey, Quarter 2, 2009*. Dublin: Central Statistics Office.

CSO (2016a). *Quarterly National Household Survey Childcare Module, Quarter 3, 2016*. Dublin: Central Statistics Office.

CSO (2016b). *Women and Men in Ireland 2016*. Dublin: Central Statistics Office. www.cso.ie/en/releasesandpublications/ep/p-wamii/womenandmeninireland2016/employment/.

CSO (2016c). *Census of Population – Profile 10 Education, Skills and the Irish Language 2016*. https://www.cso.ie/en/releasesandpublications/ep/p-cp10esil/p10esil/.

Department of Children and Youth Affairs (2011). *ECCE Programme Guide to the Programme and the Administrative Procedures – For Service Providers and Parents*. www.dcya.gov.ie/docs/ECCE_Programme_Guide_to_the_Programme_and_the_Administrative/1550.htm.

Department of Children and Youth Affairs (2015). *Public Consultation Document: Future Investment in Early Years and School-Age (After-School and Out-of-School) Care and Education Services – Primer*. Dublin: Department of Children and Youth Affairs.

Department of Education and Science (1999). *Ready to Learn – White Paper on Early Childhood Education*. Dublin: Stationery Office.

Department of Enterprise, Trade and Employment (2003). *National Employment Action Plan Ireland, 2003–2005*. Dublin: Stationery Office.

Department of Finance (2003). www.finance.gov.ie.

Department of Finance (2004). www.finance.gov.ie.

Department of Justice, Equality and Law Reform (2003). *McDowell Announces Further Grants for the Development and Support of the Childcare Sector*. Press Release, 23 May.

Department of Justice, Equality and Law Reform (2007). *National Women's Strategy 2007–2016*. Dublin: The Stationery Office.

Department of the Taoiseach (2003). *Sustaining Progress – Social Partnership Agreement 2003–2005*. Dublin: Stationery Office.

Downes, J. (2006). Creche inspections find numerous breaches. *Irish Times*, 28 November.

Employment Equality Agency (1996). *Introducing Family Friendly Initiatives in the Workplace*. Dublin: Employment Equality Agency.

European Commission. (2006). *The Demographic Future of Europe – From Challenge to Opportunity*. Brussels: Commission of the European Communities.

European Commission/EACEA/Eurydice (2019). *Key Data on Early Childhood Education and Care in Europe – 2019 Edition*. Eurydice Report. Luxembourg: Publications Office of the European Union.

Eurostat (2002). *Labour Force Survey*. Luxembourg: Eurostat.

Eurostat (2006). *Population Statistics*. Luxembourg: Office for Official Publications of the European Communities.

Eurostat (2018). *Births and Fertility in 2016: Women in EU Have First Child on Average at 29*. News Release 52/2018, 28 March.

Expert Working Group on Childcare (1999). *National Childcare Strategy – Report of the Partnership 2000 Expert Working Group on Childcare*. Dublin: The Stationery Office.

Fagnani, J. (2000). *Un travail et des enfants. Petits arbitrages et grands dilemmes*. Paris: Bayard Ed.

Fagnani, J. (2002). Why do French women have more children than German women? Family policies and attitudes towards childcare outside the home. *Community, Work and Family*, 5 (1), 103–119.

Fagnani, J. (2007). Family policies in France and Germany: Sisters or distant cousins? *Community, Work and Family*, 10 (1), 39–56, February.

Fahey, T. and Fitzgerald, J. (1997). *Medium Term Report*. Dublin: Economic and Social Research Institute.

Fanning, B. (2003). The construction of Irish social policy (1953–2003). *Administration*, 51 (1–2), 3–18.

Fine-Davis, M. (1979). Social-psychological predictors of employment status of married women in Ireland. *Journal of Marriage and the Family*, 47 (1), 145–158.

Fine-Davis, M. (1983a). *Women and Work in Ireland: A Social Psychological Perspective*. Dublin: Council for the Status of Women.

Fine-Davis, M. (1983b). Mothers' attitudes toward childcare and employment: A nationwide survey. In: Working Party on Childcare Facilities for Working Parents, *Report to the Minister for Labour*. Dublin: Stationery Office, pp. 73–168.

Fine-Davis, M. (1988a). Changing gender role attitudes in Ireland: 1975–1986. Vol. I: Attitudes Toward the Role and Status of Women, 1975–1986. In: *First Report of the Second Joint Committee on Women's Rights* (Pl. 5609). Dublin: The Stationery Office, May.

Fine-Davis, M. (1988b). Changing gender role attitudes in Ireland: 1975–1986. Vol. II: Issues Related to Equal Employment Opportunity. In: *Second Report of the Second Joint Committee on Women's Rights* (Pl. 5673). Dublin: The Stationery Office, June.

Fine-Davis, M. (1989). *The Economic and Social Benefits of Childcare in the Workplace*. Dublin: Irish Congress of Trade Unions.

Fine-Davis, M. (2004). The childcare policy debate in Ireland. *Administration*, 52 (2), 36–56.

Fine-Davis, M. (2007). *Childcare in Ireland Today*. Briefing Paper to the Irish Congress of Trade Unions. www.ictu.ie/download/pdf/briefing_paper_on_childcare_final_draft_14_june_2007_mfd.pdf.

Fine-Davis, M. (2015). *Childcare Policy in Ireland: Recent Developments and Comparisons with New Maltese Policy*. Peer Country Comments Paper – Ireland Mutual Learning Programme DG Employment, Social Affairs, Skills and Labour Mobility. Peer Review on 'Making Work Pay for Mothers', St Julian's (Malta), 18–19 May.

Fine-Davis, M. (2016). *Changing Gender Roles and Attitudes to Family Formation in Ireland.* Manchester: Manchester University Press.

Fine-Davis, M., Fagnani, J., Giovannini, D., Højgaard, L. and Clarke, H. (2004). *Fathers and Mothers: Dilemmas of the Work-Life Balance – A Comparative Study in Four European Countries.* Dordrecht, Boston and London: Kluwer Academic Publishers.

Fine-Davis, M., McCarthy, M., Edge, G. and O'Dwyer, C. (2005). *Work-Life Balance and Social Inclusion in Ireland: Results of a Nationwide Survey.* Dublin: National Flexi-Work Partnership (Centre for Gender and Women's Studies, Trinity College Dublin; IBEC; ICTU; FÁS, Age Action Ireland and Aware).

FitzGerald, G. (2007). Childcare issue reflects large social changes. *Irish Times*, 9 June, p. 16.

FitzGerald, J. (2004). *Ireland: An Ageing Multicultural Economy.* ESRI Working Paper, No. 157. Dublin: The Economic and Social Research Institute.

FitzGerald, J. (2018). Women hold the answer to tightening the job squeeze. *The Irish Times* (Business this Week), 31 August, p. 1.

Goodbody Economic Consultants (1998). *The Economics of Childcare in Ireland.* Dublin: Goodbody Economic Consultants.

Government of Ireland (1994). *First Progress Report of the Monitoring Committee on the Implementation of the Recommendations of the Second Commission on the Status of Women* (Pn. 0798). Dublin: The Stationery Office, May.

Government of Ireland (1996). *Second Progress Report of the Monitoring Committee on the Implementation of the Recommendations of the Second Commission on the Status of Women* (Pn. 2489). Dublin: The Stationery Office, March.

Government of Ireland (1999). *Third Progress Report on the Implementation of the Recommendations of the Second Commission on the Status of Women* (Pn. 6821). Dublin: The Stationery Office, March.

Hayes, N. (2002). *Children's Rights – Whose Right? A Review of Child Policy Development in Ireland.* Studies in Public Policy: 9. Dublin: The Policy Institute at Trinity College Dublin.

Hayes, N. (2006). *A Decade of Reflection – Childhood Care and Education in Ireland: 1996–2006.* Dublin: Centre for Social and Educational Research.

Hayes, N. and O'Flaherty, J. (1997). *A Window on Early Education in Ireland: The First National Report of the IEA Preprimary Project.* Dublin: Dublin Institute of Technology.

Holmquist, K. (2003). 'Vision-led' leader sees teaching as an art: Countdown to teachers' conferences. *Irish Times*, 21 April, p. 4.

Horgan, D. (2001). Childcare in Ireland: Themes and issues. *Irish Journal of Applied Social Studies*, 2 (3), 104–117. doi:10.21427/D72H9D. https://arrow.dit.ie/ijass/vol2/iss3/8.

Hynes, B. O. (2012). *Designed to Benefit Whom? An Evaluation of Irish Early Childhood Education and Care Policy Using Policy Design Theory.* PhD dissertation, Dublin Institute of Technology, Dublin.

IBEC (1998). *Helping the Childcare Industry to Grow Up.* Dublin: Irish Business and Employer's Confederation.

IBEC (2004). *Education for Life – The Challenge of the Third Millennium.* Education Policy Document. Dublin: IBEC.

IBEC/ICTU Subcommittee (2005). *Quality Childcare from a Social Partnership Perspective.* Report by an IBEC/ICTU Sub-Committee Prepared in the Context of Sustaining Progress.

ICTU (2002a). *Identifying Members' Childcare Needs*. Congress Report on Survey of Childcare Practices. Dublin: ICTU.

ICTU (2002b). *Congress Calls for Action on Childcare*. News Release, 17 April. Dublin: ICTU.

ICTU (2006). *Market Has Failed to Deliver on Care – New Infrastructure of Care an Urgent Priority*. News Release, 1 June. Dublin: ICTU.

Irish Times (2019). The Irish Times view on poverty rates: Lone parents' struggles. *The Irish Times*, 6 March.

Kelleher, L. (2019). Childcare costs here among the most expensive in Europe. *Irish Independent*, 8 July, p. 12.

Kiely, G. (1999). Introduction: From colonial paternalism to national partnership: An overview of Irish social policy. In: G. Kiely, A. O'Donnell, P. Kennedy and S. Quin (Eds.), *Irish Social Policy in Context*. Dublin: University College Dublin Press, pp. 1–11.

Kohler, H. P., Billari, F. C. and Ortega, J. A. (2002). The emergence of lowest-low fertility in Europe during the 1990s. *Population and Development Review*, 28 (4), 641–680, December.

Langford, S. (1999). *The Childcare Challenge*. Proceedings of the SIPTU National Women's Forum – 1999 – The Legal, Social and Economic Position of Women on the Verge of a new Century and Millennium, Equality Unit, SIPTU, Dublin, pp. 66–73.

Lunn, P., Fahey, T. and Hannan, C. (2009). *Family Figures: Family Dynamics and Family Types in Ireland, 1986–2006*. Dublin: The Economic and Social Research Institute and the Family Support Agency.

Mahon, E. and Bailey, J. (2015). The incomplete revolution: Development of childcare policies in Ireland. In: D. Kutsar and M. Kuronen (Eds.), *Local Welfare Policy Making in European Cities*. Social Indicators Research Series 59. Dordrecht: Springer.

McGinnity, F., Murray, A. and McNally, S. (2013). *Mothers' Return to Work and Childcare Choices for Infants in Ireland*. Dublin: The Stationery Office.

Mol, D. (2002). Innovations in the Netherlands. In: M. Fine-Davis, H. Clarke and M. Berry (Eds.), *Fathers and Mothers: Dilemmas of the Work-Life Balance – Conference Proceedings*. Dublin: Centre for Gender and Women's Studies, Trinity College.

Monks, T. (2015). Personal communication with Mr. Tony Monks. Department of Children and Youth Affairs, Dublin, 1 May.

Munton, T., Mooney, A., Moss, P., Petrie, P., Clark, A. and Woolner, J. (2002). Part A: Review of International Research on the Relationship Between Ratios, Staff Qualifications and Training, Group Size and the Quality of Provision in Early Years and Childcare Settings. In: *Research on Ratios, Group Size and Staff Qualifications and Training in Early Years and Childcare Setting*. Thomas Coram Research Unit Institute of Education, University of London.

National Council for Curriculum and Assessment (NCCA) (2009). *Aistear: The Early Childhood Curriculum Framework*. Dublin: NCCA.

National Economic and Social Forum (NESF) (2005). *Early Childhood Care and Education*. Report 31. Dublin: National Economic and Social Forum.

National Women's Council of Ireland (2001). *Creating Opportunities . . . Making Choices. Women and Work*. Report from the NWCI Millennium Project. Dublin: National Women's Council of Ireland.

National Women's Council of Ireland (2005). *An Accessible Childcare Model*. Dublin: National Women's Council of Ireland.

O'Brien, C. (2006). New standards for childcare workers planned. *Irish Times*, 9 May, p. 7.

OECD (2003). *Babies and Bosses – Reconciling Work and Family Life*. Vol. 2: Austria, Ireland and Japan. Paris: Organisation for Economic Cooperation and Development.

OECD (2004). *Education at a Glance*. Paris: Organisation for Economic Cooperation and Development.

OECD (2006). *Starting Strong II: Early Childhood Education and Care*. Paris: Organisation for Economic Cooperation and Development.

OECD (2019). *Family Database*. OECD – Social Policy Division – Directorate of Employment, Labour and Social Affairs. www.oecd.org/els/family/database.htm. Last updated 2 April 2019.

Punch, A. (2007). *Marriage, Fertility and the Family in Ireland – A Statistical Perspective*. Presidential address from Central Statistics Office to the Statistical and Social Inquiry Society of Ireland, Dublin, 31 May.

Report on the National Forum for Early Childhood Education (1998). Dublin: The Stationery Office.

Russell, H., Grotti, R., McGinnity, F. and Ivan Privalko, I. (2019). *Caring and Unpaid Work in Ireland*. Dublin: Irish Human Rights and Equality Commission and the Economic and Social Research Institute.

Russell, H., McGinnity, F., Callan, T. and Keane, C. (2009). *A Woman's Place: Female Participation in the Irish Labour Market*. Dublin: The Equality Authority and the Economic and Social Research Institute.

Russell, H., McGinnity, F., Fahey, E. and Kenny, O. (2018). *Maternal Employment and the Cost of Childcare in Ireland*. Dublin: Economic and Social Research Institute.

Second Commission on the Status of Women (1993). *Report to Government*. Dublin: The Stationery Office.

Smith, K. (2019). The commodification of childcare. Letter to the Editor, *The Irish Times*, 27 July, p. 13.

Tusla (2018a). *Tusla Annual Report 2017 of Tusla Child and Family Agency's Early Years Inspectorate*. Dublin: Tusla.

Tusla (2018b). *Quality and Regulatory Framework: Full Day Care Service and Part-Time Day Care Service*. Dublin: Early Years Inspectorate, Tusla.

Villa, P. (2002). *Family and Work Can Be Made Compatible? The European Experience*. National and European Meeting: Which "Kind" of Reconcilation? Family, Labour and Gender: Balances and imbalances, Turin, 28–29 August.

Williams, J., Murray, A., McCrory, C. and McNally, S. (2013). *Growing Up in Ireland – National Longitudinal Study of Children. Development from Birth to Three Years-Infant Cohort*. Dublin: Economic and Social Research Institute, Trinity College and the Department of Children and Youth Affairs.

Working Group on Childcare Facilities for Working Parents (1994). *Report to the Minister for Equality and Law Reform*. Dublin: Stationery Office.

Working Party on Child Care Facilities for Working Parents (1983). *Report to the Minister for Labour*. Dublin: Stationery Office.

Yeates, P. (2001). Childcare costs have more than doubled since 1998. *The Irish Times*, 6 August, p. 7.

Chapter 7

Work-life balance and well-being

Background

Work-life balance is a subject which has been increasingly recognised, internationally and in Ireland, as an important social policy issue (e.g., Humphreys et al., 2000; Drew, 2003; Fagnani, 2005; Russell et al., 2007; Scott and Plagnol, 2012; Eurofound, 2017, 2018). Esping-Andersen argues that "it is in large part the changing role of women that explains the new household structure, our altered demographic behaviour, the growth of the service economy and, as a consequence, the new dilemmas that the advanced societies face." Most European countries, he claims, "have failed to adapt adequately to the novel challenges and the result is an increasingly serious disequilibrium" (Esping-Andersen, 2004, p. v). As a result, the issue of how to combine employment and family responsibilities is a concern for most of the populace at some stage in their lives.

Russell et al. (2007) have pointed out that the rapid economic growth which took place in Ireland was accompanied by a strong surge in the number of women in employment. This, in turn, led to a significant increase in the proportion of dual-earner families. These changes brought the issue of reconciliation between work and family life to the fore. The authors noted that these changes took place "in a policy climate where state support for caring is low, and Government policy is predicated on there being one female carer in the home to care" (p. 3). Russell et al. (2009) argued that the increase in work-life conflict had more to do with this increase in the spread of the dual-earner household than to long working hours. In this context they note that "there has been a transformation of the division of paid labour within households." Whereas in 1994, the single-breadwinner model was the most common form for couples, by 2000 this model applied to just 36%. More recent analysis of 2005 data from the EU SILC study indicated that this proportion fell further in the period 2000–2005 – to just 31% of couples, while the proportion of dual-earner couples remained the same at approximately 50% (Ibid., pp. 62–63). These findings make it clear that combining work and family life, including caring responsibilities, is a trend which has been increasing, yet "there is also evidence that the gender distribution of unpaid work and caring has not adapted to this rapid change in the paid work sphere" (Ibid.; McGinnity and Russell, 2008).

As Del Boca and Locatelli (2006) concluded, after carrying out an analysis of numerous studies on the effects of social policies on women's fertility and employment in Europe, "social policies have a very relevant role in reducing the incompatibility between employment and child rearing" (p. 24). While childcare policies are crucial to reconciling work and family life, so too are other work-life balance policies, such as flexible working.

For Irish parents the interaction between the workplace and other aspects of life is becoming increasingly complex as working parents endeavour to balance responsibilities. This is further aggravated by the fact that there has been no statutory child-care policy in Ireland until very recently (see Chapter 6) with public provision for the 0–3 age group extremely limited. Working arrangements are still not sufficiently flexible to enable parents and carers to fulfil their roles as workers and as carers. Rigid nine-to-five working hours, which are very common, lead to a myriad of problems, including scheduling problems and a lack of synchronicity in dropping off and picking up children from crèches, childminders and schools.

While certain flexible working policies have appeared, Drew et al. (2003) found that the take up of available work-life balance policies in Ireland tended to be "highly gendered," and employees often find that barriers exist to taking up flexible working arrangements. The fact that certain work-life balance policies or arrangements were taken almost exclusively by women helps confirm and solidify the belief that work-life balance is only for mothers of young children and not applicable to all. On the other hand, workers from countries that offer public provision of childcare (e.g., Denmark and France) report that it is significantly easier to combine their jobs with their family lives and have a much higher level of gender equality in the workplace (Fine-Davis et al., 2004).

Work-life balance has been a concern of the European Community for some time. The Commission initially tried to have a maternity directive which would require all member states to provide a certain amount of maternity leave. However, this policy did not get full support of all the countries and hence the proposal had to be withdrawn (European Commission, 2015), as was the case some years earlier when the EU was considering a childcare directive (Cohen and Korintus, 2017). Instead they decided to focus on work-life balance, which included many different measures including flexible working, parental leave, etc. (Eurofound, 2017, 2018). In June 2019 the European Council adopted a new directive on work-life balance for parents and carers "which aims to increase the participation of women in the labour market and the take-up of family-related leave and flexible working arrangements" (European Council/Council of the European Union, 2019).

In this chapter attitudinal data concerning people's attitudes to flexible working and work-life balance will be presented from a nationwide Irish survey (Fine-Davis, McCarthy, Edge and O'Dwyer, 2005a), as well as a cross-national comparative study of the work-life balance of working parents in four European countries – Ireland, France, Italy and Denmark (Fine-Davis, Fagnani, Giovannini, Højgaard & Clarke, 2004). In addition, more current Irish attitudes to work-life balance issues will be included from a more recent study (Fine-Davis, 2016). The relationship between work-life balance policies and employee well-being cross-culturally will be a particular focus. These findings continue the emphasis on well-being which was initially addressed in Chapter 4.

The Work-Life Balance Project

In 2002–2005, the Centre for Gender and Women's Studies, Trinity College Dublin, carried out a major four-year project – the Work-Life Balance Project – under the auspices of the European Union to examine the relationship between flexible working and work-life balance in the Irish population (Fine-Davis et al., 2005a). This project was funded by the European Social Fund through the EQUAL Community Initiative, administered by the Irish Department of Enterprise, Trade and Employment. The aim of the project was both to examine and promote flexible working as a mechanism to facilitate work-life balance and social inclusion. The project focused on three main target groups: working parents and carers, older people and people with mental health problems, for whom flexible working could potentially be essential in facilitating social inclusion in the workforce as well as work-life balance. This work was carried out in collaboration with several other Irish organisations:

- Irish Business and Employer's Confederation (IBEC)
- Irish Congress of Trade Unions (ICTU)
- FÁS, the National Training Authority
- Age Action Ireland, a national advocacy agency for older people
- Aware, a national voluntary agency supporting people with depression

In the course of this project, several different activities were undertaken. These included a series of pilot projects in companies where various forms of flexible working were piloted and evaluated through research. Through a Working Party of Employers, including 17 companies in the public, private and NGO/community sectors, pilot projects were designed for the various target groups. The results of this research, which were both qualitative and quantitative in nature, were published in a report entitled: *The Effects of Flexible Working on Work-life Balance and Social Inclusion: An evaluation of a series of pilot projects* (Fine-Davis, McCarthy, O'Dwyer, Edge, and O'Sullivan, 2005c). The evaluation of these pilot projects demonstrated the value of flexible working patterns in achieving work-life balance for the target groups.

A second pilot project carried out by the Work-Life Balance Project was in the area of childcare. Given the importance of childcare to facilitating the reconciliation of work and family life it was a natural area for the project to address. The way we addressed it was to focus on men in childcare. It is well known that most childcare workers, and indeed most primary teachers, are female. For this reason, most children do not have regular access to male role models except for their father. It is well established that male role models can play a very important part in the development of gender-role attitudes and behaviour in children. It is these gender-role attitudes which lead to adult attitudes and behaviour which are the very things helping to create the work-life balance problems which we have today, including the lack of equal division of labour in the household and the attitudes concerning appropriate gender-role behaviour in the workplace, including attitudes to flexible working.

The Work-Life Balance Project ran a pilot project to recruit more men into childcare, in collaboration with FÁS (the National Training Authority) and a number of childcare providers in both the public and private sectors. This pilot aimed to promote non-stereotyped role models in the childcare sector in order to foster the development of egalitarian gender-role attitudes and behaviour in children. It was hoped that seeing men in caring roles at such an early stage would help to instil fundamental ideas of equality in children, including the notion that men can be carers. This is a critical piece in the overall strategy to overcome traditional gender roles and the persisting dual burden which women carry. It is only through the development of values of equality at an early age that male and female children will grow up with such values of sharing and equality in the workplace and the home. The results of this work are presented in *Men in Childcare: Promoting Gender Equality in Children – Evaluation of a Pilot Project* (Fine-Davis, O'Dwyer, McCarthy, Edge, O'Sullivan and Wynne 2005d).

A third strand of the overall Work-Life Balance Project involved a study of people with mental health problems in relation to their issues surrounding employment. A separate survey was carried out on this subject population to explore their particular experiences and needs in relation to social inclusion in the workplace and work-life balance. This research conducted mainly with people with depressive illnesses shows how important employment opportunities are for this group – therapeutically, economically and psychologically. Previous studies have shown that the highest rates of unemployment are among people with mental health difficulties. This study highlights the critical role of flexible working arrangements in helping this group remain in employment. The results of this study were published in a report entitled *Mental Health and Employment: Promoting Social Inclusion in the Workforce* (Fine-Davis, McCarthy, Edge, and O'Dwyer, 2005b).

Nationwide survey of attitudes to flexible working arrangements

All of these pieces of work, described above, both action-oriented and research-oriented, both qualitative and quantitative, fed into the development of a nationwide attitudinal survey. In order to more fully understand the needs of people in relation to work-life balance and social inclusion in the labour force, it was necessary to carry out a broad spectrum survey of attitudes and experiences of the population as a whole. Because the focus of this book is primarily on women, and particularly working mothers, we shall restrict ourselves to presenting some of the key findings of the study which relate to this group, while also including data relevant to working parents generally.

The sample of the survey was a nationwide representative sample of 1,212 adults over the age of 18. Of the total sample, 679 were employed. Full details of the sampling are contained in Chapter 2, Method.

Apart from childcare and leave policies, such as maternity leave, paternity leave and parental leave, etc., the main policy which can help workers to achieve work-life balance is flexible working. In the following section we present findings from a nationwide survey of Irish adults in relation to their attitudes towards flexible working for men and women, as well as related work-life balance issues.

Before presenting the results of the attitudinal research, it may be of interest to see what the prevalence of flexible working was for the employed people in our nationwide sample.

Availability and take-up of flexible working

Just over a third (36.5%) of all respondents stated that they had "a fair amount" or "a great deal" of flexibility in their jobs. However, 27.1% had none at all, and a further 16.7% only had very little. Respondents working in private companies were more likely to state that they had "a fair amount" or "a great deal" of individual flexibility in their job (42.0%), while only 20.0% of respondents working in the community/NGO sector stated the same. Those working in the public sector fell somewhere in between, with 24.5% saying that they had either a fair amount or a great deal of flexibility. Those who managed staff were more likely to indicate that they had more flexibility than those who did not manage staff.

Respondents were asked to indicate whether a variety of forms of flexible working were available to them in their workplaces and whether or not they themselves availed of each one. The results showed that flexible working hours, including flexi-time and personalised hours, appeared to be the most popular form of flexible working among all employed respondents.

Part-time working, half-time or less, was only available to approximately a quarter of all employed respondents and was taken up by 31% of these. However, it was much more likely to be available to women than to men (41.9% vs. 17.9%) and more women than men were likely to take it up (41.6% of women vs. 15.7% of men) (Table 7.1). Part-time work (half-time or more) was also only available to about one quarter of the sample – though again it was more likely to be available to women (36% vs. 14.2% of men). However, roughly equal proportions of men and women availed of it (approximately one quarter of whom it was available to) (Table 7.2).

Job-sharing was available to just one-fifth of employees (32.2% of women and 15.5% of men). It was less popular than part-time working, being taken up by only 14.7% of people who were offered it. However, many more women

Table 7.1 Availability and take-up of part-time working (half-time or less), among employed respondents, by gender

Availability	*Male (n = 390) %*	*Female (n = 270) %*	*Total (N = 660) %*
Yes	17.9	41.9	27.7
No	80.5	54.8	70.0
Don't know	1.5	3.3	2.3
Total	**100.0**	**100.0**	**100.0**
Respondent availing	*Male (n = 70) %*	*Female (n = 113) %*	*Total (N = 183) %*
Yes	15.7	41.6	31.7
No	84.3	58.4	68.3
Total	**100.0**	**100.0**	**100.0**

Source: Fine-Davis et al. (2005a), Table 3.33, p. 63.

Table 7.2 Availability and take-up of part-time working (more than half-time), among employed respondents, by gender

Availability	*Male (n = 387) %*	*Female (n = 267) %*	*Total (N = 651) %*
Yes	14.2	36.0	23.1
No	84.2	61.0	74.8
Don't know	1.6	3.0	2.1
Total	**100.0**	**100.0**	**100.0**
Respondent availing	*Male (n = 56) %*	*Female (n = 96) %*	*Total (N = 152) %*
Yes	23.2	24.0	23.7
No	76.8	76.0	76.3
Total	**100.0**	**100.0**	**100.0**

Source: Fine-Davis et al. (2005a), Table 3.3, p. 63.

job-shared than men (22.4% of those to whom it was available vs. only 3.4% of men) (Table 7.3).

Flexi-time was available to just a quarter of all employed respondents, but was taken up by 62.4% of those who had the opportunity to avail of it (56.6% of women and 67.9% of men) (Table 7.4). Similarly, personalised hours were available to just 18.5% of employed respondents, but taken up by 67% (60% of women

Table 7.3 Availability and take-up of job-sharing among employed respondents, by gender

Availability	*Male (n = 389) %*	*Female (n = 264) %*	*Total (N = 653) %*
Yes	15.2	32.2	22.1
No	82.3	63.6	74.7
Don't know	2.6	4.2	3.2
Total	**100.0**	**100.0**	**100.0**
Respondent availing	*Male (n = 58) %*	*Female (n = 85) %*	*Total (N = 143) %*
Yes	3.4	22.4	14.7
No	96.6	77.6	85.3
Total	**100.0**	**100.0**	**100.0**

Source: Fine-Davis et al. (2005a), Table 3.35, p. 63.

Table 7.4 Availability and take-up of flexi-time among employed respondents, by gender

Availability	*Male (n = 390) %*	*Female (n = 271) %*	*Total (n = 661) %*
Yes	20.5	28.8	23.9
No	78.7	69.0	74.7
Don't know	0.8	2.2	1.4
Total	**100.0**	**100.0**	**100.0**
Respondent availing	*Male (n = 81) %*	*Female (n = 76) %*	*Total (n = 157) %*
Yes	67.9	56.6	62.4
No	32.1	43.4	37.6
Total	**100.0**	**100.0**	**100.0**

Source: Fine-Davis et al. (2005a), Table 3.37, p. 64.

and 73% of men). Other forms of flexible hours were also popular – taken up by 60% of those who had the opportunity to avail of them.

Tele-working/working from home was not widely available to respondents, being offered to just 8.3% of respondents, although the level of take-up was high – about 60% (75% of men to whom it was available and 48.3% of women) (Table 7.5). Term-time (in which employees have the summer off to spend with children who are home from school, with income for 10 months spread over 12)

Table 7.5 Availability and take-up of working from home (e-working, tele-working) among employed respondents, by gender

Availability	*Male (n = 389) %*	*Female (n = 273) %*	*Total (N = 662) %*
Yes	6.2	11.4	8.3
No	93.6	87.2	90.9
Don't know	0.3	1.5	0.8
Total	**100.0**	**100.0**	**100.0**
Respondent availing	*Male (n = 24) %*	*Female (n = 29) %*	*Total (N = 53) %*
Yes	75.0	48.3	60.4
No	25.0	51.7	39.6
Total	**100.0**	**100.0**	**100.0**

Source: Fine-Davis et al. (2005a), Table 3.41, p. 65.

was also available to very few (5.5%), but for those to whom it was available, a relatively high proportion availed of it: 25.9% of women and 44.4% of men.

These figures suggest that when various modes of flexible working are made available to employees, they are in many cases likely to avail of them. The figures also reflect the variety of modes of flexible working which can meet needs of different employees. It is interesting that our study reinforces the results of Drew et al. (2003) to the extent that women are more likely to avail of part-time working, whereas men are more likely to favour modes of flexible working which are not as intrusive in the normal full-time routine and presumably do not significantly affect their income or promotion prospects as directly, such as flexible hours and tele-working. While term time was not widely available, it is interesting to note the high take-up by men, suggesting that this may be a mode which suits men and enables them to combine work with family life.

Factor analysis: exploration of the dimensionality of attitudes to flexible working

In the survey all respondents were asked their attitudes about various aspects of flexible working. The survey included 26 attitudinal items reflecting various views on flexible working. These were presented on seven-point Likert scales, ranging from "strongly disagree" to "strongly agree." The responses to these statements were factor analysed to identify underlying dimensions in the items. This analysis showed that there were seven statistically and psychologically interpretable dimensions or factors which emerged from the analysis, each of which reflects a cluster of attitudes relating to flexible working. These are shown in Table 7.6 and described below.

Table 7.6 Factor analysis of attitudes to working arrangements (N = 1,212)

Item No.		*Varimax rotated loading*
Factor I: Support for family-friendly workplaces		
5.	There should be a certain amount of paid leave in the case of a child's illness, so that parents do not need to use their own sick leave/leave time.	.77
9.	Working hours should be more flexible so that men and women can better meet family needs.	.58
12.	Employers should make a special effort to accommodate the needs mothers of young children face in balancing their work and family life.	.69
20.	Employers should make a special effort to accommodate the needs fathers of young children face in balancing their work and family life.	.72
22.	Fathers should have a right to take paternity leave on the birth or adoption of a new baby.	.63
% Variance: 18.3%	Cumulative % variance: 18.3%	Cronbach's alpha .78
Factor II: Belief that flexible working is compatible with fatherhood, management and company success		
2.	Employers benefit too if workers are enabled to balance work and family life through flexible working.	.47
10.	Men who work flexible hours can be just as serious about their career as anyone else.	.55
11.	People who have flexible working should be entitled to the same opportunities for promotion as those working more regular hours.	.66
18.	More men need to take on flexible working in order to spend more time caring for their families.	.48
21.	Women who work flexible hours can be just as serious about their careers as anyone else.	.59
26.	Part-time working/job-sharing should be available to managers as well as to non-managers.	.60
% Variance: 10.6%	Cumulative % variance: 28.9%	Cronbach's alpha: .70
Factor III: Belief that flexibility hampers career success		
15.	Women who work part-time or job-share are usually less serious about their careers.	.63
16.	You put your career on hold when you work part-time/job-share.	.73

Item No.		Varimax rotated loading
17.	To get ahead, employees have to work over and above normal hours.	.63
24.	The reality is that if men worked part-time or job-shared, they would be seen as less serious about their careers.	.46
25.	To be viewed favourably by management, employees have to put their job ahead of family or personal life.	.56
% Variance: 5.8%	Cumulative % variance: 34.6%	Cronbach's alpha: .65
Factor IV: Belief that flexible working is more suited to women		
6.	Working flexible hours is a more suitable option for women than men.	.82
13.	Working part-time/job-sharing is a more suitable option for women than men.	.83
% Variance: 5.3%	Cumulative % variance: 39.9%	Cronbach's alpha: .68
Factor V: Belief that employees resent colleagues who take maternity leave / use flexible time		
7.	Many employees are resentful when women take maternity leave.	.77
14.	Other staff often resent a colleague taking flexible time.	.68
% Variance: 4.3%	Cumulative % variance: 44.2%	Cronbach's alpha: .49
Factor VI: Negative perceptions of flexible working		
1.	While certain forms of flexible working such as part-time or job-sharing are a good idea, the reality is that they are a luxury most people can't afford.	.73
3.	Other employees often have to pick up the slack when their colleagues work flexibly.	.52
8.	While employers might like to facilitate workers' needs for flexible working, the reality is that they have a business to run.	.57
% Variance: 4.3%	Cumulative % variance: 48.5%	Cronbach's alpha: .44

(Continued)

Table 7.6 (Continued)

Item No.		*Varimax rotated loading*
Factor VII:	**Positive attitudes to flexible working hours**	
19.	*Workplaces function best when everyone comes in at the same time and leaves at the same time.	–.59
23.	Rigid working hours (e.g., 9 to 5) are often unnecessary and can lead to considerable stress for some people.	.52
% Variance: 4.0%	Cumulative % variance: 52.6%	Cronbach's alpha: .39

*Reversed composite score
Source: Fine-Davis et al. (2005a), Table 3.59, pp. 79–80.

Factor I, *support for family-friendly workplaces*, contains five items and is a rather global dimension, as first factors in factor analyses often are. It expresses positive attitudes to a variety of family-friendly policies, including flexible working, maternity leave and paternity leave, etc. It includes such items as "working hours should be more flexible so that men and women can better meet family needs" and Employers should make a special effort to accommodate the needs mothers of young children face in balancing their work and family life. It also includes items expressing support for meeting the needs of fathers for work-life balance, e.g., Employers should make a special effort to accommodate the needs fathers of young children face in balancing their work and family life and "fathers should have a right to take paternity leave on the birth or adoption of a new baby." This global factor explains the greatest per cent variance of all of the seven factors (18.3%) and its Cronbach alpha is also high (.78), indicating a high degree of reliability. Cronbach alpha is a coefficient of reliability of the internal consistency of a set of items, indicating how closely related they are as a group. A high Cronbach alpha is often used along with other evidence, such as factor analysis, to see if the items are measuring an underlying construct.

Factor II, *belief that flexible working is compatible with fatherhood, management and company success*, juxtaposes several ideas and challenges some common myths. This six-item factor expresses the view that flexible working is compatible with fatherhood, being a manager and the success of the company. It includes such statements as "men who work flexible hours can be just as serious about their career as anyone else," "part-time working/job-sharing should be available to managers as well as to non-managers," and "employers benefit too if workers are enabled to balance work and family life through flexible working." It explains the next highest per cent variance (10.6%) of all the factors and also has a high Cronbach alpha (.70).

Factor III, *belief that flexibility hampers career success*, expresses the view that flexible working is a barrier to or negatively impacts on career success. It contains five items, including: "you put your career on hold when you work part-time/job-share" and "the reality is that if men worked part-time or job-shared, they would be seen as less serious about their careers," etc. It explains less variance than Factors I and II (5.8%), but its Cronbach alpha (.65) indicates that it is a reliable measure.

Factor IV expresses the view that flexible working is more suitable for women, e.g., "working flexible hours is a more suitable option for women than men" and "working part-time/job-sharing is a more suitable option for women than men." This factor also explains relatively less variance than the first two factors (5.3%), but its Cronbach alpha of .68 indicates it is a reliable measure.

Factor V expresses the view that people resent other colleagues who use maternity leave or flexible working.

Sometimes attitudes cluster in such a way that positive attitudes cluster together on one factor and negative attitudes cluster together on another factor, even on the same issue. Thus, whilst some of the other factors included positive attitudes to flexible working (e.g., Factor I and Factor VII), Factor VI, *negative perceptions of flexible working*, contains statements which solely express negative attitudes or reservations concerning flexible working, such as "while certain forms of flexible working such as part-time or job-sharing are a good idea, the reality is that they are a luxury most people can't afford," and "other employees often have to pick up the slack when their colleagues work flexibly."

Factor VII, *positive attitudes to flexible working hours*, measures attitudes to working times. Those who are high on the factor express support for flexible working hours and tend to agree with the statement that "rigid working hours (e.g., 9 to 5) are often unnecessary and can lead to considerable stress for some people," whereas those who are "low" on the factor tend to agree with the statement that "workplaces function best when everyone comes in at the same time and leaves at the same time."

The last three factors each explained just over 4% of the variance and their Cronbach alphas were in the range of .39–.49, indicating they are not as reliable measures as were the first four factors. Nevertheless they are interesting in elucidating and adding to our understanding of the different attitudinal components of flexible working. Overall the seven factors explained 52.6% of the variance, which is quite respectable in social attitude research.

Levels of support for flexible working in the sample

Analysis of the level of agreement or disagreement with the items described earlier revealed very strong support for flexible working patterns in the Irish population, as shown in Table 7.7. The vast majority (80–90%) supported the statements in Factor I, *support for family friendly workplaces*. A large majority (70–90%) also

Table 7.7 Attitudes to working arrangements: percentage responses to items grouped by factor (N = 1,212)

Item	DISAGREE Strong	Moderate	Slight	D. K., etc.	AGREE Slight	Moderate	Strong
Factor I: Support for family-friendly workplaces							
1. There should be a certain amount of paid leave in the case of a child's illness, so that parents do not need to use their own sick leave/leave time.	3.4	3.7	3.7		54	21	13
	10.8%			**1.3 %**	**88%**		
2. Working hours should be more flexible so that men and women can better meet family needs	4	3.6	2		44.2	27.2	18.5
	9.6%			**.7 %**	**89.9%**		
3. Employers should make a special effort to accommodate the needs mothers of young children face in balancing their work and family life	2.7	3.2	2.4		46.7	28.4	15.8
	8.3%			**.7 %**	**91%**		
4. Employers should make a special effort to accommodate the needs fathers of young children face in balancing their work and family life	4.2	5	6.2		25	29.2	30
	15.4%			**.6 %**	**84%**		
5. Fathers should have a right to take paternity leave on the birth or adoption of a new baby.	4	4.2	4.4		17	21.4	47.8
	12.6%			**1.2 %**	**86.2%**		
Factor II: Belief that flexible working is compatible with fatherhood, management and company success							
1. Employers benefit too if workers are enabled to balance work and family life through flexible working.	2	3.2	3.3		16.3	29.6	44.4
	8.5%			**1.3 %**	**90.2%**		

2. Men who work flexible hours can be just as serious about their career as anyone else.	DISAGREE			D. K., etc.	AGREE		
	Strong	Moderate	Slight		Slight	Moderate	Strong
	2	2.3	4.2		12.6	26	52
	8.5%			**1.1 %**	**90.4%**		
3. People who have flexible working should be entitled to the same opportunities for promotion as those working more regular hours.	DISAGREE			D. K., etc.	AGREE		
	Strong	Moderate	Slight		Slight	Moderate	Strong
	5	4	6.1		15.3	25.2	43.8
	15.1%			**.7%**	**84.2%**		
4. More men need to take on flexible working in order to spend more time caring for their families.	DISAGREE			D. K., etc.	AGREE		
	Strong	Moderate	Slight		Slight	Moderate	Strong
	6.3	7.8	14		25	25.4	19.3
	28.1%			**2%**	**69.7%**		
5. Women who work flexible hours can be just as serious about their careers as anyone else.	DISAGREE			D. K., etc.	AGREE		
	Strong	Moderate	Slight		Slight	Moderate	Strong
	1.1	3	4.4		15.6	26.6	49
	8.5%			**.4 %**	**91.2%**		
6. Part-time working/job-sharing should be available to managers as well as to non-managers.	DISAGREE			D. K., etc.	AGREE		
	Strong	Moderate	Slight		Slight	Moderate	Strong
	6	4.7	7.6		18.2	28.4	34
	18.3 %			**.7%**	**80.6%**		
Factor III: Belief that Flexibility hampers Career Success							
1. Women who work part-time or job-share are usually less serious about their careers.	DISAGREE			D. K., etc.	AGREE		
	Strong	Moderate	Slight		Slight	Moderate	Strong
	31.6	20.3	18.7		12.5	11	5
	70.6%			**1.1 %**	**28.3%**		
2. You put your career on hold when you work part-time/job-share.	DISAGREE			D. K., etc.	AGREE		
	Strong	Moderate	Slight		Slight	Moderate	Strong
	15.2	16	16		22.7	18.5	10
	47.2 %			**1.6%**	**51.2%**		

(Continued)

Table 7.7 (Continued)

3. To get ahead, employees have to work over and above normal hours.	DISAGREE			D. K., etc.	AGREE		
	Strong	Moderate	Slight		Slight	Moderate	Strong
	8.3	8	11		21.5	22.8	27.6
	27.3%			**.8 %**	**72%**		
4. The reality is that if men worked part-time or job-shared, they would be seen as less serious about their careers.	DISAGREE			D. K., etc.	AGREE		
	Strong	Moderate	Slight		Slight	Moderate	Strong
	11.2	13.3	14.3		23	19.4	17.8
	38.8 %			**1.2%**	**60%**		
5. To be viewed favourably by management, employees have to put their job ahead of family or personal life.	DISAGREE			D. K., etc.	AGREE		
	Strong	Moderate	Slight		Slight	Moderate	Strong
	10.4	9	11.8		22.3	20	25.4
	31.2%			**1.2%**	**67.6%**		
Factor IV: Belief that flexible working is more suited to women							
1. Working flexible hours is a more suitable option for women than men.	DISAGREE			D. K., etc.	AGREE		
	Strong	Moderate	Slight		Slight	Moderate	Strong
	9.5	10	8.3		17.6	22.6	30.8
	27.8 %			**1.3%**	**71%**		
2. Working part-time/job-sharing is a more suitable option for women than men.	DISAGREE			D. K., etc.	AGREE		
	Strong	Moderate	Slight		Slight	Moderate	Strong
	8	9	9.4		20.7	25	27.5
	26.4%			**.7 %**	**73%**		
Factor V: Belief that employees resent colleagues who take maternity leave / use flexible time							
1. Many employees are resentful when women take maternity leave.	DISAGREE			D. K., etc.	AGREE		
	Strong	Moderate	Slight		Slight	Moderate	Strong
	23	18	17		15.6	12	11.8
	58 %			**2.7%**	**39.3%**		

2. Other staff often resent a colleague taking flexible time.	DISAGREE			D. K., etc.	AGREE		
	Strong	Moderate	Slight		Slight	Moderate	Strong
	9	12.7	19.2		28.2	16.4	10.6
	40.9%			**4.1 %**	**55.2%**		
Factor VI: Negative perceptions of flexible working							
1. While certain forms of flexible working such as part-time or job-sharing are a good idea, the reality is that they are a luxury most people can't afford.	DISAGREE			D. K., etc.	AGREE		
	Strong	Moderate	Slight		Slight	Moderate	Strong
	7.2	9.6	8.4		19.2	29	25.2
	25.2%			**1.3 %**	**73.5%**		
2. Other employees often have to pick up the slack when their colleagues work flexibly.	DISAGREE			D. K., etc.	AGREE		
	Strong	Moderate	Slight		Slight	Moderate	Strong
	9.3	15	14.8		20.8	21.4	17.2
	39.1%			**1.6 %**	**59.3%**		
3. While employers might like to facilitate workers' needs for flexible working, the reality is that they have a business to run.	DISAGREE			D. K., etc.	AGREE		
	Strong	Moderate	Slight		Slight	Moderate	Strong
	2.8	4.4	8		23.4	29.3	30.8
	15.2%			**1.2%**	**83.6%**		
Factor VII: Positive attitudes to flexible working hours							
1. Workplaces function best when everyone comes in at the same time and leaves at the same time.	DISAGREE			D. K., etc.	AGREE		
	Strong	Moderate	Slight		Slight	Moderate	Strong
	18.7	21	15.7		13	12.2	18.7
	55.4%			**.8 %**	**43.8%**		
2. Rigid working hours (e.g., 9 to 5) are often unnecessary and can lead to considerable stress for some people.	DISAGREE			D. K., etc.	AGREE		
	Strong	Moderate	Slight		Slight	Moderate	Strong
	8.3	9	14.8		20.2	19.3	26.7
	32%			**1.7%**	**66.2%**		

Source: Fine-Davis et al., (2005a), Table 3.60, pp. 83–88.

endorsed the statements in Factor II, *belief that flexible working is compatible with fatherhood, management and company success*.

However, the attitudes expressed *vis à vis* the items in Factor III indicate that people think that flexible working can hamper career success. Just over half (51.2%) agreed with the statement "you put your career on hold when you work part-time/job-share." Respondents were also likely to think that "to get ahead, employees have to work over and above normal hours" (72% agreed). However, only a minority (28.3%) felt that women who worked part-time or job-shared were less serious about their career. In contrast though, a majority (60%) felt that "the reality is that if men worked part-time or job-shared, they would be seen as less serious about their careers." This illustrates that men are perceived to be at a disadvantage if they work part-time or job-share, while women are much less likely to be seen this way. These attitudes reflect the ambivalence which people have on this issue. On the one hand, they are supportive of flexible working patterns. Yet, on the other hand, when it comes to part-time working, this is seen as hampering career success for all, but mostly for men. Attitudes to part-time working are clearly related to gender; for women it not seen as a hindrance, for men it is. Data from a more recent study of Irish adults of childbearing age, carried out in 2010, found that the levels of agreement with these items were very similar (Fine-Davis, 2016). In this study, a higher proportion (79%) agreed that "to get ahead, employees have to work over and above normal hours." A higher proportion (57%) also agreed that "you put your career on hold when you work part-time/job-share." An identical proportion (60%) agreed that "if men work part-time or job-share, they are seen as less serious about their careers."

Furthermore, the attitudes in Factor VI, *negative perceptions of flexible working*, show that a majority have negative attitudes to flexible working for several other reasons. Firstly, while it is seen as a good idea, it is also seen as a "luxury that most people cannot afford" (73.5% agreed). A large majority (83.6%) also endorsed the statement that "while employers might like to facilitate workers' needs for flexible working, the reality is that they have a business to run." Finally, almost 60% felt that "other employees often have to pick up the slack when their colleagues work flexibly." So these are some of the countervailing attitudes which modify the overall positive attitudes to flexible working.

In spite of this, a majority (66.2%) felt that "rigid working hours (e.g., 9 to 5) are often unnecessary and can lead to considerable stress for some people" and a majority (55.4%) did not believe that "workplaces function best when everyone comes in at the same time and leaves at the same time," indicating support for a more flexible working environment in relation to the start and end of the working day.

Demographic determinants of attitudes to flexible working

While it is important to have an understanding of the attitudes of the sample as a whole, representing the attitudes of the whole country, it is also important to understand how different groups in the population feel about flexible working. In particular, it is of interest to see to what extent men and women differ on these issues. This is so because as of now it is women who are more likely to work part-time and to job-share in Ireland and the extension of such arrangements to men would make it more likely that work and domestic life could be shared more equally. In some countries, notably the Netherlands, part-time working is more common both for men and women, but in Ireland it is women who are significantly more likely to work part-time.

Thus we looked at whether or not there were differences in attitudes to flexible working on the basis of gender as well as on the basis of three other demographic characteristics of respondents, namely (1) employment status (employed vs. non-employed), (2) socio-economic status (low vs. high) and (3) age (18–34, 35–49 and 50+). Table 7.8 presents the results of a four-way analysis of variance which measured the main effects of these demographic variables on attitudes to flexible working. The dependent variables in the analysis were composite scores (summary scores) computed for each respondent summarising their attitudes on each of the factors. Thus, a respondent will have had five responses to items on Factor I and six responses to items on Factor II. Instead of dealing with these responses to individual items, we create a summary of their responses to all the items on a factor and use this as the input to the analysis of variance. Thus, we have just seven scores per respondent, representing their views on each factor, which represent the underlying dimensions among the items. These "composite scores" are more reliable and robust than individual items. The four demographic variables of gender, employment status, socio-economic status and age constituted the independent variables.

Table 7.8 presents these results. When we look at the first column, which presents the results for gender, it may be seen that there were significant differences on six of the seven factors. The strongest effect was on Factor II, showing that women were more likely than men to believe that flexible working is compatible with fatherhood, management and company success ($F = 51.85$; $p \leq .001$). The female mean score of 5.87 (out of a possible 7) indicates moderate agreement with the items on Factor III, (*belief that flexibility hampers career success*) while the male mean of 5.45, while also reasonably high, reflects attitudes between slight and moderate agreement. A significant gender difference was also revealed in relation to Factor VII, *positive attitudes to flexible working hours*. This showed that women were more strongly in favour of flexible working hours than men were ($F = 52.42$; $p \leq .001$). Women were also more strongly in favour of family-friendly workplaces (Factor I) ($F = 29.68$; $p \leq .001$), though men were also, just to a slightly lesser degree.

On the other hand, men were more likely to agree with the items on Factor VI, which measured *negative attitudes to flexible working*, such as "while certain forms of flexible working such as part-time or job-sharing are a good idea, the reality is that they are a luxury most people can't afford," "other employees often have to pick up the slack when their colleagues work flexibly," and "while employers

Table 7.8 Analysis of variance: main effects of four demographic variables on factors measuring attitudes to working arrangements (N = 1,212)

Factor	*Gender*		*Employment status*		*Socio-economic status*		*Age*		
	Male (n = 538)	*Female (n = 547)*	*Employed (n = 621)*	*Not employed (n = 464)*	*Low (n = 754)*	*High (n = 331)*	*18–34 (n = 299)*	*35–49 (n = 300)*	*50+ (n = 486)*
I. Support for family-friendly workplaces	**F = 29.68*****		**F = 13.25*****		**F = 15.67*****		**F = 26.53*****		
	5.63	5.99	5.9	5.7	5.88	5.66	6.02	6.1	5.5
II. Belief that flexible working is compatible with fatherhood, management and company success	**F = 51.85*****		**F = 19.81*****		F = 0.422 ns		**F = 15.16*****		
	5.45	5.87	5.75	5.53	5.63	5.73	5.71	5.96	5.44
III. Belief that flexibility hampers career success	**F = 14.09*****		**F = 8.35****		F = 0.02 ns		F = 0.09 ns		
	4.36	4.07	4.13	4.33	4.23	4.17	4.16	4.18	4.27
IV. Belief that flexible working is more suited to women	**F = 8.83****		**F = 31.41*****		**F = 7.77****		**F = 10.62*****		
	5.01	5.3	4.9	5.5	5.27	4.89	4.8	4.99	5.48
V. Belief that employees resent colleagues who take maternity leave / use flexible time	F = 3.01 ns		**F = 4.13***		F = 1.01 ns		F = 0.91 ns		
	3.82	3.99	3.81	4.03	3.95	3.81	3.77	3.9	3.99
VI. Negative perceptions of flexible working	**F = 9.09****		F = 0.162 ns		F = 1.66 ns		F = 2.5 ns		
	5.13	4.9	5.03	4.98	5.05	4.94	5.09	4.86	5.06
VII. Positive attitudes to flexible working hours	**F = 52.42*****		**F = 21.85*****		**F = 17.59*****		**F = 7.5****		
	4.13	4.83	4.64	4.26	4.31	4.86	4.43	4.63	4.08

Source: Fine-Davis et al. (2005a), Table 3.61, p. 89.

* ≤ .05
** ≤ .01
*** ≤ .001

might like to facilitate workers' needs for flexible working, the reality is that they have a business to run." It should, however, be said that agreement with these items was not as strong as it was on the more positive attitudes to flexible working. The mean scores for both men and women were about 5 on this factor indicating just slight agreement, but men were on average significantly more likely to hold these attitudes (male mean of 5.13 vs. female mean of 4.9) ($F = 9.09$; $p \leq .01$). Counter-intuitively, perhaps, women were more likely to think that flexible working was more suited to women than to men ($F = 8.83$; $p \leq .01$), as one might expect men to more strongly hold this view. This may relate to the fact that women are used to women working part-time and they may also be more conscious of childcare and domestic work, which women are more likely to carry out and have to balance with employment. The fact that men were *less* likely to think that flexible working was more suited to women may indicate an open mind on this subject and a readiness for greater flexibility in their own work.

The employed were more supportive of flexible working in all of its dimensions than were the non-employed, which may relate to their greater experience of it.

There were mixed results based on socio-economic status (SES). It did not have as strong an effect as gender and employment status. On the one hand there was somewhat more support for family friendly workplaces from people of lower socio-economic status ($F = 15.67$; $p \leq .001$), though this group was more likely to think that flexible working was more suitable for women ($F = 7.77$; $p \leq .01$). Those of higher socio-economic status were more in favour of flexible working hours ($F = 17.59$; $p \leq .001$).

Age was a significant determinant of four of the seven factors in the direction of younger people being more in favour of flexibility in the workplace. In some cases the middle age group (35–49) was the most supportive, for example in the case of Factor II (*belief that flexible working is compatible with fatherhood, management and company success*) ($F = 15.16$; $p \leq .001$). This makes sense since it is this age group which can best relate to all of these issues. The oldest age group (50+) was least likely to express support for family-friendly workplaces ($F = 26.53$; $p \leq .001$), least likely to hold positive attitudes to flexible working hours ($F = 7.5$; $p \leq .01$) and most likely to think that part-time working was more suited to women ($F = 10.62$; $p \leq .001$). This is explainable on the basis of less experience of flexible working on the part of older people and also a general tendency for older people to hold more traditional attitudes. The fact that the youngest age group (18–34) was highly supportive of family-friendly workplaces indicates that it is ready for a new kind of workplace which embodies policies which support both fathers and mothers.

Attitudes to flexible working: cross-cultural comparisons

Prior to carrying out the Irish survey of attitudes to work-life balance, we collaborated in a cross-cultural study to examine attitudes to work-life balance of parents of young children in four European countries – Ireland, France, Italy and Denmark (Fine-Davis, Fagnani, Giovannini, Højgaard and Clarke, 2004). The methodology of this study was described in Chapter 2, Method. All of the respondents in this study were employed, living with a spouse/partner and had at least one child under six years of age; hence work-life balance issues were likely to be quite salient for them. This study offered an opportunity to compare Irish attitudes with those of three of our European neighbours. There are some similarities in the items used in this somewhat earlier cross-cultural study (carried out in 2001) and in the subsequent Irish nationwide study carried out in 2004/5, since we replicated some of the most successful items from the earlier study.

Perceived attitudes towards men working part-time or job-sharing

One of the ways in which men and women can combine work and family is to work part-time or to job-share. This practice is widespread for women in many countries. Indeed, women make up the majority of part-time workers and they are also more likely to avail of job-sharing options than are men. It was one of the aims of the cross-cultural study to see if there were barriers to men availing of family-friendly options such as these. Hence, we asked the question: "To what extent do you agree that in your workplace. . .

> men who participate in available work-family programmes (e.g., job-sharing, part-time work) are viewed as less serious about their career than those who do not participate in these programmes."

This is quite close to the item we have already discussed in relation to the Irish nationwide study ("the reality is that if men worked part-time or job-shared, they would be seen as less serious about their careers").

We found that there was a significant difference between the four countries in response to this statement. French and Irish participants both agreed that men who participate in available work-family programmes (e.g., job-sharing or part-time work) are viewed as less serious about their career than those who do not, whereas both the Italians and the Danes disagreed. There was a significant interaction effect between country and socio-economic status (SES) indicating that in three of the countries – Ireland, France and Denmark – higher-SES respondents were more likely to agree with the statement, whereas in Italy there was no such effect of class. The social class difference was quite pronounced in France and Ireland, where higher-SES subjects had mean scores of 6 (out of 7) in France and 5.9 in Ireland, whereas lower-SES respondents had scores of 4.2 in France and 4.3 in Ireland. This trend was not evident in Denmark where higher-SES respondents had a mean of just 3.5 and lower-SES respondents a mean of 2.9. Thus the French and the Irish high-SES respondents tended to strongly agree with the statement, whereas the high-SES Danes tended to slightly disagree. Lower-SES Irish and

Table 7.9 Men in work-family programmes perceived as "less serious" about career: mean scores by country and SES (N = 400)

	France	*Italy*	*Denmark*	*Ireland*	*Total*
Low SES	4.2	2.1	2.9	4.3	**3.4**
High SES	6.0	2.1	3.5	5.9	**4.5**
Total	**5.1**	**2.1**	**3.2**	**5.1**	**3.9**

(1 = "strongly disagree"; 7 = "strongly agree")
Country: $F = 56.13$, $df = 3$, $p \leq 0.001$
SES: $F = 29.01$, $df = 1$, $p \leq 0.01$
Country x SES: $F = 4.35$, $df = 3$, $p \leq 0.005$

Source: Fine-Davis et al. (2004), Table 9.22, p. 155.

French were neutral and lower-SES Danes, like their higher-SES counterparts, tended to slightly disagree, reflecting the greater acceptability of male participation in flexible working in Denmark. The Italian data was very similar to that of the Danish and in fact more strongly in the direction of disagreement with the notion that men who engaged in part-time work or job-sharing were less serious about their career (see Table 7.9).

Perceived attitudes towards women working part-time or job-sharing

In general, the participants from all countries disagreed that women who participate in available work-family programmes (e.g., job-sharing, part-time work) are viewed as less serious about their career than those who do not, except for the Irish, who tended to agree slightly (see Table 7.10). Despite the overall disagreement with the statement, those in low-SES jobs were more likely to disagree than those in high-SES jobs. When looking more closely at the groups who agreed with the statement, it is evident that it was the French and Irish high-SES participants. The Irish mean of 5.8 out of a potential 7 indicates that the high-SES Irish respondents tended to moderately agree that women who participate in job-sharing or part-time work are viewed as less serious about their career. This is comparable to the mean score obtained among high-SES Irish respondents concerning men (see Table 7.9).

When we examine gender differences in attitudes across all the four countries, as shown in Table 7.11, it is apparent that males are significantly more likely to think men who take engage in part-time work or job-sharing are less serious about their careers than females who do so ($t = 5.74$; $p \leq .001$). While females in all countries are less likely overall to think anyone (male or female) is less serious about their career if they work part-time or job-share, they too think men who do so are less serious than females who do ($t = 4.29$; $p \leq .001$). These attitudes on the part of men, but also, to a lesser extent, on the part of women, are likely to

Table 7.10 Women in work-family programmes perceived as "less serious" about career: mean scores by SES and country (N = 400)

	France	*Italy*	*Denmark*	*Ireland*	*Total*
Low SES	3.2	2.0	2.1	3.7	**2.7**
High SES	4.6	2.0	2.9	5.8	**3.8**
Total	**3.9**	**2.0**	**2.5**	**4.7**	**3.3**

(1 = "strongly disagree"; 7 = "strongly agree")
Country: $F = 45.12$, $df = 3$, $p \leq 0.001$
SES: $F = 32.02$, $df = 1$, $p \leq 0.001$
Country x SES: $F = 5.66$, $df = 3$, $p \leq 0.001$

Source: Fine-Davis et al. (2004), Table 9.24, p. 156.

Table 7.11 Perceived attitudes towards men vs. women in work-family programmes: mean scores by country and sex (N = 400)

Sample	*Means*		*Statistics*		
	Men in work-family programmes	*Women in work-family programmes*	*t*	*df*	*Sig.*
France	5.2	3.9	6.09	92	$p \leq 0.001$
France – males	5.6	3.9	6.37	46	$p \leq 0.001$
France – females	4.7	3.8	2.63	45	$p \leq 0.01$
Italy	2.1	2.0	0.92	99	n.s.
Italy – males	2.0	1.8	1.57	49	n.s.
Italy – females	2.2	2.1	0.06	49	n.s.
Denmark	3.2	2.5	4.01	96	$p \leq 0.001$
Denmark – males	3.7	2.9	2.96	47	$p \leq 0.005$
Denmark – females	2.8	2.1	2.69	48	$p \leq 0.01$
Ireland	5.1	4.7	2.40	99	n.s.
Ireland – males	5.2	5.0	0.75	49	n.s.
Ireland – females	5.1	4.4	2.60	49	$p \leq 0.01$
All countries	3.9	3.3	7.08	389	$p \leq 0.001$
All countries – males	4.1	3.4	5.74	194	$p \leq 0.001$
All countries – females	3.7	3.1	4.29	194	$p \leq 0.001$

Source: Fine-Davis et al. (2004), Table 9.25, p. 158 (1 = "strongly disagree"; 7 = "strongly agree").

create a distinct barrier to men taking up this kind of employment, which could potentially facilitate greater work-life balance for them and their partners.

When looking at respondents' views more specifically by country and by gender we see that French and Danish participants, particularly the men, thought there was a difference in how men and women were perceived – men who participated in work-family programmes were more likely than women to be perceived as not taking their careers seriously. The Italians did not see a difference between how men and women were perceived in this regard and, interestingly, neither did Irish males. These attitudes, by country and separately for men and women within each country, are presented in Table 7.11.

The most striking impressions from the data in this section as well as related sections of the study were that the attitudes of the Italians and the Danes appeared to reflect the most accepting and relaxed workplace cultures, compared with the French and the Irish. In general the French tended to agree with the statements more than participants of the other countries – that there was resentment when people took advantage of work-family measures and they were expected to put work above family. The Irish also agreed to some extent that there were these pressures in their workplaces. Those in high-SES jobs as well as those in the private sector tended to perceive the most pressures of this type. Male participants perceived more pressure about men regarding work-family measures. On many of the statements most participants disagreed except for French participants in high-SES jobs, who were the group most likely to feel this sort of pressure. The group that appeared to feel the least pressure was female participants in low-SES jobs. On the other hand, they have fewer occupational opportunities and therefore may have lower expectations. While this study had a relatively small sample overall, the findings nevertheless provide interesting comparisons. They also support findings that we saw in the larger Irish study carried out just a few years later.

Ease vs. difficulty in combining work and family life: cross-cultural comparisons

In the four-country study of work-life balance (Fine-Davis et al., 2004), we examined how working parents with young children reconciled two major areas of their lives, namely work and childcare. Our major focus was on key dependent measures of well-being. These included a measure of ease vs. difficulty in combining work and family life as well as several classic measures which have been widely used in social indicators research, i.e., satisfaction with work, health, partner/spouse, family life and life in general. We also included two measures related to time which cross the boundary of family and work and have major implications for reconciliation, namely (1) the extent to which parents' working schedules create problems with their childcare arrangements and (2) parents' ideal working schedule.

We examined the predictors of successfully – or unsuccessfully – combining work and family life for the combined four-country sample and then for males and females separately.

We then examined country differences in well-being, as well as the correlates of the different measures of well-being, drawing upon the key sets of variables presented earlier, including time variables, attitudes in the workplace, extent of help received, etc. Policies in the workplace, such as potential and actual flexibility and overall "family friendliness" of the workplace were also examined in relation to the various measures of perceived well-being.

Ease vs. difficulty in reconciling work and family

Participants were asked how easy or difficult it was for them to combine their work with their family lives. They responded on a six-point scale, ranging from 1 = "very easy" to 6 = "very difficult."

As may be seen in Table 7.12, 56.8% of all parents said it was easy to combine work and family life, whereas 43.2% said it was difficult. However, these were nuanced into three levels each, such that 4% said it was "very easy," 15.9% said it was "easy" and 36.9% said it was "somewhat easy" (36.9%). On the other side of the continuum, 30.6% said it was "somewhat difficult", 8.3% said it was "difficult" and 4.3% said it was "very difficult."

Irish women and Italian women were more likely than other groups to say it was "difficult" or "very difficult," with 22% in these two countries saying this was the case, compared with Danish women, of whom just 4% gave these two extreme responses. These findings are not surprising given that both Italy and Ireland are relatively more traditional societies in comparison to France and Denmark and in fact an analysis of the actual number of hours of unpaid domestic work carried out by women in the 28 EU countries in 2016 found that Ireland and Italy were in the top nine countries whereas Denmark and France were in the lowest nine countries, with Irish women carrying out 38 hours per week and Danish women 22.5 hours per week (Russell et al., 2019). In spite of all of the unpaid work performed by Irish women, Irish men were also more likely to say combining work and family was difficult or very difficult (18%), whereas Italian men were much less likely to do, with just 4% giving these responses (Table 7.12). These issues are discussed more fully in Chapter 8.

Further analysis, using one-way analysis of variance, confirmed that there were significant differences between the four countries in terms of the ease or difficulty in combining work and family life. This was much easier in Denmark than in the other three countries and it was also more difficult for those in higher occupational status jobs, which may be related to the generally greater pressure which was found to exist for people in these jobs (see Table 7.13).

Predictors of ease vs. difficulty in combining work and family life: country comparisons

A large number of potential predictor variables were examined in a series of multiple regression analyses to try to identify which variables were most significant in predicting ease vs. difficulty in combining work and family life. When looking at the total sample, male and female, for all four countries, we found that many of the things one might have expected to be significant were not, like age, education and number of children. However, among the most important factors was found to be time. The length of one's partner's commuting time was particularly important ($p \leq .001$). The longer the commuting time, the less time

Table 7.12 Ease vs. difficulty in combining work and family life: percentage distributions by country and sex (N = 400)

	France %		*Italy* %		*Denmark* %		*Ireland* %		*All countries* %		
	M	*F*	*M*	*F*	*M*	*F*	*M*	*F*	*M*	*F*	*Total*
Very easy	0.0	2.1	2.0	2.0	12.0	2.0	6.0	6.0	5.0	3.1	4.0
Easy	6.0	6.4	6.0	6.0	24.0	32.0	26.0	22.0	15.5	16.3	15.9
Somewhat easy	48.0	48.9	58.0	20.0	32.0	44.0	24.0	20.0	40.5	33.2	36.9
Somewhat difficult	34.0	29.8	30.0	50.0	26.0	18.0	26.0	30.0	29.0	32.1	30.6
Difficult	10.0	6.4	2.0	16.0	6.0	2.0	12.0	12.0	7.5	9.2	8.3
Very difficult	2.0	6.4	2.0	6.0	0.0	2.0	6.0	10.0	2.5	6.1	4.3
Total	**100.0**	**100.0**	**100.0**	**100.0**	**100.0**	**100.0**	**100.0**	**100.0**	**100.0**	**100.0**	**100.0**

Source: Fine-Davis et al. (2004), Appendix Table A65, p. 283.

Table 7.13 Ease vs. difficulty in combining work and family life: mean scores by country and SES

	France	*Italy*	*Denmark*	*Ireland*	*Total*
Low SES	3.4	3.5	2.7	3.2	**3.2**
High SES	3.7	3.7	3.2	3.7	**3.5**
Total	**3.5**	**3.6**	**2.9**	**3.4**	**3.4**

(1 = "very easy"; 6 = "very difficult")
Country: $F = 7.54$, $df = 3$; $p \leq 0.001$
SES: $F = 10.25$, $df = 1$; $p \leq 0.001$

Source: Fine-Davis et al. (2004), Table 10.2, p. 181.

they would be around to help with the family. The importance of time was also expressed in the item "do the hours you work create problems in your child care arrangements?" The more this was true for people, the more difficulty they had in combining work and family life ($p \leq .001$). Not surprisingly, the more hours a person worked per week the more difficulty they also had in combining work and family (see Table 7.14a).

Another very significant predictor was the amount of help a person received with domestic responsibilities. The more help one got, the easier it was to combine work and family ($p \leq 0.001$). Attitudes in the workplace were also very important. Most important was a feeling that one's colleagues accepted one's childcare responsibilities. A feeling that one's manager accepted one's childcare responsibilities also helped a lot and was significantly related to ease in combining work and family. For example, if one felt that in a pinch one could bring one's child to work for a little while if childcare arrangements broke down, this helped a great deal. If working parents felt that this was accepted by colleagues in particular, but also by their managers, they were more likely to say that combining work and family was easier. Such behaviour was more likely to be considered acceptable in Denmark, as opposed to Ireland, France and Italy. As this question was tapping a relatively sensitive issue, it is interesting that it was a good predictor, as it clearly is tapping into the acceptance of childcare responsibilities in the workplace culture.

All countries: males only

Looking at the data for males only in the four countries, it was found again that if the hours one works create problems in one's childcare arrangements, the more likely one is to have difficulty combining work and family life. Not surprisingly, the longer the working week, the greater the difficulty. Also important was colleagues' acceptance of one's childcare responsibilities, as manifested in the item concerning acceptability of bringing a child to work say for an hour if one had difficulty in childcare arrangements (Table 7.15a).

Table 7.14a Predictors of ease vs. difficulty in combining work and family life: multiple regression for all countries, total sample males and females (N = 400)

	Predictor variables	*Beta*	*Sig.*
1.	Age	0.03	–
2.	Level of education	–0.01	–
3.	Partner's education	0.02	–
4.	Occupational status	0.14	–
5.	Partner's occupational status	0.06	–
6.	Own commuting time	0.10	–
7.	Partner's commuting time	0.16	***
8.	Length of work week	0.16	**
9.	Length of partner's work week	–0.05	–
10.	Number of children	–0.02	–
11.	HELPINDEX Index of help with domestic responsibilities	–0.25	***
12.	Acceptability of arriving late / leaving early		
12a.	among your colleagues	0.09	–
12b.	your managers	–0.10	–
13.	Acceptability of bringing child to work		–
13a.	among your colleagues	–0.31	***
13b.	your managers	0.20	–
14.	How well the following people take into account your responsibility for a child:		
14a.	your colleagues	–0.02	–
14b.	your immediate supervisor	–0.10	–
14c.	your employer	0.07	–
15.	Extent to which the hours you work create problems with childcare arrangements	0.29	***

R = 0.54, R^2 = 0.292, Adj R^2 = 0.252, Standard Error = 0.96

Source: Fine-Davis et al. (2004), Table 10.6, p. 186.

Table 7.14b ANOVA for total equation

	Sum of squares	df	*Mean square*	F	*Sig.*
Regression	928.99	19	6.79	7.41	***
Residual	313.45	342	0.91		
Total	**442.44**	**361**			

Source: Fine-Davis et al. (2004), Table 10.6a, p. 186. * $p \leq .05$ ** $p \leq .01$ *** $p \leq .001$

All countries: females only

What were the key predictors of successfully combining work and family for women? Again time was a crucial factor. One's own commuting time was significant, as was one's partner's. The shorter the commuting time, the easier it was to combine work and family. Women whose hours created problems with their

Table 7.15a Predictors of ease vs. difficulty in combining work and family life: multiple regression for all countries, males and females (males, N = 200 and females, N = 200)

		Males		Females	
	Predictor variables	*Beta*	*Sig.*	*Beta*	*Sig.*
1.	Age	0.00	–	0.06	–
2.	Level of education	–0.13	–	0.15	–
3.	Partner's education	0.01	–	–0.02	–
4.	Occupational status	0.11	–	0.08	–
5.	Partner's occupational status	0.22	*	0.00	–
6.	Own commuting time	0.03	–	0.15	*
7.	Partner's commuting time	0.17	*	0.18	**
8.	Length of work week	0.22	***	0.13	–
9.	Length of partner's work week	–0.06	–	–0.08	–
10.	Number of children	–0.00	–	–0.00	–
11.	HELPINDEX Index of help with domestic responsibilities	–0.05	–	–0.16	*
12.	Acceptability of arriving late / leaving early		–		–
12a.	among your colleagues		–	0.07	–
12b.	your managers	–0.13	–	0.02	–
13.	Acceptability of bringing child to work				
13a.	among your colleagues	–0.37	**	–0.28	*
13b.	your managers	0.25	–	0.18	–
14.	How well the following people take into account your responsibility for a child:				
14a.	your colleagues	0.02	–	–0.12	–
14b.	your immediate supervisor	0.04	–	–0.25	**
14c.	your employer	0.08	–	0.07	–
15.	Extent to which the hours you work create problems with childcare arrangements	0.36	***	0.20	**

Males: R = .583, R^2 = .34, Adj R^2 = .259, Standard Error = .92
Females: R = .59, R^2 = .35, Adj R^2 = .275, Standard Error = .97

Source: Fine-Davis et al. (2004), Table 10.7, p. 188.

Table 7.15b ANOVA for total equation

		Sum of squares	*df*	*Mean square*	*F*	*Sig.*
Male	Regression	67.62	19	3.56	4.20	***
	Residual	131.32	155	0.85		
	Total	198.94	174			
Female	Regression	83.87	19	4.17	4.72	***
	Residual	156.29	167	0.94		
	Total	240.16	186			

Source: Fine-Davis et al. (2004), Table10.7a, p. 188. *p ≤ .05 **p ≤ .01 ***p ≤ .001

childcare arrangements also had more difficulty reconciling work and family life. The amount of help women received was also significantly related to successfully combining work and family. The less help they received from their partner, the more difficulty they experienced combining work and family life – the more help they received the easier it was. Finally, colleagues' attitudes were also important, as were those of the woman's immediate supervisor. The more accepting the attitudes concerning the woman's childcare responsibilities, the easier she found it to combine work and family (Table 7.15a).

Results for Ireland

The factors that were significant in the all country data were also significant for Ireland and in most cases even more significant. The most significant factors for Irish parents were:

- partner's commuting time
- the number of hours worked per week
- the amount of help received with domestic chores and childcare at home
- the extent to which one's hours create problems with childcare arrangements

The multiple regression for Ireland explained a greater degree of variance in the dependent measure than did the multiple regressions for the all country data (see Table 7.16). In the Irish data set, 39% of the variance in the dependent measure was explained, based on the adjusted R^2. Again the total equation was highly significant.

Satisfaction and well-being: four country comparisons

In addition to examining the dependent measure of ease vs. difficulty in combining work and family life, we also examined several standard satisfaction measures, such as satisfaction with health, work, partner and life in general. When using a measure such as life satisfaction as the dependent variable in a multiple regression, we were not as successful in predicting it from the work-life measures in the study. We found that the measure ease vs. difficulty in combining work and family life was a much more satisfactory dependent measure in this research.

However, we did find interesting country differences in the measures of satisfaction as well as significant correlations between the satisfaction measures and other measures relating to the workplace and to childcare, which we shall present here.

In looking at the results for the satisfaction measures, it may be seen that the highest levels of satisfaction with health, work, partner and life in general were obtained in Denmark. Ireland was similar to Denmark in relation to satisfaction with partner and had the second highest mean scores on the other three

Table 7.16a Predictors of ease vs. difficulty in combining work and family life: multiple regression for Ireland only (N = 100)

	Predictor variables	*Beta*	*Sig.*
1.	Age	0.06	–
2.	Level of education	0.07	–
3.	Partner's education	0.02	–
4.	Occupational status	0.09	–
5.	Partner's occupational status	–0.02	–
6.	Own commuting time	–0.06	–
7.	Partner's commuting time	0.31	***
8.	Length of work week	0.31	***
9.	Length of partner's work week	–0.07	–
10.	Number of children	–0.06	–
11.	HELPINDEX Index of help with domestic responsibilities	–0.46	***
12.	Acceptability of arriving late/leaving early		
12a.	among you and colleagues	0.21	–
12b.	by managers	–0.14	–
13.	Acceptability of bringing child to work		
13a.	among you and colleagues	–0.35	*
13b.	by managers	0.29	–
14.	How well the following people take into account your responsibility for a child:		
14a.	Colleagues	0.02	–
14b.	Immediate Supervisor	–0.18	–
14c.	Employer	0.24	–
15.	Extent to which the hours you work create problems with childcare arrangements	0.48	***

$R = .71$, $R^2 = .50$, Adj $R^2 = .39$, Standard Error = 1.03

Source: Fine-Davis et al. (2004), Table 10.8, p. 190.

Table 7.16b ANOVA for total equation

	Sum of squares	*df*	*Mean square*	*F*	*Sig.*
Regression	91.82	19	4.83	4.57	***
Residual	93.03	88	1.06		
Total	184.85	107			

*≤ .05 **≤ .01 ***≤ .001

Source: Fine-Davis et al. (2004), Table 10.8a, p. 190.

measures. The mean scores for the four countries were significantly different from each other with the Danish clearly the highest. There were no significant country differences on satisfaction with family life (Table 7.17). The greater satisfaction which is apparent in the Danish data may reflect three things: (1) the relatively equal distribution of working hours between the men and women, as well as more

Table 7.17 Summary table of satisfaction levels: mean scores by country (N = 400)

Satisfaction with:	*France*	*Italy*	*Denmark*	*Ireland*	*Sig.*
Health	4.5	4.5	**5.1**	4.7	$p < 0.001$
Work	4.3	4.4	**4.9**	4.6	$p < 0.005$
Family life	4.9	5.1	5.2	5.2	N.S.
Partner	5.0	5.0	**5.3**	**5.4**	$p < 0.005$
Life in general	4.6	4.9	**5.4**	5.1	$p < 0.001$

(1 = "very dissatisfied"; 6 = "very satisfied")

Source: Fine-Davis et al. (2004), Table 10.16, p. 195.

equal distribution of work in the home; (2) a high level of relatively affordable public day care provision and a high degree of paid maternity and parental leave and (3) a workplace culture with a relatively relaxed and permissive attitude towards reconciling work and family life. It is thus clear that the nature of the Danish workplace, the greater public provision of childcare facilities and the greater sharing of roles in the home are reflected in higher levels of well-being in several spheres on the part of the Danish respondents (Højgaard, 2002).

Subsequent to examining country differences in well-being, we then explored relationships between the various satisfaction measures and various work and childcare-related variables. There was a consistent pattern of correlations indicating that the more favourable the working environment, the greater the well-being. For example, the more an employer/supervisor is perceived as taking account of one's childcare responsibilities, the greater not only is the employee's work satisfaction, but also the greater the satisfaction with his/her partner and with his/her life in general. The greater the potential flexibility at work the greater is one's work satisfaction, but not only that – greater potential flexibility is also significantly related to satisfaction with one's health and one's life in general (Table 7.18). In contrast, *actual* flexibility was not significantly related to well-being. What this suggests is that the freedom to have flexibility has a salutary effect on health, even though one may not need to use that freedom.

Satisfaction with one's childcare arrangements was also found to be significantly related to all measures of well-being. Conversely, if one's hours created problems with one's childcare arrangements this was significantly related to dissatisfaction in all areas – from health, to work, to relationship with partner, to life in general. Thus, it is clear that workplace characteristics and work-life balance supports, such as childcare, are significantly related to several key areas of working parents' well-being, far beyond those which might be expected.

Implications of the findings

The results provide an analysis of parents' dilemmas and coping strategies in balancing work and family life in four countries of the EU. In particular the

Table 7.18 Relationships between variables related to workplace and childcare and measures of well-being: correlations for all countries, males and females (N = 400)

Variables related to workplace and childcare	*Measures of well-being: satisfaction with:*				
	Health	*Work*	*Family life*	*Relationship with spouse/partner*	*Life*
Satisfaction with childcare arrangements	0.14**	0.13**	0.28***	0.25***	0.23***
How well supervisor takes account of childcare responsibilities	0.11*	0.35***	0.12*	0.14**	0.25***
Potential flexibility at work	0.18***	0.21***	0.05	0.11*	0.18***
Actual flexibility at work	.09	.10*	−.08	−.06	.03
Hours worked create problems with childcare arrangements	−0.16***	−0.23***	−0.25***	−0.17***	−0.27***
Ease/difficulty combining work and family life	−0.25***	−0.23***	−0.38***	−0.22***	−0.33***

*$p \leq 0.05$
**$p \leq 0.01$
***$p \leq 0.001$

Sources: Fine-Davis et al. (2004), Tables 10.20, p. 202, Table 10.23 p. 206, 10.26, p. 212.

significant predictors of ease vs. difficulty in balancing work and family life were identified as well as the work-life balance correlates of key measures of subjective well-being.

The findings clearly illustrate the pressure that working parents are under, particularly in relation to time. Ways need to be found to reduce this pressure so that people can have more satisfying lives, which successfully integrate their working lives and their private lives. Time flexibility in the workplace appears to be particularly important. It would also be helpful if employees did not feel such a sense of pressure to work over and above the normal hours to get ahead. Equally, the attitudes in the workplace were found to be very important. Supportive attitudes on the part of colleagues, supervisors and employers appear to make a great deal of difference to the success of working parents in balancing work and family. Long working hours and long commuting times add to the difficulties. Policies need to be found, including greater availability of flexible working hours and improved transportation policies to reduce these stresses on working parents.

Women are still bearing the major responsibility for childcare and domestic chores. While men think they are sharing these, women often do not perceive it like that. This unequal division of labour in the household adds additional stress to women to that which they already have in balancing work and family and dealing with often unsupportive attitudes in the workplace. In particular, attitudes towards flexible working patterns, including part-time work and job-sharing, need to be given more status, so they are not seen as hindering men's and women's career development.

In a report from the Irish Business and Employers Confederation (IBEC, 2003) entitled *A Business Vision for Ireland: The New Decade*, IBEC refers to six drivers of competitiveness. One of these is quality of life. The report points out that

> for the Irish economy to continue to develop, business needs to make the best use of the talents of as many people as possible. Therefore employers should recognise the changing social structure in which a modern workforce operates, and the social and personal benefits of balancing work with other dimensions of people's lives. To be successful, business must embrace the approach of family-friendly and work/life balance policies, while understanding that such policies need to reflect business requirements.
>
> (p. 24)

This view is to be welcomed, though the last caveat is, of course, often a stumbling block. However, increasingly, businesses are realising that family-friendly policies in fact have positive effects on the "bottom line," since they produce committed and loyal workers who more than pay the company back in productivity, reduced absenteeism, reduced turnover, etc.

The time has come for these aspirations to become realities so that (1) working parents do not continue to be squeezed by pressures of work and domestic responsibilities, (2) we don't lose the talent of our women workers who often leave the workforce because they don't have sufficient social supports to enable them to continue to contribute to the labour market and (3) men can participate in their children's development and not be made to feel less manly or threatened in their careers by doing so.

Moreover, recent data from a study of Irish men and women in the childbearing age group (Fine-Davis, 2011, 2014, 2016) examined attitudes to social policies relevant to family formation. This study found that 61% felt that "if people had flexible working conditions, this would make it more likely that they would have more children." Similarly, 85% said that "if people have to spend a lot on childcare they are more likely to have fewer children." In light of the falling birth rate in Ireland, which has decreased 50% from an average of four children per woman in 1970 to less than two children per woman in 2016, it is important to take cognisance of such attitudes. Ireland's dependency ratio is increasing with the ageing of the population and the decreasing birth rate, and hence it is important to be sure to have social policies which do not discourage working people in the childbearing age group from having children.

This study showed strong support for flexible working arrangements and strong support for the introduction of paternity leave. The notion of part-time working for both parents in order to facilitate co-parenting and making maternity leave available to either parent were more controversial, but the levels of support for these policies suggest that changes are underway which signal a readiness for greater sharing of childcare between men and women.

Thus, while there was an expressed wish for greater "co-parenting" among a sizeable proportion of the sample, part-time working and job-sharing were seen as leading to career disadvantages, particularly for men, and people felt that they must work long hours to get ahead in their careers. Thus, while many might wish to work part-time or job-share in order be able to better share childcare, this was not seen as an appealing option from a career point of view. In light of high childcare costs it is likely that it is also problematic from an economic point of view. It is evident that people feel financial pressure to pay for childcare costs and this is preventing them from having as many children as they might like. It was evident greater state provision of childcare was the policy which people of childbearing age most strongly supported in order for them to have the number of children they would like and in order to achieve work-life balance.

The findings underscore the need for social policy which addresses the dilemmas faced by young people who want to start families, while at the same time fulfilling their own needs for autonomy and development. Provision of necessary social supports such as childcare and greater availability of flexible ways of working that are compatible with parenthood are essential if men and women are to be able to function as workers and parents. Unless society facilitates childrearing by fathers as well as mothers, women will continue to face dilemmas which prevent them from forming stable family relationships and having the number of children that they ideally wish to have.

The recent coronavirus pandemic has forced many people all over the world, not least in Ireland, to work from home and to rely on technology to help get work done. This is a natural social experiment in tele-working and related forms of flexible working. It is to be hoped that once this health crisis is over, society will have learned that work can still get done with more flexible ways of working and hopefully new patterns of working will emerge which will help people to better balance work and family life.

References

Cohen, B. C. and Marta Korintus, M. (2017). Making connections: Reflections on over three decades of EU initiatives in Early Childhood Education and Care (ECEC). *Early Years*, 37 (2), 235–249. doi:10.1080/09575146.2016.1181050.

Del Boca, D. and Locatelli, M. (2006). *The Determinants of Motherhood and Work Status: A Survey*. Discussion Paper Series. Bonn: Forschungsinstitut zur Zukunft der Arbeit Institute for the Study of Labor.

Drew, E., Humphreys, P. and Murphy, C. (2003). *Off the Treadmill: Achieving Work Life Balance*. Dublin: National Framework Committee for the Development of Family Friendly Policies.

Esping-Andersen, G. (2004). Preface. In: M. Fine-Davis, J. Fagnani, D. Giovannini, L. Højgaard and H. Clarke (Eds.), *Fathers and Mothers: Dilemmas of the Work-Life*

Balance – A Comparative Study in Four European Countries. Dordrecht, Boston and London: Kluwer, pp. v–vii.

European Commission (2015). *Delivering for Parents: Commission Withdraws Stalled Maternity Leave Proposal and Paves the Way for a Fresh Approach*. Press Release, Brussels, 1 July.

European Council/Council of the European Union (2019). *Better Work-Life Balance for Parents and Carers in the EU: Council Adopts New Rules*. Press Release. www.consilium.europa.eu/en/press/press-releases/2019/06/13/better-work-life-balance-for-parents-and-carers-in-the-eu-council-adopts-new-rules/.

Eurofound (2017). *Work – Life Balance and Flexible Working Arrangements in the European Union*. Dublin: Eurofound.

Eurofound (2018). *Striking a Balance: Reconciling Work and Life in the EU*. Luxembourg: Publications Office of the European Union.

Fagnani, J. (2005). The 35-hour laws and the work and family life balance in France. In: A. Hegewisch, J. C. Williams, S. Buri, E. Vogelheim, M. Still, R. Bispinck, D. Barnett, A. Heron, J. Fagnani, H. Seifert, J. Morris, W. Lochmann and B. Reissert (Eds.), *Working Time for Working Families: Europe and the United States*. Washington, DC: Friedrich-Ebert-Stiftung, pp. 81–120.

Fine-Davis, M. (2011). *Attitudes to Family Formation: Findings from the Nationwide Study*. Dublin: Social Attitude and Policy Research Group, Trinity College and Family Support Agency.

Fine-Davis, M. (2014). Gender role attitudes, family formation and well-being in Ireland. In: L. Eckermann (Ed.), *Gender, Lifespan and Quality of Life: An International Perspective*. Vol. 53: Social Indicators Research Series. New York and Heidelberg: Springer, pp. 203–227.

Fine-Davis, M. (2016). *Changing Gender Roles and Attitudes to Family Formation in Ireland*. Manchester: Manchester University Press.

Fine-Davis, M., Fagnani, J., Giovannini, D., Højgaard, L. and Clarke, H. (2004). *Fathers and Mothers: Dilemmas of the Work-Life Balance – A Comparative Study in Four European Countries*. Dordrecht, Boston and London: Kluwer Academic Publishers.

Fine-Davis, M., McCarthy, M., Edge, G. and O'Dwyer, C. (2005a). *Work-Life Balance and Social Inclusion in Ireland: Results of a Nationwide Survey*. Dublin: National Flexi-Work Partnership (Centre for Gender and Women's Studies, Trinity College Dublin; IBEC; ICTU; FÁS, Age Action Ireland and Aware).

Fine-Davis, M., McCarthy, M., Edge, G. and O'Dwyer, C. (2005b). *Mental Health and Employment: Promoting Social Inclusion in the Workforce*. Dublin: National Flexi-Work Partnership (Centre for Gender and Women's Studies, Trinity College Dublin; IBEC; ICTU; FÁS, Age Action Ireland and Aware).

Fine-Davis, M., McCarthy, M., O'Dwyer, C., Edge, G. and O'Sullivan, M. (2005c). *The Effects of Flexible Working on Work-Life Balance and Social Inclusion: An Evaluation of a Series of Pilot Projects*. Dublin: National Flexi-Work Partnership (Centre for Gender and Women's Studies, Trinity College Dublin; IBEC; ICTU; FÁS, Age Action Ireland and Aware).

Fine-Davis, M., O'Dwyer, C., McCarthy, M., Edge, G., O'Sullivan, M. and Wynne, K. (2005d). *Men in Childcare: Promoting Gender Equality in Children – Evaluation of a Pilot Project*. Dublin: National Flexi-Work Partnership (Centre for Gender and Women's Studies, Trinity College Dublin; IBEC; ICTU; FÁS, Age Action Ireland and Aware).

Højgaard, L. (2002). The Danish experience. In: M. Fine-Davis, H. Clarke and M. Berry (Eds.), *Fathers and Mothers: Dilemmas of the Work-Life Balance – Conference Proceedings*. Dublin: Centre for Gender and Women's Studies, Trinity College Dublin, pp. 39–49.

Humphreys, P. C., Fleming, S. and O'Donnell, O. (2000). *Flexible Working in the Public Service*. Dublin: Institute of Public Administration.

IBEC (2003). *A Business Vision for Ireland: The New Decade*. Dublin: Irish Business and Employers Confederation.

Jacobs, J. A. and Gerson, K. (2004). *The Time Divide: Work, Family and Gender Inequality*. Massachusetts: Harvard University Press.

McGinnity, F. and Russell, H. (2008). *Gender Inequalities in Time Use: The Distribution of Caring, Housework and Employment Among Women and Men in Ireland*. Dublin: The Equality Authority and the Economic and Social Research Institute.

Russell, H., Grotti, R., McGinnity, F. and Privalko, I. (2019). *Caring and Unpaid Work in Ireland*. Dublin: Irish Human Rights and Equality Commission and the Economic and Social Research Institute.

Russell, H., McGinnity, F., Callan, T. and Keane, C. (2009). *A Woman's Place: Female Participation in the Irish Labour Market*. Dublin: The Equality Authority and the Economic and Social Research Institute.

Russell, H., O'Connell, P. J. and Frances McGinnity, F. (2007). *The Impact of Flexible Working Arrangements on Work-Life Conflict and Work Pressure in Ireland*. Working Paper No. 189. Dublin: Economic and Social Research Institute.

Scott, J. and Plagnol, A. C. (2012). Work-family conflict and well-being in Northern Europe. In: J. Scott, S. Dex and A. Plagnol (Eds.), *Gendered Lives: Gender Inequalities in Production and Reproduction*. Cheltenham: Edward Elgar, pp. 174–205.

Chapter 8

Implications for men, gender relations and social policy

Introduction and overview

In the preceding chapters we looked at those factors which precipitated women's entry into the labour force in the 1970s and beyond (Chapter 3). We also noted that this massive social change was largely accounted for by the entry of married women, a large proportion of whom were mothers (Chapter 6). We saw that employment had a beneficial effect on married women, both in terms of their physical and mental health (Chapter 4). However, discrimination in the workplace as well as by the educational system was a barrier which impinged on women's successful progress in the labour force (Chapter 5). Even though legislation for equal pay and equal opportunity was passed in the mid-1970s, women continued to experience discrimination. In fact, women were more likely to report discrimination in the workplace and by the educational system *after* the equality legislation was passed, suggesting that this legislation had heightened women's awareness of discrimination. However, surprisingly, our research showed that women were *less likely* to think they were discriminated against than others thought they were. We interpreted this as a *denial of discrimination* on the part of women, a phenomenon which has been noted in other research, notably by Crosby (1984) in the United States at about the same time. Fortunately, as time moved on, women's perceptions of discrimination decreased as the effects of the equality legislation kicked in.

Nevertheless, other obstacles faced and still face women in the workplace, notably the lack of accessible and affordable childcare (Chapter 6) and the lack of flexible working policies (Chapter 7), both of which should ideally support them in their dual role of mother and worker. Moreover, as we saw in Chapter 7, not only are policies lacking, but prevailing attitudes are also an inhibiting factor concerning the acceptability of men taking up flexible working policies when they do exist.

In this chapter we explore the implications of these findings for men, for relationships between men and women and for social policy. In this context we also explore one of the pivotal issues in the couple relationship, namely the role of men in domestic work and childcare and the sharing of this unpaid work between men and women. We begin by looking at the extent to which men and women share unpaid domestic work in the home, both in Ireland (e.g., Fine-Davis, McCarthy, et al., 2005; McGinnity and Russell, 2008; Russell et al., 2019) and cross-culturally (e.g., Bianchi et al., 2000; Giovannini, 2002; Fine-Davis et al., 2004; McMunn et al., 2019; European Institute for Gender Equality, 2019; Russell et al., 2019). We then look at the issue of men in childcare, an area where gender equality could also be enhanced, thus promoting less gender-stereotyped role models to children at an early age. In the course of these discussions we bring in views of scholars of both genders, noting particularly the views of male scholars who have addressed the issue of male involvement in promoting gender equality.

The role of men in domestic work: cross-cultural comparisons

The increasing labour force participation of women, particularly of those in the childbearing years, has been accompanied by increasing needs for childcare, flexible working arrangements and greater demands for equality in the workplace. The challenge which still faces even the most advanced of the EU member states is how to facilitate more egalitarian sharing of roles, that is – how to relieve women of the double burden of employment and domestic duties, while encouraging men to take an active part in family and domestic life.

In her groundbreaking book, *The Second Shift*, Hochschild (1989) introduced a concept which has now become part of the vernacular. One of the underlying problems in relation to women's equality at work and overall well-being is the fact that they indeed have a "second shift." At the end of the day's work, the working woman goes home to a second job – a second shift – which involves domestic work and childcare. The issues which Hochschild raised in 1989 were alluded to in the initial pages of the first Report of the Commission on the Status of Women in Ireland (1972), which noted that

> apart from attitudes of managements to the recruitment and training of women in employment there is a broader question of traditional male attitudes to women's role in society and male reluctance to accept women as an equal partner on either a social or domestic level.
>
> (p. 13)

While it is less surprising to read this in relation to the Ireland of 1972, when it was written, it is more surprising that the underlying point being made regarding "male reluctance to accept women as an equal partner on either a social or domestic level" is still relevant today, almost fifty years later.

A lack of equity on the domestic level has been documented in numerous studies both in Ireland and in other countries over many years. We shall highlight some of the key trends in Ireland, as well as refer to some cross-cultural research which has included Ireland.

An important study which measured men and women's comparative time use was carried out in Ireland in 2005 (McGinnity and Russell, 2008). It used the method of time use diaries, which is considered the "gold standard" of data collection in this area (Russell et al., 2019). This study of 1,000 Irish men and women asked participants to record a wide range of their activities and how much time was spent on each. The results showed that men carried out significantly less domestic work and childcare than women did (McGinnity and Russell, 2008). For example, "only 19 per cent of men report any cleaning on weekdays compared to 71 per cent of women" (Ibid., p. 40) – a situation which remained essentially the same on weekends. In relation to cooking or food preparation, less than a third of men reported carrying out this activity, whereas 74% of women did. The authors found that "similar gender differences emerge for shopping/errands with close to 50 per cent of women participating in these activities on both weekdays and weekend days compared to 22 per cent of men on weekdays and 29 per cent on weekend days" (Ibid.). These findings are reproduced here in Table 8.1 from McGinnity and Russell (2008, Table 4.9, p. 41).

The data show that women spent, on average, one hour and 18 minutes per day cleaning on weekdays, whereas men spent on average just 12 minutes per day. The male contribution equates to just 15% of the women's work. Women spent on average one hour and nine minutes per weekday cooking compared with 16 minutes spent by men. The male rate again constitutes a fraction (23%) of the female rate. While men spent more time on DIY, this did not compensate for the long hours women put in on cooking, cleaning and shopping (Ibid., pp. 40–42).

Commenting on their earlier research (McGinnity and Russell, 2008), Russell et al. (2019) said that "those in the 25–44 age group had the highest unpaid workload holding other factors constant. The study also found that women's unpaid work time was more responsive to the presence of children and their paid work time than men's. Moreover, the researchers added that "a partner added more to women's workload than men's" (Russell et al., 2019, p. 19).

At roughly the same time period as McGinnity and Russell's (2008) study, another Irish study examined the amount of time that men and women spent carrying out domestic tasks and caring activities (Fine-Davis, McCarthy, et al., 2005). This study, utilising a survey methodology with a nationwide representative sample of 1,212 adults over 18, also found that time spent on domestic tasks and caring was related to gender as well as to the age of respondents. The average amount of time respondents spent on domestic and caring activities was 24.6 hours per week, with women spending more time than men. Women aged between 31 and 49 spent the most amount of time (46 hours) and men aged 18–30 the least (7.9 hours) (Fig. 8.1).

The time respondents spent on caring and domestic tasks was also related to their employment status, although both employed and non-employed women spent significantly longer than men in both categories. Employed women spent 26.6 hours, compared with 42.3 hours reported by non-employed women. In

Table 8.1 Participation in and duration of housework weekends and weekdays

	Weekdays				*Weekend day*			
	Clean	*Cook*	*DIY*	*Shop*	*Clean*	*Cook*	*DIY*	*Shop*
	% participating				% participating			
All	46	52	21	37	45	50	22	38
Men	19	29	23	22	22	32	29	29
Women	71	74	19	52	67	67	16	46
Significance	***	***	*	***	***	***	***	***
	Time spent by participants (hh:mm)				Time spent by participants (hh:mm)			
All	1:39	1:23	1:40	1:19	1:19	1:29	2:15	1:43
Men	1:02	0:55	2:01	1:13	0:56	0:55	2:35	1:33
Women	1:49	1:33	1:15	1:21	1:29	1:39	1:39	1:49
Significance	***	***	***	n.s.	***	***	**	*
*	Time spent all (hh:mm)				Time spent all (hh:mm)			
All	0:45	0:43	0:21	0:29	0:39	0:40	0:30	0:39
Men	0:12	0:16	0:28	0:16	0:18	0:12	0:44	0:27
Women	1:18	1:09	0:14	0:42	1:00	1:07	0:15	0:50
Significance	***	***	***	***	***	***	***	***

Note: If two activities are recorded simultaneously the time is recorded for both activities. Therefore the total time includes care as a primary activity and as a secondary activity and therefore should be seen as an upper estimate of time spent on housework. Stars refer to statistical significance of gender differences using Pearson's chi-square test for the proportion participating and ANOVA for the time spent (see Appendix B for further details).

***$p < 0.001$; **$p < .01$; *$p < .05$.

Source: McGinnity and Russell (2008), Table 4.9, p. 41. Reproduced here with kind permission of the authors.

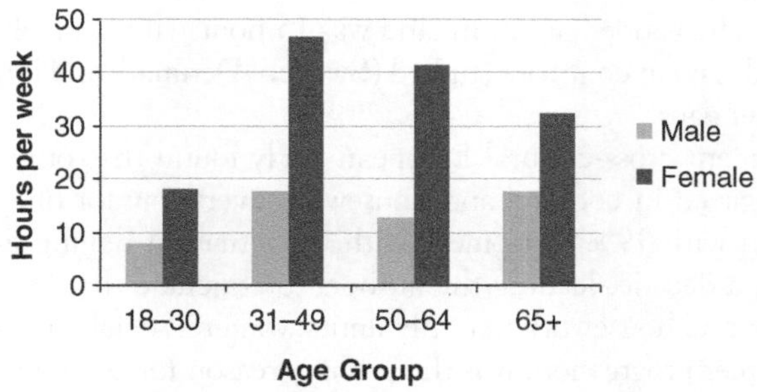

Figure 8.1 Average number of hours respondents spent on caring and domestic tasks per week, by age group and gender of respondent

Source: Fine-Davis, McCarthy, et al. (2005), Fig. 3.9, p. 38.

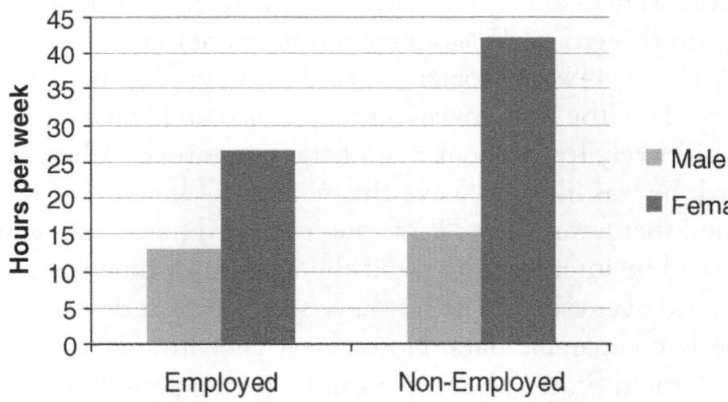

Figure 8.2 Average number of hours respondents spent on caring and domestic tasks by employment status and gender of respondent

Source: Fine-Davis, McCarthy, et al. (2005), Fig. 3.10, p. 39.

contrast, employed men spent just 12.8 hours per week on caring and domestic tasks per week, while non-employed men spent 15.1 hours (Figure 8.2).

Russell et al. (2019) carried out a more recent analysis of time spent on care and housework based on data from the European Quality of Life Survey (EQLS). In this study individuals were asked direct questions about how much time they spent either daily or weekly on housework and caring. Their results showed that Irish women spend approximately 38 hours doing unpaid work per week. The authors commented that "this places women in Ireland amongst the three countries with the highest levels of unpaid work time along with Romania and Malta. At the other end of the scale, women in Denmark did an average of just 22.5 hours of unpaid work" (Russell et al., 2019, p. 46). Not only were Irish women more likely to carry out a greater number of hours of unpaid work, but the gender gap between the hours put in by women vs. those put in by men was the seventh highest among the 28 EU countries compared. In contrast Sweden had the smallest gender gap of just 7.2 hours, whilst Greece had the greatest

(20.2 hours). The gender gap in Ireland was 15 hours (Ibid., pp. 49–51). In general the Scandinavian countries studied (Sweden, Denmark and Finland) had the smallest gender gaps.

Another recent cross-cultural European study found that only 34% of European men engaged in cooking and housework every day for one hour or more in comparison with 79% of women, with the situation having barely changed in more than a decade, leading the authors to conclude that "the unalleviated burden of care and housework not only limits women's social and personal development or career progression, it is the primary reason for economic inactivity or part-time work (European Institute for Gender Equality, 2019, p. 48).

A recent British study examined gender differences in domestic work, focusing on differences in employment status of the respondents (McMunn et al., 2019). This study involved analysis of data from more than 8,500 couples interviewed in the U.K. Household Longitudinal Study in 2010–11. Overall, almost half of the couples surveyed were dual-earners, with both members tending to be employed full-time. Within this group, 45% of men did no more than four hours of housework a week, whilst 44% of women worked between 10 and 19 hours. Even among couples where the woman was more qualified and had a more demanding job, she was still likely to do about half of the housework. Where the man was better qualified, he was likely to leave the majority of housework to his partner. The study found that fewer than 7% of couples shared housework equally.

While it would be interesting to see if the amount of time spent in domestic work had changed over time, we do not have such a time series for Ireland which provides directly comparable data. However, it is of interest to have a look at data from the United States which spans quite a long period of time, with four points in time: 1965, 1975, 1985 and 1995 (Bianchi et al., 2000). These data show that women's time spent in housework *decreased* linearly from 30 hours per week in 1965 to 23.7 hours in 1975, 19.74 hours in 1985 and 17.47 hours in 1995, which the authors said was a reflection of their increased participation in the labour force. At the same time men's contribution to housework *increased* linearly from 4.88 hours per week in 1965 to 7.23 hours in 1975, 9.75 hours in 1985 and 9.95 hours in 1995. Yet while women's work decreased and men's increased, women still carried out approximately twice as much as men 30 years later. The authors noted that the overall amount of housework carried out decreased over time, suggesting that people were adjusting their lifestyles through the use of cleaning services, having meals out, ordering meals in, etc. Bianchi et al.'s (2006) more recent work reinforces the finding that less time is being spent on housework and that mothers have made time for both work and family by "multitasking."

Sharing of domestic chores and childcare: male-female perceptions and cross-cultural comparisons for Ireland, Denmark, France and Italy

While the previously cited studies have compared the relative contribution of men and women to domestic work, other studies have looked also at the extent to which men and women share such activities and the perceptions of how much of such work the partner does. *Fathers and Mothers: Dilemmas of the Work-Life Balance*, a cross-cultural comparative study of working parents in four European countries (Denmark, France, Italy and Ireland), compared mothers and fathers in terms of who did what in the household and the reciprocal perceptions of who carried out which activities (Fine-Davis et al., 2004). All of the respondents in the study were (1) employed (2) living in a couple with a partner/spouse and (3) had at least one child under six. In designing the items in this area, we drew upon the work of Giovannini and Ventimiglia (1994), Zanatta (1999) and Haas (1993).

Respondents were asked to indicate who *usually* carried out 12 different domestic and childcare activities during weekdays, including, "shopping for food," "preparing meals," "cleaning," "playing with the child/ren," etc. The responses could be: "me," "my partner," "both of us" or "other." The last option was chosen so infrequently on all but two of the measures (washing/ironing and cleaning) that it is not included in the analyses except in those two cases. It should be borne in mind that, as we did not interview couples, the male and female responses do not reflect reciprocal perceptions in couples. We are merely examining male and female respondents about themselves and their partner; their actual partners did not take part in this study.

We present here percentage responses for each of the items by country and sex. As the response categories are nominal, we carried out Chi-square analyses by sex for each country and for all countries together. The study found that mothers carried out significantly more of the domestic and child-care tasks in the home than fathers did in all of the four countries. There were also large and systematic discrepancies between male and female perceptions of who did what. Fathers were more likely to think *both* of the partners carried out tasks than mothers did. Mothers were more likely to report that *they* carried out the tasks. Where fathers excelled was in relation to taking care of the children. This was true in the case of feeding, bathing, taking to school/crèche and changing nappies/dressing children. But most of all, it was true in the case of playing with the children. Eighty-five per cent of men in the combined all country sample said that both they and their partner played with the children. A similar proportion of women agreed that this was a shared activity. The following three tables illustrate this pattern; however, it was apparent in the case of many more items. An examination of the individual country data indicates that this is a cross-cultural trend, although there are national differences. For example, there is more concordance in France, but less so in Ireland, Denmark and Italy. Giovannini (2002) discusses this phenomenon, noting that it corroborates previous work by Bimbi and Castellano (1990), Ventimiglia (1996, 1999), and Giovannini (1998).

In relation to Ireland, it may be seen in Table 8.2 that 54.2% of Irish women said they prepared the meals, but only 38% of men said "my partner does." Men were more likely to say "both of us" – a response given by 44% of men, but only 37.5% of women. Eighteen per cent of men thought they were the one who mainly made the meals, but only 8.3% of women said that their partner usually

Table 8.2 Who usually prepares meals: percentage distributions by country and sex (N = 400)

	France %		*Italy* %		*Denmark* %		*Ireland* %		*All countries* %	
	M	F	M	F	M	F	M	F	M	F
Me	12.5	51.0	2.0	63.3	34.0	72.0	18.0	54.2	16.7	60.2
My partner	54.2	16.3	49.0	4.1	32.0	10.0	38.0	8.3	42.9	9.7
Both of us	33.3	32.7	49.0	32.7	34.0	18.0	44.0	37.5	40.4	30.1
Total	**100.0**	**100.0**	**100.0**	**100.0**	**100.0**	**100.0**	**100.0**	**100.0**	**100.0**	**100.0**
	$\chi^2 = 21.17$ df = 2 $p \leq 0.001$		$\chi^2 = 48.34$ df = 2 $p \leq 0.001$		$\chi^2 = 15.04$ df = 2 $p \leq 0.001$		$\chi^2 = 18.41$ df = 2 $p \leq 0.001$		$\chi^2 = 92.90$ df = 2 $p \leq 0.001$	

Source: Fine-Davis et al. (2004), Table 8.6, p. 106.

Table 8.3 Who usually manages home life: percentage distributions by country and sex (N = 400)

	France %		*Italy* %		*Denmark* %		*Ireland* %		*All countries* %	
	M	F	M	F	M	F	M	F	M	F
Me	0.0	46.0	6.0	60.0	0.0	70.0	10.0	60.0	4.0	59.8
My partner	48.0	4.0	32.0	0.0	50.0	0.0	30.0	6.0	40.5	2.0
Both of us	52.0	50.0	62.0	40.0	50.0	30.0	60.0	34.0	55.5	38.2
Total	**100.0**	**100.0**	**100.0**	**100.0**	**100.0**	**100.0**	**100.0**	**100.0**	**100.0**	**100.0**
	$\chi^2 = 41.64$ df = 2 $p \leq 0.001$		$\chi^2 = 40.46$ df = 2 $p \leq 0.001$		$\chi^2 = 62.50$ df = 2 $p \leq 0.001$		$\chi^2 = 29.45$ df = 2 $p \leq 0.001$		$\chi^2 = 173.32$ df = 2 $p \leq 0.001$	

Source: Fine-Davis et al. (2004), Table 8.8, p. 108.

made the meals. Sixty per cent of women thought they were the ones who mainly managed the household, whereas 60% of men thought it was "both of us" and just 34% of women thought it was "both of us" (Table 8.3).

Table 8.5 a-d presents additional data for Ireland. As can be seen, 60% of the mothers said that they were the main one who usually shopped for food. This compared with 36% of men who said their partner did. Thus, there is a 24% discrepancy in perceptions. Similarly, 48% of men said "both of us," whereas only 28% of women gave this response, again reflecting a rather great disparity.

As noted earlier, the one area in which men and women were in agreement was in relation to playing with children. Ninety per cent of Irish men said that both they and their partner played with the children. A similar proportion of women agreed that this was a shared activity (Table 8.4). These high percentages were true of all of the four countries, with slight variations.

Table 8.4 Who usually plays with the children: percentage distributions by country and sex (N = 400)

	France %		*Italy* %		*Denmark* %		*Ireland* %		*All countries* %	
	M	*F*	*M*	*F*	*M*	*F*	*M*	*F*	*M*	*F*
Me	4.0	4.1	22.0	12.0	8.2	0.0	6.0	2.0	10.5	4.5
My partner	4.0	4.1	2.0	6.0	6.1	20.4	4.0	5.9	4.0	9.0
Both of us	92.0	91.8	76.0	82.0	85.7	79.6	90.0	92.2	85.5	86.4
Total	**100.0**	**100.0**	**100.0**	**100.0**	**100.0**	**100.0**	**100.0**	**100.0**	**100.0**	**100.0**
	$\chi^2 = 0.00$ df = 2 n.s.		$\chi^2 = 2.59$ df = 2 n.s.		$\chi^2 = 7.88$ df = 2 $p \leq 0.05$		$\chi^2 = 1.23$ df = 2 n.s.		$\chi^2 = 8.65$ df = 2 $p \leq 0.01$	

Source: Fine-Davis et al. (2004), Table 8.12, p. 112.

Table 8.5 Who usually carries out household and childcare tasks: percentage responses of Irish fathers and mothers

a. Shopping for food

	Ireland (N = 100)	
	Male %	*Female %*
Me	16	60
My partner	36	12
Both of us	48	28
Other	0	0
Total	**100**	**100**

$\chi^2 = 21.3$ df = 2 $p \leq 0.001$

b. Washing up

	Ireland (N = 100)	
	Male %	*Female %*
Me	28	32
My partner	10	16
Both of us	58	50
Other	4	2
Total	**100**	**100**

$\chi^2 = 1.11$ df = 2 n.s.

(*Continued*)

Table 8.5 (Continued)

c. Washing and ironing

	Ireland (N = 100)	
	Male %	*Female %*
Me	6	70
My partner	60	2
Both of us	34	24
Other	0	4
Total	**100**	**100**

$\chi^2 = 56.94$ df = 2 $p \leq 0.001$

d. Cleaning

	Ireland (N = 100)	
	Male %	Female %
Me	10	42
My partner	22	8
Both of us	64	42
Other	4	8
Total	**100**	**100**

$\chi^2 = 16.06$ df = 2 $p \leq 0.001$

Source: Fine-Davis (2005), Table 2.6, pp. 26–28.

As Giovannini (2002) points out referring to Bimbi (1990), fathers are aware of the "asymmetry" that is present in their family. However, they do not participate more and, in many cases, do not even show a willingness to change, except where childcare is concerned. Referring to Bimbi and Castellano (1990), Giovannini suggests that we face a situation in which even those fathers who would like to spend more time with their family and with their children are nevertheless satisfied with the level of their contribution to the various household activities and do not feel that they should be more involved in a domain that they do not perceive as pertaining to them.

McKeown et al. (1998) note that the international evidence on fathers' involvement suggests that while there has been some increase in participation in childcare and domestic activities, fathers' behaviour has not kept pace with changing attitudes and cultural expectations in this area (p. 425). The implication of their analysis is that

> public policy should seek to create family-friendly measures, especially in the workplace, which maximise the choices men and women have to negotiate roles and responsibilities and will allow fathers as well as mothers the time and space for childcare.
>
> (Ibid.)

Attitudes towards sharing housework

Male and female attitudes towards sharing housework

Thus, research has addressed the issue of sharing of domestic work from different angles. Analysis of time spent through the use of time diaries gives us actual figures concerning how much time men and women spend on domestic work. Attitude surveys give us another perspective, but the results of the two methods tend to reinforce each other.

In the context of a nationwide study of attitudes to changing gender roles, family formation and relationships, 1,404 Irish men and women in the child-bearing age group were asked about their attitudes to housework among other things (Fine-Davis, 2016). This study identified a new factor which taps a cluster of attitudes towards sharing domestic work. This factor, which included several attitudinal items, was called *Perceived male reluctance to share housework* (Fig. 8.3). The first item was: "while men recognise that women have to spend less time on housework, they don't recognise that they have to contribute more than they used to." There was overall majority agreement (60%) with the statement, though a major gender difference – with just 48% of men agreeing with the item and 73% of women agreeing. This is supported by responses to another item on the factor – "there's an awful lot of lip service paid to 'sharing responsibilities,' but it's still a man's world at the end of the day" – to which 52% agreed. Again there was a large discrepancy in male and female responses: while 64% of women agreed with the statement, only 39% of men did. These findings indicate that men think they are contributing more than women think they are – a phenomenon which

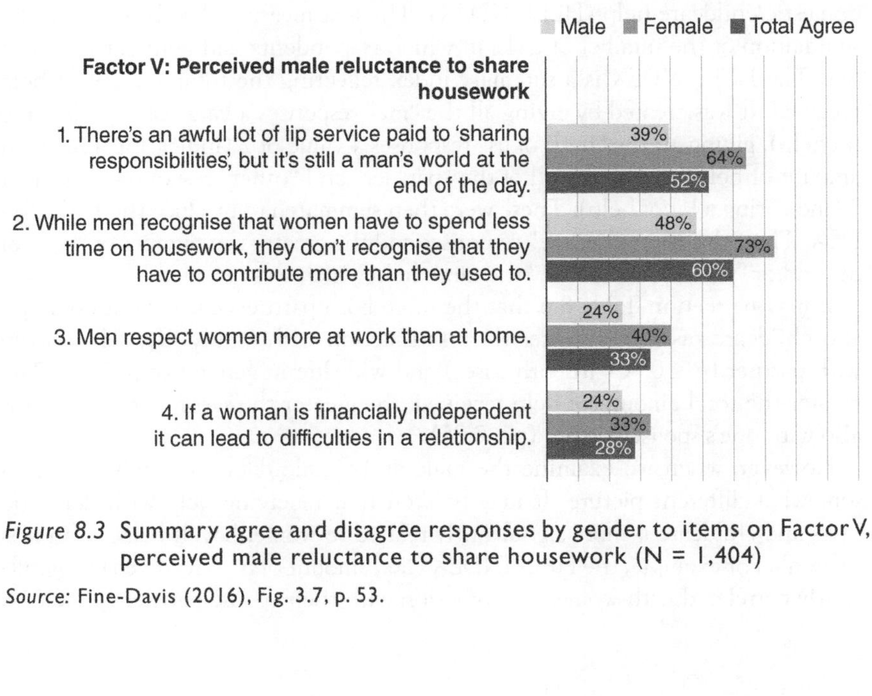

Figure 8.3 Summary agree and disagree responses by gender to items on Factor V, perceived male reluctance to share housework (N = 1,404)

Source: Fine-Davis (2016), Fig. 3.7, p. 53.

we have just observed cross-culturally in France, Denmark, Italy and Ireland in a previous study (Fine-Davis et al., 2004). The co-loading of various items on this factor found that the issue of housework was linked in people's minds with men's respect for women, suggesting that a lack of helping may be related to a lack of respect. While most people (55%) disagreed with the statement "men respect women more at work than at home," 33% agreed with it, with women more likely to do so – 40% of women felt this way, while only 24% of men did so. These findings would appear to echo the view cited earlier in the *Report of the First Commission on the Status of Women (1972)* to the effect that there is a "male reluctance to accept women as an equal partner" at least on the "domestic level." While there are clear divergences in views of men and women on these issues, nevertheless a significant proportion of women do not feel that they are as respected at home as women are in the workplace and this attitude is connected with attitudes about a lack of equality in sharing housework (Fine-Davis, 2016).

The relationship between sharing housework/help with housework and well-being

In the cross-cultural study referred to previously (*Fathers and Mothers: Dilemmas of the Work-Life Balance*) (Fine-Davis et al., 2004), two indices were computed which tallied how much help a person received with housework and childcare. We then looked at the relationship between these indices and various measures of well-being for the four countries as a whole.

It will be recalled that respondents were asked who carried out each of twelve household and childcare activities: "me," "my partner," "both of us" or "other." Specifically, we looked at the "both of us" measure and the total amount of domestic/childcare help (HELPINDEX). The first measure ("both of us") is the summation of the number of tasks in which respondents said both carried them out. The HELPINDEX is a summary index reflecting the total amount of help received. It was created by giving all the "me" responses a value of 1 (indicating no help), giving all the "both of us" responses a value of 2 (indicating a medium amount of help) and giving all of the "partner" and "other" responses a value of 3 (indicating a lot of help). These were then summated to produce the HELPINDEX. Thus, the fewer the "me" responses and the greater the number of "both of us" and/or "partner" or "other," the more help which was received.

It may be seen in Table 8.6 that the more both partners carried out domestic and childcare tasks the greater their satisfaction with family life, relationship with partner ($p \leq 0.001$ in both cases) and with life in general ($p \leq 0.05$). The greater the total amount of help received, the greater the satisfaction there was also with one's spouse/partner ($p \leq 0.05$).

However, when we examine the male and female data separately, we see a somewhat different picture. It may be seen that receiving help with domestic tasks and childcare is more significantly related to women's well-being than it is to men's. For example, the HELPINDEX (i.e., amount of help received) is significantly correlated with women's satisfaction with their spouse/partner ($p \leq 0.01$),

Table 8.6 Relationships between variables related to domestic help/childcare and measures of well-being: correlations for all countries, males and females (N = 400)

Variables related to domestic help / childcare	*Measures of well-being: satisfaction with:*				
	Health	*Work*	*Family life*	*Relationship with spouse/ partner*	*Life*
Number of domestic/childcare tasks carried out by "both of us"	0.05	–0.01	0.18***	0.22***	0.10*
HELPINDEX Total amount of domestic/ childcare help	–0.04	0.03	0.06	0.11*	–0.04

*$p \leq 0.05$ **$p \leq 0.01$ ***$p \leq 0.001$

Source: Adapted from Fine-Davis et al. (2004), Table 10.20, p. 204.

Table 8.7 Relationships between variables related to domestic help/childcare and measures of well-being: correlations for all countries, females only (N = 200)

Variables related to domestic help / childcare	*Measures of well-being: satisfaction with:*				
	Health	*Work*	*Family life*	*Relationship with spouse/ partner*	*Life*
Number of domestic/childcare tasks carried out by "both of us"	0.01	–0.00	0.17**	0.23***	0.14*
HELPINDEX Total amount of domestic/ childcare help	0.01	0.07	0.12	0.17**	0.10

*$p \leq 0.05$ **$p \leq 0.01$ ***$p \leq 0.001$

Source: Adapted from Fine-Davis et al. (2004), Table 10.21, p. 205.

whereas it is not significantly related at all for men (Table 8.7 and 8.8). It can also be seen that the more *both* partners carry out domestic tasks and childcare, the more likely women are to report feeling satisfied with their family life ($p \leq 0.01$), with their spouse/partner ($p \leq 0.001$) and with their life in general ($p \leq 0.05$) (Table 8.7). For men, there are also significant positive correlations with satisfaction with partner and family life, but these relationships are not as strong as they are for women ($p \leq 0.05$) and there is no relationship with overall life satisfaction for men as there is for women (Table 8.8).

Thus it is clear from all of the studies cited here that women carry out more domestic tasks and childcare in the home than their partners do. This is even the

Table 8.8 Relationships between variables related to domestic help/childcare and measures of well-being: correlations for all countries, males only (N = 200)

Variables related to domestic help / childcare	*Measures of well-being: satisfaction with:*				
	Health	*Work*	*Family life*	*Relationship with spouse/ partner*	*Life*
Number of domestic/ childcare tasks carried out by "both of us"	0.11	−0.02	0.16*	0.16*	0.08
HELPINDEX Total amount of domestic/ childcare help	−0.08	0.06	−0.04	−0.05	−0.05

*$p \leq 0.05$ **$p \leq 0.01$ ***$p \leq 0.001$

Source: Adapted from Fine-Davis et al. (2004), Table 10.22, p. 206.

case when women are employed outside the home and even if they are earning more than their husbands. We also see that men overestimate their own contribution to the work in the home. The research also shows that women perceive a male reluctance to share housework and this is related to the perception that men respect women more in the workplace than in the home. The lack of appreciation implied by this is further elucidated by the relationship between receiving help and well-being and conversely the relationship between not receiving help and lesser well-being.

Men and caring

The notion of "men and caring" can be seen to encompass many different aspects. It can include caring for one's partner, for one's own children and children in general, not to mention caring for oneself, one's parents and siblings, friends and people in general. However, we shall limit our focus here to caring for partners, children and children in general.

The role of men in caring at home: caring for partners, caring for children

As we have seen in the preceding sections of this chapter, research both in Ireland and cross-culturally has shown consistently that men do not contribute to the domestic and childcare tasks as much as women do and women consequently have a significantly greater dual burden (e.g., Hochschild, 1989; Eurostat, 2001; Villa, 2002; Fine-Davis et al., 2004; McGinnity and Russell, 2008; Scott and Plagnol, 2012; Russell et al., 2019). This undoubtedly contributes to the twin track system in which women are more likely to choose, of necessity, flexible arrangements involving shorter hours (Drew et al., 2003), a fact which contributes to women's lesser likelihood of reaching higher levels in their career and hence lower earnings over their lifetime, as well as smaller pensions, as a result. As we have also seen, men are not only behaviourally less inclined to do their fair share of domestic work, but they also are attitudinally less inclined to do so to the extent that their female counterparts may feel that men do not pull their weight. This can lead to resentment and is even one of the causes of divorce (Scott and Plagnol, 2012; Ruppanner et al., 2018). A study using Swedish data from the 2009 Young Adult Panel Study (N = 1,057 couples) matched with Swedish register data (2009–2014) found that women who reported performing more housework were less likely to be satisfied with their relationships and were more likely to consider breaking up. These unions were also more likely to dissolve (Ibid.). On the contrary, when men do contribute to household work, their female partners' well-being significantly increases, as shown earlier in Table 8.7.

A number of male voices, including psychologists, sociologist, economists and public servants, among others, have commented on this issue (e.g., McKeown et al., 1998; Hearn, 2001, O'Callaghan, 2002; Esping-Andersen, 2004). Hearn (2001), who has theorised about the role of men in relation to gender roles and equality policy, points out that

> so often men's avoidance of caring has been the defining feature of "being men." This is a *structural* question in terms of women doing more caring work, both in private and in public. Caring is not generally seen as a normal part of boyhood and manhood, so a challenge to men's responsibilities is how to make caring a more taken-for-granted feature of boys and men.
>
> (p. 16)

As O'Callaghan (2002) points out, "Further advances by women and mothers in particular may depend on the extent to which fathers take up their caring responsibilities, thus freeing up mothers to achieve their potential in the workplace. That may be the greatest challenge facing us, as we frame family friendly policies in the future" (p. 85).

Some authors have observed that the revolution in women's roles has resulted in women changing while men are staying the same. For example the noted sociologist Gosta Esping-Andersen believes that

> the societal revolution that latter-day women are bringing about is mainly spurred by radical change in women's own life course behaviour. When one studies the life course behaviour of Europeans over the past 30–40 years, one is struck by an amazing asymmetry: beginning with educated women and eventually extending to most, we detect a clear masculinisation of female biographies. Women are converging with men in educational attainment, in participation rates and, especially, in life-long employment. The amazing thing is that women have done all the changing while men stubbornly cling

> to a life course model that closely resembles that of their fathers and grandfathers . . . no workable social equilibrium can materialise unless we somehow begin to also reconstruct the male life course.
>
> (Esping-Andersen, 2004, p. vi)

Hochschild (1989) also observed this phenomenon when she pointed out that there is "a broader social tension – between *faster-changing women and slower-changing men*" (p. 205).

Hearn (2001) concurs, arguing that "to transform gender relations, and specifically men's continued dominance of much social life, means not only changes in what women do and what women are but also that men have to change too. This lesson is hard for many men to hear, even harder for men to act on in politics, policy development and personal practice" (p. 5). He further goes on to say that "men in management and Government have responsibilities to move from resistance to facilitate men's caring for others. These responsibilities are fundamental in the creation of gender equality at work and at home" (p. 15).

As we saw in Chapter 7, attitudes of male workers towards work-life balance issues are complex and not always apparently consistent. While men are less likely to take up flexible options such as part-time work and job-sharing, our research has shown that 82% of Irish fathers of young children would like to spend more time with their families (Fine-Davis et al., 2004). It is thus apparent that further in-depth research on male attitudes needs to be conducted to examine the conflicts and contradictions apparent among male working fathers. We still do not know how to facilitate men to contribute more to sharing of domestic and childcare responsibilities given their apparent wish to spend more time with their families. Secondly, we need to learn more about the attitudes of senior managers and their staff in order to understand how to facilitate greater flexibility in working patterns and arrangements among male and female staff at all levels. As Hearn (2001) suggests:

> The central importance of "work," still usually meaning paid work, for many men has been well established. . . . Work is a source of power and resources, a central life interest, and a medium of identity. It is also a means of ordinary *everyday yet structural resistance* to gender equality.
>
> (p. 11)

The key role of managers in supporting flexible working policies is one which has not obtained sufficient awareness. Hearn (2001) says that

> managers have the responsibility of overseeing and underwriting the behaviour of other men in their charge. Equal opportunities policies can be a way of both implementing greater equality and containing more radical demands for change. Men in management and Government have responsibilities to move from resistance to facilitate men's caring for others. These

> responsibilities are fundamental in the creation of gender equality at work and at home.
>
> (p. 15)

The role of men as childcare workers

Men can contribute to childcare not only through their roles as fathers in the home, but also through their participation as professionals in childcare centres. Currently most childcare workers are women, as are most primary school teachers. This sends a clear message to young children that caring and teaching children is a female activity, not a male one. As Hearn (2001) points out:

> Boys and men learn *not* to care for others, and changing this is an important part of the project of socialisation, for example, in the education of boys at home and in school. This should be a major policy development – in nurseries and schools, by Government and education authorities.
>
> (p. 17)

McKeown et al. (1998) in a review of research concerning fathering in an international context found that

> the more extensive a father's involvement with his children the more beneficial it is for them in terms of cognitive competence and performance at school as well as for empathy, self-esteem, self-control, life-skills and social competence; these children also have less sex-stereotyped beliefs and a more internal locus of control.
>
> (p. 423)

We can extrapolate that a "fathering presence" in childcare centres might also have such beneficial effects. An increase in the proportion of men undertaking this kind of work would help to promote non-stereotyped role models in the childcare sector which would be expected to foster the development of more egalitarian gender-role attitudes and behaviour in children. By seeing men in caring roles at such an early stage, children would begin to develop fundamental ideas of equality, including the notion that men can be carers. As part of its Gender Equality Program, the European Commission established a Network on Childcare to help with reconciliation of work and family life (Peeters, 2007). In 1996 the network set a target of 20% male workers in childcare that had to be reached by 2006. According to Peeters (2007), campaigns and other initiatives were successful in Denmark, Norway, Sweden, the U.K. and Belgium, but no European country had reached the target at that point.

A pilot research project was carried out in Ireland to promote gender equality in children as part of a larger project on work-life balance, supported by the EU EQUAL Programme (Fine-Davis, McCarthy, et al., 2005; Fine-Davis, O'Dwyer, et al., 2005). The Men in Childcare pilot project was carried out in order to introduce an innovative approach to gender mainstreaming at the early stages of a child's life when attitudes to gender roles are being formed. The project was developed to highlight the need to desegregate a gendered profession and was the first of its kind to be to be carried out in an Irish context. The research showed that having male childcare workers was perceived as positive by centre managers, parents and most importantly, by children (Fine-Davis, O'Dwyer, et al., 2005). The value and importance of including men as childcare workers has also been recommended by the National Economic and Social Forum (NESF) (2005) in its Forum Report on Childcare. In its report, the NESF agreed that there should be more opportunities for men to work in the early childhood care and education field "so as to increase the diversity of experience of young children in play and learning and, ultimately, to improve the outcomes for children" (p. 92).

This is a critical piece in the overall strategy to overcome traditional gender roles and the persisting dual burden which women carry. It is only through the development of ideas of equality at an early age that male and female children will grow up with notions of sharing and equality in the workplace and the home.

However, one of the main problems the research identified is that there are not enough men coming forward to pursue childcare as a career (Fine-Davis, O'Dwyer, et al., 2005). It is clear that it will be necessary to target young men, probably in schools, to encourage them to go into childcare. Those men who are already in the profession find it very satisfying. However, it was necessary for them to overcome the stereotyped view that this was a woman's job. Research has shown that childcare workers do not perceive that their profession is highly valued. This is reflected in low salaries in the profession. All of these issues, together with the need for more training of childcare workers, need to be addressed in order to provide the quality of childcare that children deserve.

Social policies to facilitate male caring: parental leave and paternity leave

One of the areas of policy which has discriminated against men and mitigated against their equal participation in the family and in particular with childcare has been the uneven allocation of leave for childbirth. Maternity leave has long been available to women when they give birth and it has been extended over time. Paternity leave has not been available in the same way and in Ireland it has been non-existent until very recently. While paternity leave is common in the Scandinavian countries, other countries have been slow to follow.

Esping-Andersen (2004) believes that we not only need policies to support working mothers, but we need to create policies that help to include men in the caring role:

> . . . a truly workable and positive social equilibrium needs more than public support for mothers. It needs, somehow or other, to equalize the employment

> *and* caring roles of men and women alike. The conclusion I draw . . . is that policies that help reconcile women's dual role are, perhaps, necessary but they are not sufficient. To be also sufficient, we need policies that will make it more attractive and possible for men to dedicate themselves to their families.
>
> (p. v)

It is this philosophy which underlies policies such as paternity leave and flexible working, as well as, of course, all modes of flexible working. Currently, mothers are entitled to 26 weeks' paid (statutory) maternity benefit, plus an additional 16 weeks unpaid, as well as a further 18 weeks of unpaid parental leave. Fathers are also eligible to take 18 weeks of unpaid parental leave. However, fathers were not entitled to any paid paternity leave until 2016.

Public attitudes in Ireland have been positive towards the idea of paternity leave for many years, as we saw was the case with childcare. In a nationwide survey of the Irish population conducted in 2005 the vast majority of respondents, 86.1%, felt paternity leave should be a legal entitlement (see Table 8.9). A slightly higher percentage of females than males thought so (88.2% and 83.8% respectively).

Of those who felt paternity leave should be a legal entitlement, 31.1% thought it should last from one to two weeks, 32.4% thought it should last from three to four weeks and 16.5% thought it should last from five to six weeks. A further 13.2% thought it should last anywhere from two to six months. Only 6% thought it should be less than one week. Thus, the vast majority of the nationwide sample (63.5%) thought there should be a legal entitlement to paternity leave which would last somewhere between one and four weeks (see Table 8.10). As may be seen in this table, men and women had very similar views on this matter.

Ninety-five per cent of respondents felt that at least some paternity leave should be paid – 60.5% stated that all paternity leave should be paid and 34.6% part of it (see Table 8.11).

It has taken a long time for paternity leave to become a statutory right in Ireland. In 2016 paternity leave was introduced for the first time, giving men two weeks off on the birth of a child. Similar in kind to the maternity benefit

Table 8.9 **Percentage of respondents who agree/disagree that paternity leave should be a legal entitlement, by gender of respondents**

	Male (*n* = *587*) %	*Female* (*n* = *603*) %	*Total* (*N* = *1,190*) %
Yes	83.8	88.2	86.1
No	9.0	7.8	8.4
Don't know	7.2	4.0	5.5
Total	**100.0**	**100.0**	**100.0**

Source: Fine-Davis, McCarthy, et al. (2005), Table 3.9, p. 33.

Table 8.10 Recommended duration of paternity leave, by gender of respondent

	Male (594) %	*Female (611) %*	*Total (N = 1,041) %*
Less than 1 week	5.6	6.3	6.0
1–2 weeks	31.7	30.6	31.1
3–4 weeks	33.7	31.1	32.4
5–6 weeks	16.0	16.7	16.3
2–3 months	9.6	8.1	8.8
4–6 months	2.8	5.9	4.4
Other	0.6	1.3	1.0
Total	**100.0**	**100.0**	**100.0**

Source: Fine-Davis, McCarthy, et al. (2005), Table 3.10, p. 34.

Table 8.11 Percentage of respondents who believe all, some or none of paternity leave should be paid

	Male (n = 594) %	*Female (n = 611) %*	*Total (N = 1,205) %*
No, none of leave paid	6.0	3.9	4.9
Yes, part of leave paid	32.0	36.9	34.6
Yes, all of leave paid	62.0	59.2	60.5
Total	**100.0**	**100.0**	**100.0**

Source: Fine-Davis, McCarthy, et al. (2005), Table 3.11, p. 34.

payment, new fathers are paid €245 per week. From November 2019 mothers and fathers were entitled to a further two weeks of paid parental leave. It is envisaged that there will be further increases over the following years, eventually rising to seven weeks paid parental leave over the next three years (Daly and Rush, 2018; McCrave, 2019). According to the Minister for Social Protection, this measure was being taken "to comply with EU commitments to improve the work-life balance of parents" (Hilliard, 2018).

However, Reddan (2019) points out that last year there were 61,000 births in Ireland yet only about 24,000 men took their paternity leave, a take-up rate of 39%. The obstacles are that one has to have made sufficient social contributions in order to be eligible for it. Also, not all employers top up the payment and hence many fathers cannot afford to take it up. Nor have fathers taken up the 18 weeks' unpaid parental leave either. The take-up rate has been between 10% and 20%. This is also attributed to the loss of income.

Some other countries have been more generous in relation to paternity and parental leave. For example in Norway over the last decades it has been the goal of family policy to facilitate both men and women to combine work and childcare. The length of parental leave is 49 weeks with full compensation or 59 weeks with 80% compensation. As of 1 July 2014 the mother and father have 10 weeks each as an exclusive right and the mother has a further three weeks before the child is born. The rest of the weeks can be divided at the couple's discretion. "The purpose of the quota for paternity leave ('father quota') is to encourage fathers to participate in caring for their young children" (Hardoy, 2015, p. 4; see also Blum et al., 2018).

Fagnani (2008) observes that family policies themselves are the "expression of the dominant value systems, as well as a reflection of the cultural context that plays a role in creating a more or less guilt-inducing environment for mothers who wish to work" (p. 11). Hoem (2005) concurs that it is the whole political culture of Sweden, as opposed to specific policies, that makes the country more family-, child- and woman-friendly, which may have an impact on fertility (see also Gauthier, 2007). Haas (2014) supports this view, noting that the provision of generous paternity leave in Sweden is reflected in men's greater participation in childcare and domestic activities even after the paternity leave is over. It may be that the "dominant value system" which has been prevalent in Ireland has implicitly supported women's role in the home as a carer of children (see Bradley, 2011). Bradley (2011) refers to Article 41 of the Irish Constitution which she says is "grounded in the Catholic principal of subsidiarity" which "supports a highly privatised autonomous model of family life in which the woman cares for home and children while husband acts as breadwinner" (p. 46). This view is supported to some extent by some of the continuing ambivalence towards maternal employment and the belief that mothers are the best nurturers of children (Fine-Davis, 2015). It is also reflected in the generous child benefit payments, traditionally paid to the mother, and in the disparity in leave entitlements between women and men, whereby women are entitled to extensive maternity leave benefits while men were not entitled to any paid paternity leave until 2016. However, it would appear that the times are changing. Not only is the Government planning to increase paid parental leave for both parents in forthcoming budgets, but some individual companies are offering longer periods of paid paternity leave. The move by Guinness to offer new fathers six months of paid paternity leave has been described as a "game changer" (Donnelly and Walsh, 2019, p. 1). This and similar policies offered by some employers both here and abroad are described as being a response to full employment which reflect employers' need to attract and retain employees. This set of circumstances is reminiscent of the hasty provision of childcare facilities on a widespread scale during World War II when women needed to be recruited to munitions factories when men were at war. While it is regrettable that social change sometimes comes about for economic reasons, it is nevertheless a positive development and hopefully paves the way for other employers as well as Government to follow suit.

References

Bianchi, S., Milkie, M., Sayer, L. and Robinson, J. (2000). Is anyone doing the housework? Trends in the gender division of household labor. *Social Forces*, 79, 191–228.

Bianchi, S., Robinson, J. P. and Milkie, M. A. (2006). *Changing Rhythms of American Family Life*. New York: Russell Sage Foundation.

Bimbi, F. (1990). Molteplicità dei tempi sociali; tempo quotidiano, esperienze di maternità e di paternità. In: F. Bimbi and G. Castellano (Eds.), *Madri e Padri*. Milano: Angeli.

Bimbi, F. and Castellano, G. (Eds.) (1990). *Madri e Padri*. Milano: Angeli.

Blum, S., Koslowski, A., Macht, A. and Moss, P. (2018). *International Review of Leave Policies and Research 2018*. www.leavenetwork.org/lp_and_r_reports/.

Bradley, S. (2011). *Inside the Black Box an Exploration of the Impact of Action and Activity in the Inner Spheres of Policy Making on Early Childhood Education and Care Policy*. Doctoral thesis, Dublin Institute of Technology.

Central Statistics Office. (2007). *Census 2006: Principal Demographic Results*. Dublin: Stationery Office.

Commission on the Status of Women (1972). *Report to the Minister for Finance*. Dublin: Stationery Office.

Crosby, F. (1984). The denial of personal discrimination. *American Behavioral Scientist*, 27, 371–386.

Daly, M. and Rush, M. (2018). Ireland country note. In: S. Blum, A. Koslowski, A. Macht and P. Moss (Eds.), *International Review of Leave Policies and Research 2018*. www.leavenetwork.org/lp_and_r_reports/.

Donnelly, E. and Walsh, A. (2019). Guinness game changer: Six-month paternity leave. *Irish Independent*, 23 May, p. 1.

Drew, E., Humphreys, P. and Murphy, C. (2003). *Off the Treadmill: Achieving Work Life Balance*. Dublin: National Framework Committee for the Development of Family Friendly Policies.

Esping-Andersen, G. (2004). Preface. In: M. Fine-Davis, J. Fagnani, D. Giovannini, L. Højgaard and H. Clarke (Eds.), *Fathers and Mothers: Dilemmas of the Work-Life Balance – A Comparative Study in Four European Countries*. Dordrecht, Boston and London: Kluwer Academic Publishers, pp. v–vii.

European Institute for Gender Equality (EIGE) (2019). *Gender Equality Index 2019 Work – Life Balance*. Luxembourg: Publications Office of the European Union.

Eurostat. (2001). *The Social Situation in the European Union*. Luxembourg: Office for Official Publications of the European Communities.

Fagnani, J. (2008). *The Future of Integrated Family Policy – The Long-Term Prospects: 2025/30*. Scoping Paper, Advisory Unity to the Secretary-General, International Futures Programme. Paris: OECD.

Fine-Davis, M. (2005). Work-life balance of Irish parents: A cross-national comparative study. In: G. Boucher and G. Collins (Eds.), *The New World of Work – Labour Markets in Contemporary Ireland*. Dublin: Liffey Press, pp. 17–41.

Fine-Davis, M. (2015). *Gender Roles in Ireland: Three Decades of Attitude Change*. London: Routledge.

Fine-Davis, M. (2016). *Changing Gender Roles and Attitudes to Family Formation in Ireland*. Manchester: Manchester University Press.

Fine-Davis, M., Fagnani, J., Giovannini, D., Højgaard, L. and Clarke, H. (2004). *Fathers and Mothers: Dilemmas of the Work-Life Balance – A Comparative Study in Four European Countries*. Dordrecht, Boston and London: Kluwer Academic Publishers.

Fine-Davis, M., McCarthy, M., Edge, G. and O'Dwyer, C. (2005). *Work-Life Balance and Social Inclusion in Ireland: Results of a Nationwide Survey*. Dublin: National Flexi-Work Partnership (Centre for Gender and Women's Studies, Trinity College Dublin; IBEC; ICTU; FÁS, Age Action Ireland and Aware).

Fine-Davis, M., O'Dwyer, C., McCarthy, M., Edge, G., O'Sullivan, M. and Wynne, K. (2005). *Men in Childcare: Promoting Gender Equality in Children – Evaluation of a Pilot Project*. Dublin: National Flexi-Work Partnership (Centre for Gender and Women's Studies, Trinity College Dublin; IBEC; ICTU; FÁS, Age Action Ireland and Aware).

Gauthier, A. H. (2007). The impact of family policies on fertility in industrialized countries: A review of the literature. *Population Research and Policy Review*, 26 (3), 323–346.

Giovannini, D. (1998). Are fathers changing? Comparing some different images on sharing of childcare and domestic work. In: E. Drew, R. Emerek and E. Mahon (Eds.), *Women, Work and the Family in Europe*. London and New York: Routledge, pp. 191–199.

Giovannini, D. (2002). The Italian experience. In: M. Fine-Davis, H. Clarke and M. Berry (Eds.), *Fathers and Mothers: Dilemmas of the Work-Life Balance – Conference Proceedings*. Dublin: Centre for Gender and Women's Studies, Trinity College Dublin, June, pp. 23–38.

Giovannini, D. and Ventimiglia, C. (Eds.) (1994). *Paternità e politiche per l'infanzia: Essere padri oggi* (Fatherhood and childcare policies: Being a father today). Unpublished report of research. Regione Emilia Romagna: Assessorato alla Formazione Professionale, Lavoro, Scuola e Università, Bologna.

Haas, L. (1993). Changing gender roles in Sweden. In: J. C. Hood (Ed.), *Men, Work and Family*. Thousand Oaks, CA: Sage Publications.

Haas, L. (2014). *Paid Parental Leave for Fathers? Lessons from Sweden*. Guest Lecture, Trinity College Dublin, Dublin, 21 October.

Hardoy, I. (2015). *Norway: Has Come a Long Way – And Still Strives to Improve*. Peer Country Comments Paper-NORWAY. Peer Review on 'Making Work Pay for Mothers,' Mutual Learning Programme, DG Employment, Social Affairs, Skills and Labour Mobility, St Julian's (Malta), 18–19 May.

Hearn, J. (2001). *Men and Gender Equality: Resistance, Responsibilities and Reaching Out*. Keynote Paper, Men and Gender Equality, Örebro, Sweden, 15–16 March.

Hilliard, M. (2018). Parental leave to cost State €30m a year. *The Irish Times*, 7 April, p. 7.

Hochschild, A. (1989). *The Second Shift*. New York: Avon Books.

Hoem, J. M. (2005). Why does Sweden have such high fertility? *Demographic Research*, 13 (22), 559–572.

McCrave, C. (2019). FactFind: Maternity, paternity and parental leave – How much time do new parents get? *The Journal.ie*, 23 April.

McGinnity, F. and Russell, H. (2008). *Gender Inequalities in Time Use: The Distribution of Caring, Housework and Employment Among Women and Men in Ireland*. Dublin: The Equality Authority and the Economic and Social Research Institute.

McKeown, K., Ferguson, H. and Romney, D. (1998). Fathers: Irish experience in an international context – An abstract of a report to the Commission on the Family. In: *Strengthening Families for Life. Final Report of the Commission on the Family to the Minister for Social, Community and Family Affairs*. Dublin: Stationery Office, pp. 404–454.

McMunn, A., Bird, L., Webb, E. and Sacker, A. (2019). Gender divisions of paid and unpaid work in contemporary UK couples. *Work, Employment and Society*. doi.org/10.1177%2F0950017019862153.

National Economic and Social Forum (NESF) (2005). *Early Childhood Care and Education*. Report 31. Dublin: National Economic and Social Forum.

O'Callaghan, J. (2002). Family friendly policies in Ireland. In: M. Fine-Davis, H. Clarke and M. Berry (Eds.), *Fathers and Mothers: Dilemmas of the Work-Life Balance – Conference Proceedings*. Dublin: Trinity College Dublin, University of Dublin, June, pp. 75–85.

Peeters, J. (2007). Including men in early childhood education: Insights from the European experience. *NZ Research in Early Childhood Education*, 10, 1–13.

Reddan, F. (2019). More parental leave means little at just €245 per week. *The Irish Times*, 24 April.

Ruppanner, L., Brandén, M. and Turunen, J. (2018). Does unequal housework lead to divorce? Evidence from Sweden. *Sociology*, 52 (1), 75–94.

Russell, H., Grotti, R., McGinnity, F. and Privalko, I. (2019). *Caring and Unpaid Work in Ireland*. Dublin: Irish Human Rights and Equality Commission and the Economic and Social Research Institute.

Scott, J. and Plagnol, A. C. (2012). Work-family conflict and well-being in Northern Europe. In: J. Scott, S. Dex and A. Plagnol (Eds.), *Gendered Lives: Gender Inequalities in Production and Reproduction*. Cheltenham: Edward Elgar, pp. 174–205.

Ventimiglia, C. (1996). *Paternità in controluce*. Milano: Angeli.

Ventimiglia, C. (1999). Mamme in regia, papà in panchina. *Famiglia Oggi*, 11, 18–25.

Villa, P. (2002). *Family and Work can be made compatible? The European Experience*. National and European Meeting: Which "kind" of reconcilation? Family, Labour and Gender: Balances and imbalances, Turin, 28–29 August.

Zanatta, A. L. (1999). Il coinvolgimento dei padri nella cura dei figli. *Polis*, 13 (3), 469–484.

Index

Note: Page numbers in *italic* indicate a figure and page numbers in **bold** indicate a table on the corresponding page.

For Product Safety Concerns and Information please contact our EU representative GPSR@taylorandfrancis.com Taylor & Francis Verlag GmbH, Kaufingerstraße 24, 80331 München, Germany